Politics, Ideology and Football Fandom

Football fans and football culture represent a unique prism through which to view contemporary society and politics. Based on in-depth empirical research into football in Poland, this book examines how fans develop political identities and how those identities can influence the wider political culture.

It surveys the turbulent history of Poland in recent decades and explores the dominant right-wing ideology on the terraces, characterised by nationalism, 'traditional' values and anti-immigrant sentiment. As one of the first book-length studies of fandom in Eastern Europe, this book makes an important contribution to our understanding of society and politics in post-Communist states.

Politics, Ideology and Football Fandom is an important read for students and researchers studying sport, politics and identity, as well as those working in sports studies and political studies covering sociology of sport, globalisation studies, East European politics, ethnic studies, social movements studies, political history and nationalism studies.

Radosław Kossakowski is Professor of Sociology and Chair of the Scientific Council of Sociology at the University of Gdańsk, Poland, where he is also Director of the Institute of Sociology.

Przemysław Nosal is Assistant Professor at the Faculty of Sociology, Adam Mickiewicz University, Poland.

Wojciech Woźniak is a Sociologist in the Department of Sociology of Social Structure and Social Change at the Faculty of Economics and Sociology, University of Łódź, Poland. He is also Chair of the Sociology of Sport Section in the Polish Sociological Association.

Critical Research in Football

Series editors:

Pete Millward, Liverpool John Moores University, UK
Jamie Cleland, University of Southern Australia
Dan Parnell, University of Liverpool, UK
Stacey Pope, Durham University, UK
Paul Widdop, Manchester Metropolitan University, UK

The *Critical Research in Football* book series was launched in 2017 to showcase the inter- and multi-disciplinary breadth of debate relating to 'football'. The series defines 'football' as broader than association football, with research on rugby, Gaelic and gridiron codes also featured. Including monographs, edited collections, short books and textbooks, books in the series are written and/or edited by leading experts in the field whilst consciously also affording space to emerging voices in the area, and are designed to appeal to students, postgraduate students and scholars who are interested in the range of disciplines in which critical research in football connects. The series is published in association with the *Football Collective*, www.footballcollective.org.uk.

Available in this series:

African Footballers in Europe
Migration, Community, and Give Back Behaviours
Ernest Yeboah Acheampong, Malek Bouhaouala and Michel Raspaud

Football in Fiction
A History
Lee McGowan

Football as Medicine
Prescribing Football for Global Health Promotion
Edited by Peter Krustrup and Daniel Parnell

Politics, Ideology and Football Fandom
The Transformation of Modern Poland
Radosław Kossakowski, Przemysław Nosal and Wojciech Woźniak

The Development of Women's Soccer
Legacies, Participation and Popularity in Germany
Henk Erik Meier

https://www.routledge.com/sport/series/CFSFC

Politics, Ideology and Football Fandom
The Transformation of Modern Poland

Radosław Kossakowski, Przemysław Nosal and Wojciech Woźniak

LONDON AND NEW YORK

First published 2020
by Routledge
2 Park Square, Milton Park, Abingdon, Oxon OX14 4RN

and by Routledge
605 Third Avenue, New York, NY 10017

First issued in paperback 2021

Routledge is an imprint of the Taylor & Francis Group, an informa business

© 2020 Radosław Kossakowski, Przemysław Nosal and Wojciech Woźniak

The right of Radosław Kossakowski, Przemysław Nosal and Wojciech Woźniak to be identified as authors of this work has been asserted by them in accordance with sections 77 and 78 of the Copyright, Designs and Patents Act 1988.

All rights reserved. No part of this book may be reprinted or reproduced or utilised in any form or by any electronic, mechanical, or other means, now known or hereafter invented, including photocopying and recording, or in any information storage or retrieval system, without permission in writing from the publishers.

Trademark notice: Product or corporate names may be trademarks or registered trademarks, and are used only for identification and explanation without intent to infringe.

Publisher's Note
The publisher has gone to great lengths to ensure the quality of this reprint but points out that some imperfections in the original copies may be apparent.

British Library Cataloguing-in-Publication Data
A catalogue record for this book is available from the British Library

Library of Congress Cataloging-in-Publication Data
A catalog record has been requested for this book

Typeset in Times New Roman
by Taylor & Francis Books

ISBN 13: 978-1-03-223738-1 (pbk)
ISBN 13: 978-0-367-34452-8 (hbk)

 Printed in the United Kingdom by Henry Ling Limited

Contents

	List of figures	vi
	Acknowledgements	viii
1	Introduction	1
2	Football fans and their political engagement in Central and Eastern Europe	10
3	Socio-economic and political transformation of Poland since the collapse of communism	50
4	Football fandom in Poland in a historical perspective	69
5	The pathological 1990s: Violence, anomie and political extremism among fans	92
6	Polish political elites versus football fandom	106
7	Contemporary Polish fandom and its civic, social and political engagement	126
8	Ideology on Polish terraces	143
9	Polish national team supporters: From the politicisation to the depoliticisation of fandom	182
10	Conclusion: Football fans and politics in Poland: between universality and peculiarity	202
	Index	215

Figures

4.1 Many derby rivalries were political in pre-war period, but only in case of Wisła–Cracovia derby of Cracow, the ethnic, religious, political and class tensions were overlapping so profoundly. The photo taken during the derby match on 07 May 1939 at the Wisła stadium.   76

4.2 The unprecedented triumph against vice-World Champion Hungary came on 27 August 1939, just 4 days before German invasion of Poland. The joyful crowd in the photo carries the heroes of the day: Władysław Szczepaniak and Ernest Wilimowski. The former will spend the occupation playing in clandestine tournaments in occupied Warsaw and will play his next international game for Poland only in 1947. Meanwhile, Wilimowski, the best Polish footballer of this era, will play eight games and score 13 goals for the National team of the Third Reich.   79

5.1 Pathology was a buzzword used to describe football fandom in the late 1990s in media reports portraying fans as dangerous folk devils. The stigma was semantically reclaimed by supporters of ŁKS Łódź who proclaimed their yard in the impoverished district of the city as 'The Stronghold of Pathology'.   103

6.1 New and more restrictive rules concerning the security of the fans require all clubs to provide separate stands for away fans, regardless of the level of the competition. Consequently, at lower leagues away fans are frequently literally caged at the stands. Photo depicts away fans sector at the stadium of Garbarnia Cracow.   111

6.2 The cover of *Polityka* from 1998 with a title 'League of Hooligans' is a classic example of the narrative fuelling moral panic about football-related violence. Interestingly, the anonymous fan depicted on the photo on right ceased to be anonymous when, as a member of the radically right-wing League of Polish Families (and highly qualified lawyer), he became a Member of Parliament and subsequently a Polish Government Minister.   114

List of Figures vii

7.1 Local patriotism is frequently manifested in fans' choreographies. Łódź Fabryczna (Industrial Łódź) is the celebration of the industrial heritage of the city by fans of Widzew, the club deeply rooted in the tradition of local working class. 132

7.2 Fans of Lech Poznań celebrate their regional heritage (Wielkopolska) referring also to their distinction over the fans of other teams through reference to Magnateria, the highest estate of Polish nobility in the old days. 138

8.1 Lech 100% Anti-Antifa. The banner on Lech Poznań stands exemplifies refusal and condemnation of any groups which may be associated with left wing values. 150

8.2 Religious motifs are recurring tropes in ultras' choreographies. One of the most famous one claimed: 'God Save the Fanatics' and was displayed by Legia Warsaw fans during the friendly charity game with ADO Den Haag in 2010. 157

8.3 Mural with the inscription: "All hail the memory of Cursed Soldiers" alongside the emblem of ŁKS Łódź football club. 170

9.1 Crucial legacy of Euro 2012 was the new and very modern sport infrastructure including the National Stadium in Warsaw, pictured here. At least in case of the fandom of Polish national team, modernization of infrastructure attracted new, consumer-oriented spectators. 196

Acknowledgements

First and foremost, we wish to thank all people who helped us on every stage of working on this book. We are grateful to anonymous reviewers for inspiriting and constructive remarks, comments and suggestions. We have been provided with an excellent support by people from Routledge: Rebecca Connor and Simon Whitmore.

During the writing process we received enormous support from Piotr Styk, who is the best proof-reader and editor any author could imagine.

It is crucial to thank all people who kindly provided the feedback for the initial versions of book, in particular John Horne whose comments were the most helpful while crafting the book proposal, Peter Millward who was our first contact in Routledge, our colleagues from Sociology of Sport Section of Polish Sociological Association and Magdalena Rek-Woźniak who was the first critical reader of many parts of this book.

Personally, each of us would like to thank:

Radosław – I am grateful to all my family (Ola, Jan, Zosia, Antek, Mum, Blackie) for continual support. I would like to thank people I am working with in Academia and who conversations with are always inspiring: Dominik Antonowicz, Honorata Jakubowska, Mateusz Grodecki, Tomasz Szlendak, Mark Doidge, Seweryn Dmowski and Dorota Rancew-Sikora from my home institute. Special thanks go to Przemyslaw and Wojciech for friendly companionship through whole writing process.

Przemysław – I would like to thank my family: Agnieszka, Tosia and Olek. I did my best to not write this book during the family time… and it worked! I am grateful to my parents and brothers for everything I received from them. Special thanks to my home Faculty of Sociology at Adam Mickiewicz University in Poznan – it is a great place to work at. Finally, I want to thank Radosław and Wojciech for a very inspiring and efficient collaboration.

Wojciech – Thank you Magda, Mum, Elżbieta and Andrzej for your support and goodwill. Radek & Przemek, guys, it was a pleasure and privilege to collaborate with you!

1 Introduction

Football fans and politics

The relation between football fans and politics is a popular research topic today (Doidge, 2013; Doidge et al. 2020). Most studies on football refer – directly or indirectly – to political engagement of fans: owing to its contemporary significance for culture and society, football is a politically fragile topic and fans are perceived as politically oriented actors.

There are several ways to investigate this phenomenon. First, fans and their clubs are described as politically engaged actors, whether on the right (e.g. Lazio Rome, Beitar Jerusalem, Zenit St Petersburg or Feyenoord Rotterdam) or the left side of political spectrum (e.g. Livorno, FC St. Pauli, Rayo Vallecano or Celtic Glasgow). They voice their point of view using banners, slogans or chants. Second, supporters are also observed through the lens of their activities beyond the stadium – engagement in political protests, manifestations or boycotts. They have become collective actors with a serious impact on the structure of the social world and have important representatives of civil society activism. Third, there are approaches concentrating on fans as voters, including studies focused on their political opinions and voting decisions. Altogether, football fans and politics is a highly developed research area.

Those analyses, however, are not without their limitations. Most researchers consider only specific groups of fans, especially hooligans and ultras. Besides, fans from some countries attract more interest than others. While the world of football supporters in Western Europe (e.g. Great Britain, Germany, Italy or Spain) or the Balkans (Serbia) has been extensively explored, Central and Eastern Europe remain under-investigated.

Apart from those disparities in research, it is also worth distinguishing between different forms of supporters' political commitment. On the one hand, their political sympathies may be viewed as an important element of the identity of the club, deeply rooted in history. This is the *static element*, as the political sympathies of the team and its supporters tend to be constant and unchangeable. Although they stem from the past, they may as well define contemporary identity of the fans. This historical background makes fans of some clubs more leftist

2 *Introduction*

or more rightist, more radical or more balanced. While there are some gaps in research on these issues, studies of this kind are widely available.

On the other hand, some supporters are engaged in more specific political areas, which is the *dynamic element* of their politicisation. They take a stance on racial, ethnic or religious issues. They contest the authorities (e.g. the government, the president) or institutions (e.g. the EU, UEFA). They refer to very current issues debated on the local, national and European level: LGBT rights, the refugee crisis, islamophobia, Brexit, separatist tendencies. They comment on current politics and react to the most recent or particularly relevant issues. Considering that such more specific manifestations and the attendant forms of activity also define their political commitment, they need continuous exploration. An in-depth analysis of politicisation of football fans, then, should take into account both aspects: the historical roots and current activities. Combining these two research tracks is a challenge that this book attempts to address.

The inspiration for this book came when writing the paper on the same topic for one of the academic journals (Woźniak, Kossakowski and Nosal, 2019). Many threads seemed worthy of a further exploration and formed the basis for the preliminary structure of this book.

Political commitment of Polish fans and why it matters at all

In this book, we argue that research on the politicisation of fandom in Poland is more topical than ever. One observation which inspired us to write it concerned the easily noticeable fact that there is no political and ideological pluralism in football fandom in Poland. Although we are aware that there are people of every political colour among the thousands in the terraces of Polish stadiums, the collective expressions of political attitudes are exclusively right-wing, frequently referring to nationalism, patriotism and anti-leftist resentments. As of 2015, this lack of pluralism was mirrored in the Polish parliament, where there was no single left-wing party for the first time since re-establishment of democracy in post-socialist Poland.

This could be interpreted as a mere coincidence, if it was not for the evidence we present in this book. We attempt to show that the processes occurring in football fandom may be regarded as a symptom of those going on in Polish society and politics at large.

Political mobilisation of Polish football fans is not a new phenomenon: we present numerous examples from the pre-Second World War period and significantly less frequent cases from the communist era, when any political expression was controlled and sometimes radically suppressed. Nevertheless, it was the twenty-first century, and 2010s in particular, that saw a significant growth in the political and ideological engagement of Polish fandom. The radicalisation of fans coincided with the polarisation of the Polish political scene from 2005 onwards. This period has also been marked with the weakening of institutionalised left-wing political parties.

Introduction 3

While the level of civic engagement in Polish society during the post-communist transformation has been relatively low, fans have been active on the national and local level, taking part in demonstrations and protests over a variety of issues. Their performative activity was widely reported in the media and became hyper-visible, thus putting fans on the verge of the political scene. The growing politicisation of fandom, which culminated in the anti-government fan protests against Donald Tusk's government (2011–2015), went largely unnoticed by most scholars. As Kerstin Jacobsson and Elżbieta Korolczuk (2019) show, they adopted a narrow understanding of 'the political' and did not see some social and political activism in the country as a fully legitimate part of civil society. Mainstream media almost unequivocally condemned football fans' political manifestations and declared that stadiums should not become a venue of such actions.

We argue that processes observed in football fandom, mostly composed of young males, and its relations to mainstream politics and establishment may be treated as a proxy for diagnosing the general political mood, particularly among younger cohorts. The processes observed in the stands preceded a significant shift towards the right and the rise of support for anti-establishment movements observed in all elections held since 2015. There is a high level of support for conservative values in society and a significant shift towards nationalism among the young cohorts of Poles. As proved by a recent (April 2019) large surveys of young (18–30 years of age) Poles, there is also a growing gender gap in the ideological and political stances between young females and males. The latter, who form the most significant cohort of active football fandom, are getting more and radicalized in their political choices, refusal of left-liberal values and their conservative views on the issues like: abortion, LGBT rights, gender equality or acceptance of refugees (Pacewicz, 2019a; 2019b). Politically steered media campaigns against refugees, as well as the Polish government's refusal to accept the quota of refugees assigned to Poland by the European Commission, most probably increased anti-immigration attitudes in society. Therefore, the politicisation and conservative mobilisation of fandom observed since the early 2000s could be viewed as a harbinger of structural processes occurring in Polish politics.

It seems that the political mobilisation of fans was not a mere reaction against more repressive policing adopted in order to tackle football-related violence. It was also directed against the hosting of UEFA Euro finals in 2012 and the large scale of expenditures involved. Their protests were unanimously ridiculed: the mainstream media and the political elite universally viewed the first Polish sport mega event as the ultimate confirmation of Poland's international prestige and a striking proof of the success of the Polish modernisation project (Burski, 2013; Woźniak, 2015). Fans, on the other hand, protested against what they perceived as unlawful suppression of free speech: they were fined and their stadiums were closed for anti-government chants and choreographies (Kossakowski, 2017; Kossakowski, Szlendak and Antonowicz, 2018).

4   *Introduction*

To some extent, their protests could be viewed as a critical reaction against the policy of 'hot water in the tap', proclaimed by Prime Minister Tusk in an interview he gave in 2010. The phrase he used was intended to capture the underlying idea of reducing tension and emotions in Polish political life, which seemed relatively successful until the landslide victory of right-wing and anti-establishment parties in 2015. That parliamentary election was also marked with the total demise of the left from the national political scene: neither new political movements, nor the traditionally powerful and well institutionalised post-communist left-wing party made it to the parliament.

Researching the process of the politicisation of fans seems important in this very moment, as it occurs also elsewhere and is particularly visible in other Central and Eastern European countries. Growing political tension all over the continent is apparent in such developments as the refugee crisis, the resurgence of nationalism in many countries, the rise of populism, Brexit and the crisis of the European Union and so on. The case of Polish football fandom and its radicalisation is not necessarily representative for the fandom all over Europe or for the reaction of the young generations towards contemporary challenges. Nevertheless, similar processes could be occurring elsewhere in various social groups and may be easily overlooked unless they are carefully observed by social scientists.

The social significance of research on football fans and politics

As has been emphasised, this book analyses the complex, multi-faceted and multi-dimensional world of football fandom in Poland. The case of Poland is an unprecedented example of unity in terms of ideological engagement and social identity cohesion.

This study presents the path of transformation and the main factors influencing the emergence and evolution of fans' political attitudes: the turbulent history of Polish society in the last decades, the conflict with government, the search for cardinal symbols and values, as well as the creation of 'Other' as an essential instrument to maintain the boundaries and social cohesion of the group. As a result of many social processes, Polish football fans have been steadfastly engaged in a conservative, right-wing model of identity. Our study offers an analysis of transformation of Polish fandom which is more embedded in the political and cultural context of Eastern Europe. As one of the first comprehensive publications devoted to this part of Europe, it could be used as a point of reference for future comparative studies.

The principal goal of this book is to introduce the topic and substantiate its wider significance not only as an issue of sociological investigation, but also as an important social and political phenomenon. The study aims to paint an in-depth picture of political engagement of Polish football fandom against the backdrop of the socio-cultural and political transformation of Polish society and economy in the last three decades. This historical change has had a significant impact on the world of Polish football fans and contributed to their political engagement.

Introduction 5

The more specific aim of this study is to provide an alternative model of transformation and modernisation of fandom related to the context of post-communist area. The objective of such an analysis is to show whether the existing typologies of football fans (mostly derived from Western European countries) could be useful for 'framing' fans from Eastern parts of Europe. Considering that the processes of modernisation and transformation of football and fandom in post-communist countries evolved differently, the implementation of available taxonomies in this context could be problematic. The discussion on categories of identity leads to the conceptualisation of a different model of transformation of fandom, one based on the case of Poland, which could be used as a frame of analysis in relation to other post-communist countries. This does not mean that the model derived from the Polish background fully corresponds to the situation in e.g. Romania, the Czech Republic or Hungary. However, the experience of modernisation and/or politicisation of fandom in Poland is much more similar to those countries than taxonomies based on the analysis of Western fandom, which has undergone significantly different processes and transformations.

Moreover, this book can be viewed as appealing to readers interested in more detailed themes in social sciences. First of all, it develops the study of football fans and fills a gap in this research field by providing Eastern European context. It offers an in-depth analysis of 'being a football fan' as a social practice in the course of particular political, historical and social transitions. In this way, it contributes to the understanding of the recent growth of right-wing sentiment in Eastern Europe and to knowledge about fandom politics in general. This context seems particularly important and timely in the European perspective, as the growth of radical right-wing/nationalist movements is clearly visible across the continent. At the same time, the study shows the weakness of left-wing discourse (using the Polish example) and the consequences of this phenomenon for football fandom and society in general. Finally, it contributes to knowledge about post-communist societies as it offers a multifaceted analysis of recent history, social transformation and political situation in Poland.

Considering the rapid and turbulent changes on the European political scene and in the internal politics of the European Union, the timing of this book seems very accurate. The growth of interest of European general public and academic circles in the state of affairs in Polish politics is visible since the parliamentary and presidential elections in 2015. The subsequent decisions of Poland's right-wing government are almost unanimously perceived by European elites as a move towards authoritarianism (or semi-authoritarianism) and/or illiberal democracy. This study, at least to some extent, contributes to the understanding of the phenomenon of support for the direction of changes proposed (or pursued) by right-wing politicians.

6   *Introduction*

In this way, this book makes a contribution to three interrelated research fields: sport, politics and transformation/modernisation themes. At the same time, it provides an analysis located at the crossroads of many other more specific areas, such as the sociology of sport, globalisation studies, East European politics, ethnic studies, social movements studies, political history and nationalism studies.

Methodology

Our book may be defined as a case study, as it focuses on a single national context. However, attempting to paint a comprehensive picture of Polish football fans and their political engagement as well as provide a broader socio-historical context of Polish society, it relies on various sources of data from various research projects (some methodological details provided in this section were also used in Woźniak, Kossakowski and Nosal, 2019).

It is a cross-sectional work, as it is not limited to one theoretical perspective or methodological tradition, but combines different approaches. It may be viewed as a critical sociological inquiry using mixed-methods research integrating qualitative and quantitative techniques. Therefore, quantitative data (from a number of independent sources) is complemented by a variety of qualitative data from in-depth interviews, content analysis and participant observation. Such a procedure does not aim to increase objectivity but rather to deepen the knowledge and understanding of the phenomenon under investigation. We follow the triangulation approach developed by Uwe Flick, who states that 'if the issue in question requires more than one approach, it may be necessary to include more than one researcher' (2017, p. 54). Our analysis includes perspectives of three researchers who are academic sociologists but approach many issues in different ways. Consequently, final conclusions presented here come as a result of numerous meetings, conversations and exchange of arguments. All the authors have benefited from the process of preparation and writing but the most important thing is that the content of the book seems to be richer, more mature and more reflexive than in the case of a single-author study.

In addition to investigator triangulation, we incorporate both qualitative and quantitative data in our analysis. It needs to be clarified, however, that the two methodological strategies were not part of one research project. The results of quantitative web-based surveys are used as a starting point and a basis for a more thorough elaboration, which mainly relies on qualitative data. We incorporate data from two online surveys. One was a quantitative survey conducted by Radosław Kossakowski in 2017 among 309 active football supporters who declared their active engagement in formal (supporters' associations) or informal social groups (e.g. ultras or hooligans) related to the club and football. The other was conducted by Sport Analytics, one of the largest Polish research agencies specialising in sport-related topics, carrying out surveys and studies for the purposes of market research and analytical

Introduction 7

support for sport organisations. This online survey was conducted in February 2017 among the supporters of clubs from Poland's top division. The final sample of 1,508 questionnaires was selected using stratified sampling from the database of 8,090 questionnaires and weighed according to the gender, age and the club supported by the respondent (on the basis of official data on match attendance in Poland's top division).

Although online surveys have their well-known limitations and cannot be considered fully representative, since both studies reveal surprising similarities it seems that they reflect the actual state of fans' preferences. At the same time, however, quantitative data allow only for some superficial insight and therefore we use a multitude of qualitative data gathered during fieldwork and supplemented with secondary sources, such as press releases, journal articles, internet forums and websites. This variety of data allows for more in-depth interpretations.

All authors engaged in participatory observation during the matches of Lech Poznań, Lechia Gdańsk, Widzew Łódź and the Polish national team. All authors had attended games played by those clubs for many years but for the purposes of our analysis we collected data from ten matches in each city. Out of all cases under consideration, we only investigated the matches during which ultras presented political content. Some observations were conducted from sectors other than ultras stands (to see all choreographies clearly) and some – from ultras stands in order to feel the atmosphere and experience of presentation of political ideas. All researchers are experienced visitors of stadiums in Gdańsk, Łódź and Poznań and they did not encounter any problems getting admitted to ultras stands. The authors also participated in many non-sporting activities undertaken by fans, e.g. political demonstrations, fans' patriotic pilgrimage to Jasna Góra Monastery in Częstochowa (the most important Roman Catholic sanctuary in Poland), the Independence March in Warsaw and others. And thirdly, data from semi-structured interviews with fans are used as well. All the quotations are marked as follows: [Club_supporter], [City_occupation], as people who are not engaged in fandom have also been interviewed. All information concerning the informants has been anonymised.

The following quotations and observations are based on research conducted under a SONATA 5 grant from the National Science Centre (Poland) (no. 2013/09/D/HS/6/00238) and a grant funded by UEFA under the UEFA Research Grant Programme, 2015/16 edition (for Radosław Kossakowski). For the purpose of the study, 52 interviews (which lasted between 20 minutes and three hours each) have been analysed – 44 informants were male and eight were female. The research sample included not only fans but also officials, journalists, representatives of football clubs and organisations cooperating with fans (e.g. NGOs). The interviews were conducted in 2013–2018.

8   *Introduction*

What is this book about?

This book consists of this Introduction (Chapter 1), eight chapters and a Conclusion. Chapter 2 is based on detailed desk research into the political engagement of fans in Central and Eastern Europe, and considers different approaches to the study of relations between fans and politics. Providing the state of art on this topic country by country, it presents the main research patterns and identifies the main gaps. Chapter 3 highlights crucial processes in Poland during the transformation. The aim here is to provide an overview of the state of affairs in the country in two major spheres: economic and social policy, as well as social divisions and party politics. Historical developments in both of them have contributed to the current shape of the Polish political scene and contemporary socio-political divisions. Chapter 4 is focused on the historical perspective. It takes into consideration the political role of Polish fans in the more distant past: under the partitions, in the pre-Second World War period and under the communist regime. Some cultural patterns from those times have influenced significantly the field of fandom in the post-1989 period. Chapter 5, in turn, provides an insight into Poland of the 1990s. The beginning of the post-socialist transformation and the introduction of market economy brought skyrocketing unemployment and pauperisation of significant segments of Polish society. In this particular context, the field of sport as well as fandom as such were abandoned as the government focused on the most pressing economic and social problems. In effect, the field of football in the 1990s was characterised by a decline in sports performance, sport-related corruption and the rule of hooligans in the terraces. Further fan activity has developed against the background of this period. Chapter 6 scrutinises the political reaction to football-related violence on the one hand, and the political mobilisation of the terraces on the other. It examines the episodes of elite-engineered moral panic and increasingly more restrictive legal regulations. Chapter 7 describes Polish fandom as it is today, focusing on its civic, social and political engagement. The largest one, Chapter 8 is devoted to ideology on the Polish terraces. The analysis makes use of various sources: survey results, interview quotes, slogans and chants. The key findings are classified into several groups: affinity with Catholicism, conservative values, re-emergence of nationalism, belated communism, anti-establishment attitudes and xenophobia. While previous chapters focus on club supporters as the most politically active group, Chapter 9 considers fans of the Polish national team and their political engagement. Covering the period between 1921 and 2019, it shows their transition from politicisation to depoliticisation. Finally, the Conclusion tries to answer three more general questions: Are fans causative agents in the political sense? Where is the left side of fandom? Is Polish fandom specific?

References

Burski, J. (2013). Euro 2012 – The end and the beginning of Polish football supporters. *Przegląd Socjologiczny*, 62(3), pp. 51–70.

Doidge, M. (2013). 'The birthplace of Italian communism': Political identity and action amongst Livorno fans. *Soccer & Society*, 14(2), pp. 246–261. https://doi.org/10.1080/14660970.2013.776471

Doidge, M., Kossakowski, R. and Mintert, S. (2020). *Ultras: The Passion and Performance of Contemporary Football Fandom*. Manchester: Manchester University Press.

Flick, U. (2017). Mantras and myths: The disenchantment of mixed-methods research and revisiting triangulation as a perspective. *Qualitative Inquiry*, 23(1), pp. 46–57, https://doi.org/10.1177/1077800416655827

Jacobsson, K. and Korolczuk, E. (2019). Mobilizing grassroots in the city: Lessons for civil society research in Central and Eastern Europe. *International Journal of Politics, Culture, and Society*. Published online ahead of print. https://doi.org/10.1007/s10767-019-9320-7

Kossakowski, R. (2017). *Od chuliganów do aktywistów. Polscy kibice i zmiana społeczna* [From hooligans to activists. Polish fans and the social change]. Kraków: Universitas.

Kossakowski, R., Szlendak, T. and Antonowicz, D. (2018). Polish ultras in the post-socialist transformation. *Sport in Society*, 21(6), pp. 854–869. https://doi.org/10.1080/17430437.2017.1300387

Pacewicz, K. (2019a). Młodzi mężczyźni są prawicowi i samotni, a młode kobiety liberalne i w związkach [Young males are right-wing and lonely, young females liberal and in relationships]. *Gazeta Wyborcza* [online]. Available at: http://wyborcza.pl/magazyn/7,124059,24700696,mlodzi-wypisali-sie-z-politycznej-wojny-starszych-maja.html [accessed 5 Aug. 2019].

Pacewicz, K. (2019b). Młodzi mężczyźni na wojnie o wartości. Dlaczego popierają Konfederację? [Young males at the war for values. Why do they support Confederation]? *Gazeta Wyborcza* [online]. Available at: http://wyborcza.pl/7,75398,24820306,mlodzi-mezczyzni-na-wojnie-o-wartosci-dlaczego-popieraja-konfederacje.html [accessed 5 Aug. 2019].

Woźniak, W. (2015). Euro 2012 i Kraków 2022. Polskie elity polityczne wobec wielkich imprez sportowych [Euro 2012 and Cracow 2022. Polish political elites towards sport mega events]. *Przegląd Socjologii Jakościowej*, 9(2): 60–83. Available at: http://przegladsocjologiijakosciowej.org/Volume30/PSJ_11_2_Wozniak.pdf [accessed 30 May 2019].

Woźniak, W., Kossakowski R., and Nosal P. (2019). A squad with no left wingers: The roots and structure of right-wing and nationalist attitudes among Polish football fans. *Problems of Post-Communism*. Published online ahead of print. 7 November 2019, DOI: 10.1080/10758216.2019.1673177.

2 Football fans and their political engagement in Central and Eastern Europe

State of the art

Introduction

The relation between football and politics has become an important topic in social sciences. In effect, there is a growing number of studies on fans' political activism. They can be classified into several groups.

The basic type of studies reflects on the general political commitment of football supporters. The authors describe fans as 'political subjects' and present different forms of their engagement (Brown, 1998; Blackshaw, 2008; Guschwan, 2016). Some works categorise fan activism as 'leftist' or 'rightist', so there is an extensive literature on left-wing (e.g. Kennedy, 2013; Kennedy and Kennedy, 2014; Spaaij and Viñas, 2013) and right-wing fans (e.g. Armstrong and Testa, 2008, 2010).

The second kind of studies frequently delivers a continental, cross-national or national analysis of fans and politics. For instance – fans and politics in Europe (De Waele, Gibril, Gloriozova and Spaaij, 2018), in Latin America (Bar-On, 1997) or in a single country, e.g. Northern Ireland (Bairner and Shirlow, 1998) or Greece (Zaimakis, 2018). A narrower concept considers particular football club as 'political', e.g. FC Sankt Pauli (Daniel and Kassimeris, 2013) or Livorno (Doidge, 2013).

A different approach is focused on a single political issue in terms of football fans' commitment. The authors explore their activism in the context of national or ethnic identity (e.g. Hayes, 2006; Barcelo, Clinton and Sero, 2015; McManus, 2015); racism (e.g. Podaliri and Balestri, 1998; Cleland and Cashmore, 2016); religion (e.g. Millward, 2008; Straton, 2015), homophobia (e.g. Cleland, 2015; Cashmore and Cleland, 2012) or legal restrictions (Tsoukala, 2009)

Some researchers also describe certain political incidents, for instance manifestations, protests or political revolutions, from the perspective of participating football fans. They investigate supporters' activism during, for example, Arab Spring in Egypt (Dorsey, 2012; Tuastad, 2014; Gibril, 2015) or the Taksim-Gezi Park protests in Turkey (Irak, 2018; Turan and Özçetin,

Football fans and their political engagement 11

2017; Battini and Koşulu, 2018). One sub-area of this field is research on political activity within the stadium and in the terraces. In this case, analysis is focused on slogans (e.g. Papoutzis et al., 2014; Stylianou and Theodoropoulou, 2013) or chants (e.g. Clark, 2006; Knijnik, 2016),

Finally, there are studies on fans as voters, where researchers try to find out how being a fan can explain voting decisions. Such analyses concern the impact of the 'fan factor' on voting in parliamentary elections (Cowley and Ford, 2016a), municipal elections (Forment, 2007) or in various referendums (Kelly, 2013; Cowley and Ford, 2016b). Besides, some investigations use surveys to ask fans about their political sympathies (Fridy and Brobbey, 2009).

To sum up this review, the Western context of these studies is significant and political activism of fans in England, Germany or Spain is explored in detail. The goal of this chapter is to provide a description of fans' political commitment in Central and Eastern Europe (hereafter: CEE).

Central and Eastern Europe

Central and Eastern Europe (CEE) is a grouping of countries with specific historical background which share some crucial features in their twenty-first century history: the experience of socialism-communism, the different ways of transition from non-democratic regimes and the diverse current conditions (Arnason, 2005; Berend, 2005). These characteristics affect the patterns of fans' political activism.

In this chapter, CEE is defined in terms of both political and geographical conditions. The analysis includes Ukraine, Belarus and Russia; the Baltic republics of Lithuania, Latvia and Estonia; Czechia, Slovakia, Hungary, Romania, Bulgaria and Moldova; Serbia, Croatia, Bosnia and Herzegovina, Slovenia, Montenegro, Macedonia, Kosovo (former Yugoslavia) and Albania. Thus, the chapter does not concern some former Soviet republics: Kazakhstan, Kyrgyzstan, Uzbekistan, Turkmenistan and Tajikistan. Besides, it omits the Transcaucasian countries of Georgia, Armenia and Azerbaijan. Although East Germany, prior to German reunification, is also sometimes described as an Eastern European country, the issue of East German fans is not considered here due to a different path of transition and problematic 'current condition'. Finally, an analysis of Polish fans can be found in Chapters 4–10.

This literature review includes studies on football fans and political activism in individual countries which are available in English: books or book chapters, journal articles, study reports and opinions of experts published in newspapers or magazines; literature on Poland can be found in a separate chapter.

Ukraine

Considering that the Ukrainian Soviet Socialist Republic was one of the largest and most significant constituent republics of the Soviet Union, football in Ukraine during this period has been studied in many aspects,

12 *Football fans and their political engagement*

including research on national team fans, which emphasised their hostility against Russia (Edelman, 1993, pp. 61–66, 98–115) and covered the topic of club supporters' political involvement in 1945–1989, e.g. Dinamo Kiev (Zeller, 2011).

The recent studies are deeply rooted in this past. Olga Ruzhelnyk compares the historical background of clubs and their past pro-/anti-Moscow stand with the map of sympathy-hostility relations between supporters in the new-born Ukraine (Ruzhelnyk, 2018). Fans are perceived as key figures of political changes, both as agents of political change impacting politics and as those influenced by events on the political scene (Ruzhelnyk, 2018, p. 311). Elena Volkava and Maciej Bartkowski stress that particularly the role of ultras exceeds the regular significance of stadium-based fandom as their political mobilisation ignited by diverse factors was very much visible all over the country (Volkava and Bartkowski, 2014).

The available studies provide an insight into today's political dilemmas of fans. On the one hand, the authors describe decisions on very specific dilemmas: contestation or co-operation with politicians-oligarchs (Veth, 2015) or fans' attitudes towards the annexation of the Crimea (Walker, 2018). On the other hand, the more general discussion concerns the division of fandom: right-wing and left-wing activism.

The right side of the stands seems to be more crowded. The Ukrainian ultras movement is formed of many far-right groups. The most important of them support Dynamo Kyiv (Dynami-131, Mobi Capitals, Young Hope, Kefirs Crew, Trudovye Rezervy, U27, Terror Family, Kids of Capital, Ultra' Fazione etc.), CSKA Kiev (CSKA-94), Karpaty Lviv (Green Lions, West Boys, Werwolf, Lviv City Firm, The Pride), Dnipro (River Sharks Firm, Barracudas, Avangard Fight Club) (see Ghosh, 2011). While most of them are strictly nationalist and anti-Russian, some also formulate racist (see Lewycka, 2012) or anti-migrant slogans (see Ghosh, 2011, p. 14). However, there are also left-wing ultras. One example is Arsenal Kiev fandom, describing themselves as anti-fascists who reject racism and hail social justice (Veth, 2013). Another case is Karpaty Lviv supporters. In 2012 they created a 'club calendar' serving the purpose of situational crime prevention. In this calendar, football players call on fans with personal quotes like: 'I use my strength only in order to win in a fair game, but not in relation to the loved ones'. In this case, the preventive measure is a declaration of contempt of domestic violence by professional players involved in the tournament, thereby distancing the aggression on the pitch from the domestic environment (Kirby, Francis and O'Flaherty, 2014).

In spite of their socio-political divisions, fans are capable of uniting in some serious situations. Maryna Krugliak and Oleksandr Krugliak describe 'the unlikely alliance of Ukrainian football ultras' in the Pavlichenko case (Krugliak and Krugliak, 2017, pp. 176–178). Dmitry Pavlichenko and his son Sergey were charged with the murder of judge Sergey Zubkov. In the judgment handed down in October 2012, Dmitry was sentenced to life

Football fans and their political engagement 13

imprisonment, and his nineteen-year-old son Sergey received a 13-year sentence. Since Sergey is an active supporter of FC Dynamo Kyiv, in 2011 Dynamo ultras began organising rallies to support him (for more on the Pavlichenko case, see Bondarenko, 2012). Another case was a march and protest against the Russian annexation of the Crimea (Gordon, 2014).

Nevertheless, the most spectacular political experience of Ukrainian fandom has been the Euromaidan movement. In 2013–2014 many of them were engaged in the protests and riots in Kiev. Most of the ultras were anti-government (Volkava and Bartkowski, 2014; Sergatskova, 2014); only some of the Odessa, Sevastopol and Donetsk fans supported Viktor Yanukovych (cf. McArdle and Veth, 2015; Portnov, 2014). The ultras provided protection for the revolutionaries in Maidan and were involved in street fights (Katchanovski, 2016). Most of them came from subcultural antifascist/football ultras networks. Arsenal Kiev supporters were particularly important. However, they cooperated with the far right in street actions:

Joining them was something of a logical step for activists with a stronger commitment to street fights than to any coherent ideology. In comments and interviews they mention different justifications for direct cooperation with the far right, for example: 'we forgot our conflicts in the face of aggressor and occupant', 'the far right do not have their own agenda in this war', 'the ultra-right, like the left, are in the minority; the majority are generally democratic or moderately patriotic people'.

(Ishchenko, 2016, p. 77)

The inter-club ultras group proclaimed an indefinite truce to promote the joint struggle against the regime. The symbolic act of unification came with the common manifesto issued by the ultras of FC Dnipro (Dnipro, called Dnipropetrovsk until May 2016), FC Zorya (Luhansk), FC Metalist (Kharkiv), FC Chornomorets (Odessa) and FC Shakhtar Donetsk, where they expressed their support of Euromaidan:

we believe that at the moment the relationship between us should be built by the principle that we are the Ukrainians in the first place. That also means that trust, mutual understanding and assistance should be in the first place as well. We call on all the Ukrainian fans, which are not members of any fan movements (not only in football) to join the truce and treat each other with no aggression regardless of the club affiliation. That is why we believe that to continue any confrontation in the fan environment at this moment – a crime against the bright future of Ukraine. From Luhansk to the Carpathians all fans are brothers to each other! Glory to Ukraine!

(Krugliak and Krugliak, 2017, p. 178)

14 *Football fans and their political engagement*

Although after the Euromaidan the truce was over (Ruzhelnyk, 2018, pp. 324–325), the most current research asks questions about the legacy of Euromaidan and further political commitment of fans (Fisun, 2014).

Belarus

A growing political role of football fans can be observed in Belarus, where they have become important actors of political contestation. Some insight into this issue is provided by Vadim Bylina, who calls fans 'a community beyond the government's control in the conditions of the authoritarian regime' (Bylina, 2015a). His analysis of Belarusian fandom stresses a pluralism of ideologies and a high degree of adaptability of football fans to political challenges (Bylina, 2015a, p. 58). He also emphasises that the government views all groups of Belarusian supporters as dangerously subversive, which makes the police control more strict or even openly violent (see Bylina, 2013a). In effect, this situation leads to a stronger consolidation of fan movements, with supporters cooperating in two principal areas.

The first is political and public protests – manifestations, boycotts, sometimes even riots, which can be addressed against national authorities; they are not very common but they happen. Dinamo Minsk ultras, right-wing and openly racist, are very active in this context (Bylina, 2013a). In 2011 the fans protested against the regime during the matches:

> fans chanted 'We Hate the Regime' and used abusive words against the police for several minutes. (…) Again in the summer of 2011, in the midst of the financial crisis and the so called 'silent protests' that swept across the country, BATE fans chanted «ШОС» (an ambiguous anti-government abbreviation which usually stands for 'let him die' or 'let him go to jail') during an away match in Lithuania against Ekranas Panevezys.
>
> (Bylina 2015a, p. 57)

Furthermore, fans protest against Russian influence on their country. Sometimes they are strictly anti-Russian, sometimes they express solidarity with Ukraine or Georgia (Bylina, 2015b). Kamil Kłysiński and Piotr Żochowski view Belarusian football fans as underestimated. They underline the prevalence of nationalist attitudes and anti-Russian hostility, sometimes expressed up to the point of personal involvement in anti-Russian struggle for the Ukrainian cause (Kłysiński and Żochowski, 2016, pp. 20–21).

The second is civic engagement – organising leisure activities (sports tournaments, concerts), involvement in charitable work, governance of local football teams, etc. One interesting example at that stage are Partizan Minsk (formerly FC MTZ-RIPO) fans. When the foreign investor left the club, the supporters raised funds to keep it alive. As it is today, Partizan is self-governed by the fans. Besides, they identify themselves as leftists, anti-racists and anti-fascists (Bylina, 2013b; Uthoff, 2013).

Football fans and their political engagement 15

To sum up, Vadim Bylina points out the political emancipation of the fandom, which is difficult to control and to monitor, unlike registered civic organisations (Bylina 2015a, p. 59). The Belarusian fandom has a very subversive political potential, although it has not yet been fully activated.

Russia

The issue of football fans and politics in the Soviet Union has been studied in great detail by many historians and social scientists. The available literature provides the analysis of the role of fans in intrarepublic relations (mainly with Ukrainians or Georgians, briefed in the previous or further subchapters) or the studies on the internal Russian relations – a general social history of football (Riordan, 1977; Sugden and Tomlinson, 2000; Edelman, 1993, pp. 44–71; Borrero, 2017; Duke and Crolley, 2014, pp. 85–95; Grant, 2014) or history of particular clubs (e.g. Edelman, 2002; 2012; 2013; Ovsepyan, 2017; Bennetts, 2009; Gloriozova, 2018, pp. 270–273). However, this section is focused on the recent political activism of Russian fans.

The frequently described political attitude of fans is violent nationalism. Russian hooligans are perceived as one of the most aggressive and the most prepared for fight in the world. They proclaim 'Russian pride' and fight for 'Russian supremacy'. The national team hooligans were reported to be aggressive at EURO 2012 (Riach, 2012) and EURO 2016 (Boffey, 2016a), and their expected behaviour was also widely discussed in connection with the World Cup in 2018. The basis of this 'national army' are hooligan groups supporting particular clubs, mainly CSKA's Moscow 'Red Blue Warriors', Spartak's 'Flint's Crew', Dynamo's 'Blue-White Dynamites' or Zenit's Sankt Petersburg 'Nevsky Front'. Apart from Russian national team matches they fight one another, and relations between Zenit, Spartak and CSKA are particularly hostile (Armstrong, 2016a; Armstrong, 2016b).

Some researchers describe Russian hooligans as 'the armed forces of national political authorities', a form of 'official nationalism' (Arnold, 2018). The interdependence between politics, business and football is recognised as a fact. Fans pursue some political goals – they give support to certain issues in the stadium or when they cause riots (Loginov, 2012; Jones, 2016; Rothfel, 2016; Boffey, 2016b; Osborne, 2016). In return, they gain political legitimisation – media support, legal protection or assistance in doing their own business (de Menezes, 2016; Boren, 2017; Gorst, 2018). Some fan leaders even become politicians, like Alexander Shprygin (cf. Gibson, 2016; Gibson and Walker, 2016). Ekaterina Gloriozova, who analyses the transformation of Russian hooligans, notes that in order to diminish collateral damage they fight in remote areas (e.g. in forests), while the authorities turn a blind eye on some of their illegal activities (Gloriozova, 2018, p. 279).

Their nationalism appears also in another context: hooligans have been the main characters in *racist incidents*, mostly involving dark-skinned players from Africa or Latin America (Arnold and Veth, 2018; Arnold, 2015). In

16 *Football fans and their political engagement*

2012 the Zenit fan club 'Landscrona' published the letter called 'Selection manifesto 12', stating as follows:

> We're not racists but we see the absence of black players at Zenit as an important tradition. (...) Dark-skinned players are being imposed on Zenit almost by force, which only brings out a negative reaction. (...) Gay players are unworthy of our great city. (...) It would allow Zenit to maintain the national identity of the club, which is the symbol of St Petersburg.
>
> (Zenit St. Petersburg fans petition club, 2012)

Besides, the studies emphasise the increasing neo-Nazi character of the hooligan movement in Russia (Parkin, 2018). Their extremist right-wing ideology is apparent from their banners, chants or slogans and violent behaviour (Glathe, 2016).

However, it is worth noting the only recognised left-side (minor) fan group – Red-White Djigits, Spartak Nalchik ultras, who call themselves 'the ultras all of Russia hates' (Petkova, 2018). The group is not important on the fan stage but gives it a touch of political differentiation.

The Baltic States: Lithuania, Latvia and Estonia

Football is not the most popular sport in the Baltic States, and especially Lithuanian and Latvian supporters prioritize basketball (Senn, 1990). In effect, the rare studies of fans' commitment usually cover this discipline (e.g. Valantinė, Grigaliūnaitė and Danilevičienė, 2017). Aldis Purs notes that 'The most central aspect of the cultish place of basketball, ice hockey and to a lesser degree football for identity is that international achievement reinforces Latvian and Lithuanian beliefs in themselves on a larger stage' (Purs, 2012, p. 170).

Apart from that there is a potential for research on football fans and politics, especially when authors explore two plots of these relations. On the one hand, the national football teams remain a widely recognised representation of the Baltic nations. It happened especially in the past that teams were used to build the nation-state awareness and anti-Soviet resistance (Sugden and Tomlinson, 2000, p. 99). As it is today, the national football team is still perceived as an important symbol, the second or third, after the basketball, hockey or volleyball squad.

On the other hand, the football ultras movement has a long history in Lithuania and Latvia. The Zalgiris Vilnus' ultras group 'Pietu IV' ('South IV') emerged in 1985 and rescued the club during the financial crisis in 2009. Dougie Brimson describes the violent behaviour of the 'Senoji Gvardija', the ultra group of FBK Kaunas from Latvia, in the early 2000s (Brimson, 2003, p. 216). A powerful ultras group, 'H-Side', supports Skonto Riga; it continues to exist despite the fact that the club went bankrupt in 2016. The condition of club supporters in Estonia is even weaker than in Lithuania or Latvia. The

Football fans and their political engagement 17

majority of fans are in Tallin and cheer FC Flora or Levadia. However, most supporters are only focused on the national team.

The Baltic states' fandom is regarded as inconsiderable and insignificant. Nevertheless, even supporters of this kind can easily engage in politics, especially in protests or other acts of contestation.

Czechia and Slovakia

The background for the present analysis of football fans and politics in Czechia and Slovakia is the historical research on the fandom in Czechoslovakia. The studies introduce a broad scope of everyday sport-based practices as acts of resistance against the communist regime. Dino Numerato writes about the 'little symbolic acts of opposition' (Numerato, 2010). Stefan Zwicker stresses the role of clubs, football idols and sports events during the Cold War period (Zwicker, 2013). This 'ordinary involvement' can also be found in today's attitudes of fans.

Czechia

The important element of the Czech fandom is its civic engagement. Numerato describes the Bohemians Prague 1905 fans as social activists (Numerato, 2017). His analysis includes a list of positive assets of their involvement: building and maintaining relationship with local communities, generating social capital, bringing rationality to governance, supervising politics (Numerato, 2017, p. 213). Besides, they saved the club during its financial crisis and struggled to keep their traditional stadium Ďolíček (Numerato, 2017, p. 217). This is the 'mundane politics' of football fans.

Apart from that, Jan Charvát pays particular attention to 'anti-fascist reputation' of Bohemians fans, which is surprising because 'a racist or even neo-Nazi orientation was exhibited by an overwhelming majority of football rowdies and especially hooligans at that time [in the 1990s]' (Charvát, 2017, p. 43). This far-left and anti-fascist attitude is unobvious in the fan community. A recent study provides evidence that many groups of Czech football hooligans are far-right sympathisers (Cenek and Smolík, 2015). In general, although the problem of hooligan violence is identified and widely described (Duke and Slepička, 2002; Smolík, 2012; Scholz, 2016), its political character is still increasing.

Many authors notice that some football ultras and hooligans proclaim right-wing extremism by racist and anti-Semitic displays (shouting, chants), using Nazi or other far-right symbols on banners, committing acts of racism or homophobia, declaring hostility to European Union or Muslims, etc. (cf. Mareš, 2012). Hooligans are called 'active proponents of extremism and radicalization' (Report on extremism, 2017).

In the context of Czech hooligan subcultures it is worth stressing that there are also entirely apolitical or far-left football hooligans. Josef Smolík,

18 *Football fans and their political engagement*

commenting on the interconnection of football hooliganism and extremism in the Czech Republic, claims that anti-social behaviour of fans may be linked to their political extremism, but no generalisations would be fully founded empirically (Smolík, 2004).

Slovakia

Political extremism is increasing also in Slovakian football. Daniela Kušnierová elaborates on this process referring to the presence of the same phenomena as elsewhere: xenophobia, anti-Semitism, nationalism and local patriotism (Kušnierová, 2014, p. 92). Exploring Spartak Trnava ultras, Kušnierová gives examples of these forms of political manifestation (pp. 92–93). Other authors also notice far-right sympathies among Slovakian ultras (Harsányi, 2005). Tomáš Nociar comments that in parallel to the weakening of the skinhead movement, the ultra-right ideology is on the rise among football fanbase (Nociar, 2012, p. 2).

The ultras and hooligans seriously involved in right-wing politics are still the minority of Slovakian fandom. However, they are the most visible and proclaim their slogans the loudest.

Hungary

Football in Hungary, despite the lack of success at the international level, is an important identity factor. In effect, it has been the subject of strong politicisation (Hadas, 2000; Földesi and Egressy, 2005). In his socio-historical overview, Gyozo Molnar shows that football was mostly used for propaganda purposes:

> Football has been used for perpetuating violence-related hegemonic values, gaining larger independence from oppression, re-establishing broken post-war diplomatic relations, conveying political propaganda and ideological superiority and stabilizing social conditions. (…) In conclusion, it can be observed that football has remained subject to political manipulation, only the angle of presentation has changed.
>
> (Molnar, 2007, p. 313)

Fan culture in Hungary is well developed: diverse in terms of locations, well-organised and quite numerous. Hungarian ultras are well-known at European stadiums: Green Monsters (Ferencváros), Ultra Red Boys Kispest (Honvéd Budapest), Ultra Viola Bulldogs (Újpest Budapest), Szívtipró Ultras Debrecen (Debrecen), Red Blue Devils '92 (Videoton Székesfehérvár), Keleti Front '92 (Nyíregyháza Spartacus). However, in terms of political sympathies they are mostly unified. All the groups – except MTK Budapest fans, who declare themselves as ideologically non-political – are right-wing, very often nationalist. They take part in patriotic manifestations and support the current government. There

Football fans and their political engagement   19

have also been racist (anti-Roma) and anti-Semitic incidents (Barna and Hunyadi, 2015, pp. 68–69).

Many fan groups also cultivate the political nostalgia for Great Hungary, the territorial restoration of pre-1920 Kingdom of Hungary, which they present on banners or in slogans and chants. Against this background, there is a conflict between Hungarian and Slovakian, Romanian and Serbian fans. The context is post-Trianon Hungarian 'lost territories', which include parts of Carpathian Ruthenia, Vojvodina and Transylvania. Judith Hamberger notes:

> The Slovak football matches are good opportunities both for Hungarians and Slovaks to express hostile feelings. The team and fans of Dunaszerda-hely FC DAC 1904 (the Slovakian name is FC DAC 1904 Dunajská Streda) which represents Hungarian Slovaks in the national championship are exposed to the nationalism of Slovak football fans.
>
> (Hamberger, 2008, p. 56)

She reports the riots which started at the end of October 2008 when Spartak Trnava played with DAC and continued on 1 November with the match of Slovan and DAC:

> The organized provocation of Hungarian football fans evoked another provocation from Slovak riot-police. After these events the Hungarian-Slovak conflict was deepened by some other events: a demonstration in Budapest, Hungarian provocations, the border blockade of extremist Hungarians. Apparently, Hungary fell into the nationalist 'trap' of the Slovak government: these extreme actions inside our borders threaten the situation of Hungarian Slovaks and render Hungarian ambitions more difficult on the international scene.
>
> (Hamberger, 2008, p. 56)

The category of the 'nationalist trap' can be useful for understanding fandom in many other CEE countries.

Romania

The relation between football fans and politics in Romania has been studied in many aspects. Historical analyses cover the pre-war (László, 2014), interwar (Faje, 2015) and communist periods (Borisov, 2015, p. 113–116). They show the state's expansion and the web of interdependences between regionalism, ethnicity, nationalism and Romanian football. Florin Faje points out two major dimensions of historical relations between fans and politics:

> First, for a century the Romanian state, under various political regimes, used football to promote and popularly disseminate its nation-building

20 *Football fans and their political engagement*

agendas. By the 1980s, this investment on the part of the state was finally delivering the goods, at both club and national team levels. Second, this period witnessed a massive shift in the politics of history, one that could not leave football unscathed. The aggressive nationalism of the late Romanian Communist regime was superseded by an equally aggressive anti-communism that tended to emphasise the supposed 'liberal' traditions of the interwar. State politics and the politics of history coupled with the Romanian footballing triumphs combined to create a nationalistic popular narrative of Romanian football, while doing away with the material and ideological developments that have made it possible.

(Faje, 2018, p. 245)

Today's research on fandom and politics in Romania is focused on three main topics. The first is football fans' political activism, which is very often expressed by violent behaviours. The old political sectarianism is still an important context of hooligan fights. It explains the present hostility between fans of Steaua, Rapid and Dinamo Bucharest (Lepădatu, 2015), or among other clubs outside the capital (Beiu, 2005). The other significant context of violence is ethno-nationalism. It includes ethnic/national (e.g. Romanian–Hungarian relations) (see Hughes, 2014) and racial aspects (e.g. the Roma people) (for example, Romania played their Euro 2016 qualifier at home with Finland behind closed doors after racist and violent behaviour of their fans during the matches against Hungary and Greece). This ideology remains the background for many acts of fan violence. Faje describes this phenomenon on the example of Cluj fandom (Faje, 2011). Nevertheless, fans also contest political authorities. They took part in the anti-corruption protests in 2012, 2017 and 2018 (Kornievych and Fedeczko, 2018), and were regarded as the trigger for their violent course.

The second topic is the tension in fans' attitudes between local activism and passive consumerism (Izzo et al., 2011). For Dino Guțu, the ultras movement is a manifestation of the pro-active and conscious search for the cultural identity by young people – 'cultural bricolage' (Guțu, 2017). Furthermore, Faje stresses the engagement of fans in the disputes about the ownership of sport clubs' names, symbols and records, e.g. Steaua Bucharest, Rapid Bucharest, Universitatea Craiova, Politehnica Timişoara (Faje 2018: 261). Remus Crețan describes Timosoara fans' resistance against the renaming of their club in the same terms (Crețan 2018). Finally, Simona Ionescu, Sorinel Voicu and Radu Gabor (2010) explore the phenomenon of Politehnica Timişoara ultras (Commando Viola Ultra Curva Sud) as an example of well-organised informal structures, an important marker of social capital.

The third topic is fandom and the legacy of transformation. Romania remains one of the very few CEE countries where the transition of football fans in the political transformation has been explored in detail, and where authors analyse the 'long shadow' of communism. Adrian Beiu presents the 'rebranding' of old politicians from communists to capitalists on the example

Football fans and their political engagement 21

of Romanian football and its fans (Beiu, 2006). Melissa McDonald considers the impact of oligarchs on the clubs and their supporters (McDonald, 2014). She describes the figure of Gigi Becali, the owner of Steaua Bucharest, and the reaction of fans to his political engagement:

> While FC Steaua fans are divided, the hooligans of the stadium, known as ultras, appreciate Becali's approach and mimic his racism through chants and posters they display at matches. In contrast, many longstanding Steaua fans have contested Becali's influence on the club. In 2007, fans, who were in disagreement with Becali's behavior, opted to write a manifesto in protest of Becali's actions that stain the longstanding pride and honour of the club. The manifesto was followed by chants at matches including 'Becali go!'. Nonetheless, the Steaua fans account for almost half of all football fans in Romania, giving Becali a constant audience.
>
> (McDonald, 2014, p. 45)

The role of former members of communist nomenklatura remains an important issue in recent studies.

In turn, Guţu examines the phenomenon of ultras football gangs' survival networks and clientelism (Guţu, 2018). He emphasises fans' adaptive skills, when in face of growing economic inequality and financial insecurity, Dinamo's ultras increasingly came to rely on goods, contacts, status and prestige flowing through informal networks of exchange developed in and around the stadium, practices that assured their belonging and hardened their loyalty and attachment to their peers and their club, often to the exclusion of outsiders.

Romanian studies on fans and politics offer one of the most comprehensive analysis of fandom in CEE. The available papers adopt different research perspectives and consider a variety of issues. Moreover, the studies on transformation provide a wider knowledge about the post-communist context.

Bulgaria

The relation between football and politics in Bulgaria has a long history. The available studies present fandom under the communist regime as the object of socialist propaganda on the one hand, and the subject of resistance on the other (Kortazov, 2012; Borisov, 2015). CSKA Sofia and Levski Sofia were the most important clubs during this period and important political agents. Georgi Georgiev comments on their political roles as follows:

> CSKA Sofia was founded by a decree of the Communist Party and was assigned to Ministry of Defense 1948 while Levski Sofia was founded in 1914 but it was assigned by the Communist Party to the State Security Department. This actuality has shaped Levski Sofia fans view of themselves as victim of a forced alliance to the Communist apparatus in contrary to their self-proclaimed bourgeoisie origin. These accusations have

22 *Football fans and their political engagement*

led to fierce rivalry where the political significance become much greater than the sport competition itself.

(Georgiev, 2017, p. 8)

Both clubs, then, have had a significant political meaning, which was even enhanced during the democratic transformation. Tihomir Bezlov, describing the story of Bulgarian football during the post-communist transition, elaborates on how clubs were used for money laundering and tax evasion practices. Violent fans were becoming street pressure groups, sometimes instrumentally used for political purposes (Bezlov, 2015, p. 102).

Current studies on Bulgarian fans confirm their politicisation. Moreover, the authors emphasise the radicalization of their behaviour: acts of violence, xenophobia or ethnic and religious intolerance have intensified over past ten years. One of the most spectacular examples of fans' radical engagement is the 'Katunitsa case'. In September 2011, in the village of Katunitsa, a mass-scale clash burst out between Bulgarians and Roma people living in the village. What triggered the fight was the death of a nineteen-year-old, run down by a minivan driven by a man close to Kiril Rashkov, a notorious 'Gypsy Baron' and rich businessman, who resided in the same village. The Bulgarian villagers rose up in rebellion – they began to destroy Rashkov's property and one of the houses in his courtyard was set on fire. Later on, the protesters were joined by fans of the Plovdiv football team and acts of vengeance continued (see Todorov, 2013, pp. 11–12). The fans also took part in the nationalist 'Lukov March', an event praising Hristo Nikolov Lukov, minister of war and the leader of the nationalist Union of Bulgarian National Legions (from 1942 to 1943), which supported Nazi Germany during the Second World War (see Todorov, 2013, pp. 11–12).

In Georgiev's opinion, this radicalisation stems from ethnic nationalism and political and economic reality. He writes that 'soccer hooliganism is an avenue for organization of lumpen proletariat along the lines of ethnic nationalist ideologies and in the process, becomes an important structural element in contemporary capitalist social relations in Bulgaria' (Georgiev, 2017, pp. 2–3). Georgiev distinguishes several crucial discourse modes: 'real Bulgarians', 'invaders', 'hordes' on the one hand, and 'same old Communists', 'cheap labour' or 'masters in Brussel' on the other (pp. 53–60). His conclusion is that nationalist actions and practices of soccer hooligans are used by the ruling class to take focus away from the economic failures (p. 66).

Moldova

Moldova remains an under-investigated territory of fans' political activism and there are not many studies on this issue. Nevertheless, two aspects of supporters' commitment appear in the analysis – internal and external.

Internal contexts concern the tension between Moldova and Transnistria, a breakaway province and unrecognised statelet. According to research

Football fans and their political engagement   23

conducted by Adam Eberhardt, regardless of its size and population (a few times smaller than that of Moldova proper), Transnistria is a crucial region for sport-related politics, with clubs backed by the separatist government and domination of Sheriff Tiraspol in domestic competitions (Eberhardt, 2011, pp. 13–14). The most widely publicised case was that of top-league football club Constructorul Chişinău, which was moved to the capital city of Transnistria and started playing in Moldova's top league as FC Tiraspol in 2002. In effect, there is a strong reluctance to Transnistrian clubs. The most visible example is the conflict between Zimbru Chişinău and Sheriff Tiraspol fans (Glennon, 2016).

The external context is affected by the relations between Moldova and Russia. On the one hand, there is an open hostility between Moldovan and Russian football fans. Russia is perceived as a former occupier and current threat. During the Moldova vs Russia game (1–2) in 2015 many home fans sang an offensive song about Russian President Vladimir Putin and some displayed flags of neighbouring Ukraine; the Moldovan federation was fined by UEFA. That situation shows anti-Russian moods among fans. Most of them stress independence and political autonomy. Some groups also proclaim sympathy to Romania as a close neighbour and a potential helping hand in accession to the European Union. On the other hand, fans from Transnistria openly support Russia.

> Sometimes, during Moldovan league games, fans of Transnistrian clubs would chant 'Russia, Russia', 'Go Russia' or 'Russia-empire', which is their way of teasing fans of the teams from Moldova proper. When the Under-21 national teams of Moldova and Russia were playing a match in November 2009 at the stadium in Tiraspol, the Moldovan team could not count on receiving support from the spectators, since most of them were either behaving passively or supporting the Russians.
>
> (Eberhardt, 2011, pp. 20–21)

This diversity of fans' sympathies is symptomatic of today's Moldova – a country with weak identity, lost between the East and the West, between Moscow and Bucharest, and, moreover, split along the Dniester (Eberhardt, 2011, p. 23).

Post-Yugoslav republics

Relations between football supporters and politics in the Balkans is probably the most explored research topic in fan studies. There is a long list of monographs and papers on this issue. They represent different disciplines (history, sociology, anthropology, political science) and focus on various historical periods (1945–1992, 1992–1995, 1995–2000, 2000–2018) or various topics (the war, nationalism, homophobia, etc.). To make the analysis clear, this

24 *Football fans and their political engagement*

subchapter is divided into seven sections – one for each republic plus one for the pre-breakup period.

Football fans in the Socialist Federal Republic of Yugoslavia (1945–1992) and during the Yugoslav Wars (1992–1995)

Research on this period mostly covers five main subjects. It is important to mention these historical aspects because their consequences are still relevant in Balkan football.

The first topic is focused on propaganda aspects of football. Stadium rivalry was a form of proliferation of the socialist idea – brotherhood, unity, cult of labour (Kajtezović, 2015; Klasić, 2017). Football promoted the concept of 'new man' (Brentin and Zec, 2017), and football clubs provided a space to develop it (Borisov, 2015, pp. 116–122). Richard Mills shows that football successes served as an illustration of the successful Yugoslav 'Third Way' (Mills, 2018a). Ana Petrov even writes about 'sport as culture' in Yugoslavia (Petrov, 2017), whereas Dejan Zec and Miloš Paunović describe the assumed role of football in integration of different nations within the Federal Republic (Zec and Paunović, 2015).

The second issue is the analysis of the most popular football clubs as the medium of local-national identity. This stream of research shows the impact of football on building nationalisms during the pre-breakup era (Mills 2013a; Andjelic 2014). Studies on that topic stress a strong relation between supporting Dinamo Zagreb, FK Sarajevo or Red Star (*Crvena Zvezda*) Belgrade (Sack and Suster 2000; Wood, 2010, pp. 5–19; Djordjević, 2016; Blasius, 2017; Tregoures, 2018, pp. 205–209) and local chauvinism. Another thing is the banal nationalism of 'own' organisational structure of football. Richard Mills mentions the slogan about the impact of domestic competitions on national awareness and state building: 'recreating the state daily – leagues, cups and newspapers' (Mills, 2013b, pp. 946–948).

The third matter concerns internal frictions amongst the nations of the Federation in the field of football (Mills, 2009). Despite the assumed pro-integration role of football, the matches served as an opportunity to proclaim hostility towards other nations or ethnic groups. In effect, sports events became the stage for violent behaviours.

In a broader context, it should be stressed that the disintegration of the Yugoslav federation in the late 1980s and early 1990s was preceded by several years of violent skirmishes between various nationalist groups (Serbs, Croats, Bosnians and so on), where fans of Red Star Belgrade ('Delije'), Hajduk Split ('Torcida'), Dinamo Zagreb ('Bad Boys Blue') or NK Rijeka ('Armada') were highly involved. Srdan Vrcan and Dražen Lalić write that

> the first armed clashes were frequently described by those participants as a direct continuation of the clashes between Croatian and Serbian fan

Football fans and their political engagement 25

groups. (…) Some of the most brutal and criminal war actions in the early stages of the civil war were committed by units full of football fans.
(Vrcan and Lalić, 1999, pp. 180–181)

The symbolic end of socialist Yugoslavia was the so-called 'Maksimir riots', serious clashes between Dinamo Zagreb and Crvena Zvezda Belgrade fans during the Yugoslav football league match at Zagreb's Maksimir stadium on 13 May 1990 (Mihailović, 1997; Djordjević, 2012; Brentin, 2015; Mills, 2018a, pp. 202–227).

The fourth concern is fans' involvement in the war. Supporters of many Yugoslav clubs took active part in military operations in 1992–1995 (Mills, 2018a, pp. 267–306). In an analysis of their involvement in the war, Srdjan Vrcan and Dražen Lalić point out the continuum from the terraces and the symbolic, ritual struggles to the trenches and the actual warfare (Vrcan and Lalić, 1999, pp. 176–179). Ivan Čolović describes the role of fans as well-prepared soldiers (Čolović, 2000). Shay Wood adds that they were 'the earliest volunteers, and thereby carried their violent inter-ethnic rivalries to the battlefields' (Wood, 2013, p. 1080). Richard Mills, who explores the role of football in the nation-building process, claims: 'Football served as an important morale-boosting activity, providing soldiers with a distraction from the front, but it also served a higher cause' (Mills, 2013b, p. 945).

As it is today, one significant aspect of fans' activity is their attention to collective memory of the war – building monuments, putting up memorial plaques, celebrating anniversaries or honouring war victims. The supporters remember especially about their fellow fans who died in the conflict (Mills, 2012; Wood, 2013, p. 1082).

The last, fifth topic is more specific because it is focused on the present rather than the past: long-term effects of the Yugoslav wars on different aspects of Balkan football. The underlying concern here is social disintegration. On the one hand, the long shadow of war affects international football relations, for instance between Serbia and Croatia or Bosnia (Djordjević, 2014, 2016; Wood, 2013, p. 1082; Djordjević and Žikić, 2016). On the other, there are ethnic or religious conflicts within domestic leagues – e.g. in Bosnia (Mills, 2010; Wood, 2013). Apart from that, the war experience blurs the lines among such categories as 'patriotism', 'nationalism', 'chauvinism' or even 'fascism' (Rudic, Milekic and Lakic, 2018).

Another important result of war legacy is the existing, well-organised system of sport, violence and politics – 'the model includes a mixture of strong ethnically and religiously-based identity politics, links to organised crime, informal ties to politicians, and a love of the game of football' (Azinovic, Bassuerne and Weber, 2011, pp. 147–148).

In conclusion, it should be stressed that the era of the Socialist Federation and the war experience still have a significant impact on current football relations in the Balkans.

26 *Football fans and their political engagement*

Serbia

Ivan Čolović views football as a relevant element of the national 'politics of symbols' in Serbia – using the everyday 'national representations' for political purposes (Čolović, 2002). Recent studies on the political activism of Serbian football fans provide information on a number of areas of their symbolic and non-symbolic commitment.

One greatly explored issue is the relation between fans and Serbian nationalism (Djordjević, 2013). A particular manifestation of nationhood is praising such persons as Slobodan Milošević, Radovan Karadzić or Ratko Mladić by waving flags or wearing t-shirts with their images (see Rudic, 2017). Nevertheless, the key area of fans' involvement is match activity – banners, slogans, chants or acts of aggression – directed against 'Others'. Stadium choreographies and violence outside the stadiums are the most visible platform for demonstrating Serbian hostility against 'other' nations of former Yugoslavia (e.g. Croats, Slovenians and Macedonians) and Albanians (Djordjević, 2014; Brentin, 2014a; Mills, 2018b, p. 296) and Kosovans (Djordjević, 2016, p. 117).

Apart from that, domestic rivalries also have political connotations. The factors of differentiation include political origins of the club (e.g. Red Star Belgrade vs Partizan Belgrade; OFK Belgrade vs RAD Belgrade) and religious aspects or ethnic/national conflicts within the Serbian state (e.g. Partizan Belgrade vs Vojvodina Novi Sad) (Zec, 2010, pp. 140–144; Mills, 2018b, pp. 293–295; Djordjević, 2016; Djordjević and Pekić, 2017, pp. 356–357). Conflict thus appears the key element of the Serbian fandom landscape.

Researchers underline the role of football fans in the socio-political transformation in the 1990s. Christian Axboe Nielsen uses football as 'a metaphor for Serbia's long journey to the rule of law' (Nielsen, 2010). He even notes that 'during the 1990s, football in Serbia to a significant extent became synonymous with organized crime and the criminalization of the Serbian state' (Nielsen, 2010, p. 87). Other authors explore political careers of fan leaders, for instance Željko 'Arkan' Ražnatović (Stewart, 2008). Besides, some scholars provide analyses concerning cases of corruption with fans in the background (Simonović, Otašević and Djurdjević, 2014) and the political 'culture of violence' (Marković, 2015). Altogether, Alexander Shea calls the universe of this mutual interdependence the 'troubling relationship between Serbian politics and football hooliganism' (Shea, 2018).

Another group of studies is focused on the political activity of right-wing fans. Many of them explore the homophobic aspects of Serbian fan environment. Nielsen analyses hooligan violence in reaction to the Gay Pride Parade in Belgrade (Nielsen, 2013). In turn, Tamara Pavasovic Trost and Nikola Kovacevic describe the overlap between football hooliganism and the extreme-right movement as reflected in people's reactions on the Internet (Pavasovic Trost and Kovacevic, 2013). Other authors provide the picture of racist (Obradovic-Wochink, 2012; Bakic, 2013, pp. 3–5; Ames, 2017), anti-Muslim (Zivanovic, 2018) or even neo-Nazi attitudes (Tomić, 2013, pp. 106–107) among Serbian fandom.

Football fans and their political engagement 27

Some researchers consider the place for left-wing fans in Serbian football. In their paper on left-wing ideology among fans, Ivan Djordjević and Relja Pekić note as follows:

> It can be concluded that the political space for alternatives is still rather narrow, and that the conditions for a full formalization of a visible left-oriented agenda have still not been met. Activism operates through the prism of ideological neutrality and a strategy of non-participation, which is still too weak to take on the dominant nationalistic ideology. This is why the values of the 'new left', especially those connected to antifascism, cannot be loudly articulated even though most of the fans would declare themselves as antifascists.
>
> (Djordjević and Pekić, 2017, p. 12)

The question of the left returns in all Balkan countries.

Concluding, it is worth noting that politics and football fans seem to be inseparable in the Serbian context. These two worlds have blurred borders, common actors and mechanisms of mutual support.

Croatia

Croatia is the next Balkan state, apart from Serbia, where the relations between fans and politics have been examined in great detail. General reflection on their political activism can be found in studies by Andrew Hodges (2018), Loïc Tregoures (2018, pp. 212–220) or Andrew Hodges with Paul Stubbs (2016), who stress that football supporters are very influential political actors in Croatia. The national team and clubs are important symbols of national (Brentin, 2013a) or local identity (Sindbæk, 2013). Moreover, since many clubs have a very specific political background (Hodges, 2018, pp. 102–116), they protect the collective memory (Perasović and Mustapić, 2014). Exploring the slogan 'Za dom – spremni!' (Ready for the Homeland), Dario Brentin writes about the triangle of 'politics–ethnicity–identity' ('ethnoidentity') (Brentin, 2014b). Other researchers describe this triangle as an integration or differentiation mechanism, even in the life of Croatian diaspora in Australia (Hughson, 2000; Hay and Gouth, 2009, pp. 831–835; Kampark, 2018). In effect, football is a significant tool for political (self)identification in Croatia.

Furthermore, fans' commitment was an important element of the socio-political transition in the 1990s. Research findings suggest that fandom has a real impact on current politics. Srdan Vrcan (2002) and Dario Brentin (2013b) describe the relation between fans and the first Croatian president, Franjo Tudjman. Fans initially supported Tudjman and helped him rise to power. In the course of time, however, the unsatisfied fandom initiated public political contestation of the president with growing political consequences. Apart from Tudjman's case, Benjamin Perasović and Marko Mustapić note that supporters have effective weapons of political protest:

28 *Football fans and their political engagement*

boycotts, petitions and demonstrations (Perasović and Mustapić, 2013); Lalić and Wood add acts of violence to the list (Lalić and Wood, 2014). All of them make fans key actors on the political stage.

Considering that fans are strongly connected with the world of politics and sport authorities, they regard sports issues as political and vice versa. Their protest against corrupt members of the national football federation had a strictly political context (Tregoures, 2017). It is worth noting that contestation activity brings together even the warring groups of fans, like Dinamo's Bad Boys Blue and Hajduk's Torcida (Perasović and Mustapić, 2017).

One important topic is fans' far-right political extremism. The existing studies provide examples of their nationalist behaviour (Brentin, 2016) or racist incidents (Obućina, 2012, p. 9). On the other hand, there is also a (little) space for left-wing fans. Andrew Hodges explores the NK Zagreb ultras group, White Angels Zagreb. He describes their anti-homophobic activity (2016a), analyses fans in the gender context (2018, pp. 117–134) and considers the relation between violence and masculinity (2016b). Another paper outlines the international solidarity of leftist fans of Dinamo Zagreb's Bad Blue Boys and Celtic Glasgow's Green Brigade (Hodges, 2016c). Moreover, an important part of fans' activity is focused on immediate issues – self-governing the local club (Ceronja, Ivkošić and Petrović, 2017) or work for the local community (Vukušić and Miošić, 2017). Tregoures and Šantek, meanwhile, analyse initiatives for changes to the legal system, for the decommercialisation of football, and for the democratisation of sporting institutions (Tregoures and Šantek, 2017). Some of these activities arise from the 'Against Modern Football' movement (Perasović and Mustapić, 2018). Although not all of them are 'leftist', they share democratic values.

To sum up, Vrcan writes about the relation between fans and politics in Croatia as follows:

> football has become an arena for the visible shift in the traditional role of a fan tribe to the role of a political actor, with the fan tribe taking over an opposition political role in challenging existing powers while opposition political parties remain docile and satisfied with acting as a token opposition, not daring to contest publicly the nationalist ideology which had long served as the basis of legitimization of the powers that be.
>
> (Vrcan, 2002, p. 73)

The question which comes from his observation is more universal: how far are fans able to be the subject rather than the object of local politics?

Bosnia and Herzegovina

The key factor which determines the relation between football fans and politics in Bosnia is post-war tension. The war left a deep mark on Bosnia and Herzegovina's territory, and there are still many remnants of the conflict

Football fans and their political engagement 29

in the public space, including football stadiums (Mills, 2016). But the military conflict meant not only armed struggle but also the collapse of Yugoslav ideology. Mills gives the example of Velez Mostar club-manifesto of 'Brotherhood and Unity' (Mills, 2010). Quoting Mills, Wood comments as follows:

> Velez, seen as representing the communist state's official ideology of the brotherhood and unity of the country's various national groups, became the target of nationalists during the fighting in Bosnia (1992–1995). In 1992, Croat nationalists established their own club, Zrinjski, and fan group; Velez came to be labelled as the 'Muslim' club. According to historian Richard Mills, Zrinjski was 'resurrected solely in the pursuit of ethnic separation, or in other words, as another vehicle from which Croat nationalists could challenge the inclusive and multiethnic values of brotherhood and unity which Velez had always claimed to uphold'.
>
> (Wood, 2013, pp. 1079–1080)

Velez still plays a key role in the political arena. The current engagement of Red Army, Velez Mostar ultras, is described by Toby Kinder (2013).

As it is today, the former war enemies, Bosnians, Serbs and Croats, coexist within one country. The state is composed of two political entities: Republika Srpska and the Federation of Bosnia and Herzegovina. Both of them have extensive autonomy and they do not have many common institutions. In result, even the united Bosnia and Herzegovina national football team is a political issue (Dedovic, 2013; Vest, 2014, pp. 87–97). Besides, for many years the two entities also had their separate domestic leagues. Although they have had a common league and common national team since 2002, research findings present tensions among fans, which have mainly socio-political background. Most incidents can be explained using the ethnic perspective. The warring fans represent one of the three groups: Bosniaks (FK Sarajevo, Zeljeznicar Sarajevo, Sloboda Tuzla, Celik Zenica), Bosnian Serbs (Borac Banja Luka) or Bosnian Croats (Zrijnski Mostar, NK Siroki Brijeg). In fact, hooligan fights remain part of political struggle for supremacy in the state (Azinović, Bassuener and Weber, 2011, pp. 57–59). The ethnic context of conflicts between fans is stressed by many authors (Özkan, 2013; Galijaš, 2014). Davide Sterchele comments that ethnicity is instrumentally used by the post-war elites to exploit the common good for private enrichment (Sterchele, 2013). Nevertheless, the intra-ethnic group tension is also the case, as illustrated by a long-term conflict between FK Sarajevo (Horde Zla – Evil Hordes) and Zeljeznicar Sarajevo (Maniacs), clubs with a different social background: the former established by political authorities under the name SD Torpedo (in homage to Torpedo Moscow), the latter formed by railway workers.

Currently, fans' commitment is often important in the process of social integration, with football serving as a platform for reconciliation (Gasser and Levinsen, 2004; Vest, 2014, pp. 142–186). In these terms, Sterchele compares the forms of religious rituals and football rituals and develops some

30 *Football fans and their political engagement*

considerations that can be applied to the general debate about inter-religious dialogue (Sterchele, 2007). Besides, supporters cooperate during political protests. Andrew Gilbert describes the decisive role played by the Sloboda Tuzla ultras in the Tuzla uprising in 2014 (Gilbert, 2018): the ultras-led mass protests forced the resignation of the regional government. All these examples show the potential of politically-related fan activism. In this way, football, which was one of the triggers of disruption, is now a tool of cooperation.

Slovenia

Slovenia is usually viewed as the most quiet and westernised state in the Balkans. The war of the 1990s did not affect it as much as other post-Yugoslav republics. After Slovenia's political secession from Yugoslavia in 1991, the new nation-state needed new symbols of national identification. Sport became one of them, but football was just one of many disciplines which played the role, along with skiing (Kotnik, 2009), basketball and handball.

Nevertheless, football fans appear in the country's public sphere. Most of them focus on supporting the national team or local clubs. They form ultras groups ('Viole' of NK Maribor or 'Green Dragons' of Olimpia Ljubljana) and prepare stadium performances. Sometimes their activity has a political context, including nationalist or xenophobic chants and banners. For example, at a football match played between a Slovenian and a Bosnian team in July 2012, Slovenian fans screamed the infamous Serb war slogan: 'Knife, wire, Srebrenica!' (Toplak and Haček, 2012, p. 16). However, Peter Stankovic stresses the paradoxes of these pro-nationalist attitudes of football fans:

> Many members of the Slovenian national team, who have performed splendidly since the late 1990s, are immigrants or, more often, second generation immigrants from other former Yugoslav regions. (…) Having contributed so much to the continuation of Slovenian nationalism since the late 1990s, the (national) team is in reality a team largely comprised of exactly those against whom contemporary Slovenian nationalism was actually aimed. This inconsistency is not interesting in purely theoretical terms; it is actually very funny to see euphoric supporters of Slovenia's national team assertively chanting at games 'Mi, Slovenci!' ('We, Slovenians!'), when at least half the team sparking such outbursts of national pride are not only of apparent non-Slovenian origin, but actually comprise those who are strongly detested by Slovenian nationalists.
>
> (Stankovic, 2005, p. 247)

Lucie Chládková mentions homophobic incidents:

> Most of the violence happened also at football stadiums where expressions such as 'Southerners' (*čefurji*) or 'poofties' (gay) were being shouted. (…) The most infamous attack came in June in 2009 during the Pride

Football fans and their political engagement 31

Parade in Ljubljana when the Café Open was assaulted by neo-Nazis. (…). The police caught three perpetrators of this attack. All were members of Green Dragons, the hooligan group of the football club Olimpija Ljubljana. All three accused refused that they are sympathisers of the far right, however the police found Nazi literature and t-shirts with neo-Nazi symbols in their homes.

(Chládková, 2014, pp. 50–52)

Another form of fans' political activism is public protests. The NK Maribor ultras participated in the Maribor protest in 2012–2013 against the political elites (Kirn, 2018). Some others contested a planned asylum centre (read more: Locals in Maribor protest, 2016). However, fan circles in Slovenia are not as active as those in Croatia or Serbia.

Montenegro

Political aspects of fandom in Montenegro have not been explored in more detail so far. This could stem from the fact that football fans over there are not very 'politically' active, with one exception.

The country did not suffer so much as Bosnia or Croatia during the war. After the conflict it became part of the State Union of Serbia and Montenegro, and declared independence in 2006. Most of the very few studies on fans' political commitment concern their violent behaviour. Hooligan incidents were recorded during national team matches, for instance a suspended match with Russia in 2015 (see Montenegro v Russia Euro 2016, 2015). Stevo Popović and Duško Bjelica claim that this form of 'supporting' Montenegro's team is a form of strengthening national identity (2014). At the club stage, the Varvari (Barbarians), Buducnost Podgorica fans, are perceived as the largest, the most political and the most violent group (Hughson and Skillen, 2014, pp. 138–139). Apart from violence, they engage in political stadium choreographies (mainly right-wing, with Celtic crosses and pro-skinhead banners) and protests against local authorities (Wilson, 2007). However, the politicisation of fandom in Montenegro is still waiting for more in-depth research.

Republic of North Macedonia

Although the Republic of North Macedonia is not a top-rated football country in the Balkans, North Macedonian fans are visible and influential. There are a number of very active groups in Skopje, Bitola, Prilep and Tetovo (Vangelovski, 2017, pp. 281–284). Their involvement in political issues is often related to ethnic conflicts, and is characterised by the antagonism between clubs of the Macedonian majority and the Albanian minority (Manasiev, 2012a). This hostility fuels violence between 'Komiti' from FK Vardar Skopje (Macedonians) and 'Sverceri' from Sloga Jugomagnat in Skopje (a club of Albanian minority) or 'Vojvodi' from FK

32 *Football fans and their political engagement*

Teteks Tetovo (Macedonians) and 'Ballistet' from Shkendija Tetovo (where Albanians are a local majority) (Saveski and Sadiku, 2012, pp. 5–6).

Ethnicity is also the key factor at play when it comes to pacts and alliances between different cities: 'Komiti' have a good relationship only with 'Vojvodi' and fight with all other groups. On the other hand, there are cases of hostility without any specific political background. For instance, the competition between Vardar Skopje and Pelister Bitola is famous in spite of hooligan engagement of 'Komiti' and 'Čkembari'. Violence, then, appears as the crucial problem of Macedonian fandom (Anastasovski, Nanev and Klimper, 2009), including the international level (Holme, 2015).

Fans are also engaged in politics in a narrow sense: they actively participate in protests and demonstrations. Aleksandar Manasiev claims that sometimes they have done this to political order (Manasiev, 2012b). The latest example is the involvement of Russian-Greek businessman Ivan Savvidi, formerly a member of the Russian parliament, who allegedly gave hundreds of thousands of euros to North Macedonian opponents of the country's proposed name change. The recipients included football hooligans who rioted in the capital. Savvidi, who moved to Greece in the mid-2000s, purchased the PAOK football club and various media outlets, and his business empire now dominates Thessaloniki, the country's second city (Cvetovska, 2018).

Other studies indicate close relations between politicians and football hooligans. Manasiev quotes one of them:

> The doors of local government, companies, and political parties are always open to us. (...) Although I've faced several charges of violent behaviour, including involvement in an attack on a police officer, I've never spent more than 10 days in custody.
>
> (Manasiev, 2012b)

Researchers notice that politicians provide protection to hooligans and in return, in some cases, they serve them as foot soldiers for particular political aims (Cvetanovski, 2018). In these terms, Tome Vangelovski underlines the significance of ultras as political actors, who can be easily mobilised by politicians, but are also capable of undertaking independent actions (Vangelovski, 2017, pp. 283–284). All these examples indicate that North Macedonia is another country where the lines between the fandom and politicians are blurred.

Kosovo

Political activism of football fans in the Republic of Kosovo is mostly oriented in one direction – against the Serbian neighbour. The history of this tension on the ground of football has been outlined by Richard Mills (Mills, 2018b, pp. 297–304). Kosovo declared independence from Serbia in 2008 and has gained diplomatic recognition of its sovereign status by 113 United

Football fans and their political engagement   33

Nations member states. Serbia refuses to recognise Kosovo as a state, although it has accepted the legitimacy of its institutions in the Brussels Agreement of 2013. Kosovo has its own domestic football league and has been member of UEFA and FIFA since 2016.

While Kosovo is still a developing country in terms of football fandom, it has well-organised groups of supporters. The relations among them reflect the existing political conflicts. The 'Plisat', FC Prishtina ultras, are pro-Albanian and anti-Serbian. On the other hand, 'Torcida 1984', KF Trepca Mitrovica supporters, declare themselves as anti-Albanian, anti-Muslim and pro-Serbian. These teams are the greatest rivals and political enemies, and the matches between them are presented as 'ethnic derbies' of the oldest ultras firms in Kosovo.

Football is also an instrument in the process of social integration. Sanije Krasniqi and Besnik Krasniqi describe a project where it is a peace-building device in the post-conflict society in Kosovo (Krasniqi and Krasniqi, 2018). Apart from that, football and its fans serve as a tool in the so-called 'sport diplomacy', whereby politicians use the national football team as a key symbol of the nation. Brentin and Tregoures note: 'The Kosovar nation-building and -branding process, emblematised through the 'soft power' of representative sport, could be increasingly used to create symbolic pressure on states that have not yet recognised Kosovo' (Brentin and Tregoures, 2016, p. 360).

The relations between fandom and terraces in Kosovo are still building up. They will probably develop and acquire new dimensions in the years to come.

Albania

Although Albania was not a member of the Socialist Federal Republic of Yugoslavia, it had a similar experience of communist regime (Vickers, 2001; Pearson, 2004) and social transformation (Gurashi, 2017; Jusufi, 2017) like former Yugoslav republics. One major difference is that football in Albania does not play such a key role as in Croatia or Serbia, even though it is the national sport (Fshazi, 2013, pp. 1023–1029). The national team played at UEFA EURO 2016, and the clubs – KF Skenderbeu Korce, FK Kukesi, or Partizani Tirani – achieve good results in European cups. The football fandom also keeps growing. The most important ultras group 'Tirona Fanatics' of FK Tirana was formed in 2006, and there are also many other groups, e.g. 'Armata e Veriut' (FK Kukesi) and 'Ultras Guerills' (Partizani Tirana).

Fan activity is mostly focused on contesting Serbia, as was the case of the famous 'drone conflict' in October 2014. During the EURO 2016 qualifier Serbia vs Albania in Belgrade, an Albanian fan flew a drone with a banner showing Kosovo as part of Greater Albania into the stadium. When the drone got close to the ground, a Serbian player ripped the flag off, provoking a fight between both teams and their fans. The match was abandoned. The incident greatly increased tensions between the Serbian and Albanian governments (Ames and Ibrulj, 2014; Baker, 2016, p. 857).

34 *Football fans and their political engagement*

Current research shows that football in Albania has been strictly politicised from its very beginning. Rrezearta Thaçi views Albanian football as a constant patriotic manifestation:

> 'Furia Albanica' has now become the national emblem, a synonym of unification, stronger than the all-inclusive national flag. A 'Furia' which in fury, encompasses all Albanians in an 'imagined community', perhaps the only permissible community for the Albanians. It seems as if those 90 minutes, make the idea for a unified nation as real as it can be, thanks to the '90 minute patriots'.
>
> (Thaçi, 2016, p. 537)

Falma Fshazi, in turn, claims that 'through football the central and local agents' tensioned relationship emerging from the Albanian central governments' understanding of the capacity to control the country – as the ability to command and influence all local actors is disclosed' (Fshazi, 2013, p. 1025). Analysing the tensions among fans, the paper shows 'how conflicts in football matches and disputes over them are also and particularly rooted in the struggle of power centre – locality, and as a production of this, in the tension locality versus locality' (p. 1033). Fshazi concludes that football in Albania is 'rather an ongoing narrative of struggle that blends individual and collective action or agency with political, economic and cultural flows and forces' (p. 1025) and 'remains an area involving spaces and possibilities of empowering local actors' (p. 1033).

Conclusion

The above literature review provides some more general conclusions about the relations between football fans and political activism in Central and Eastern Europe.

First, football remains a significant field of political contestation. It becomes a social area in which the latent mass social discontent may obtain its political articulation and expression. This is the basic mode of fans' political activism. The examples mentioned above indicate that this contestation has become more radical and violent. The stadiums provide an opportunity to proclaim with impunity: dissatisfaction with political authorities or economic conditions, ethnic/national animosities, racist/homophobic slogans. Football protesters, then, seek to change rather than preserve the current situation. Although fans rarely provide support to authorities (e.g. Hungary or Russia) or praise the status quo, they very seldom offer any 'positive programme' or engage in building the 'new order'. They opt for change but are not able to define what this change should look like. Nevertheless, it is worth noting that their contestation can also be viewed as more anti-establishment than strictly political. Their protests break out over poor living conditions, police violence or corruption affairs, and they can mostly be seen as acts against the ruling establishment rather than particular politicians.

Football fans and their political engagement 35

Second, the available studies present the political radicalisation of the terraces. Their authors underline the growing extremism of football fans – both in terms of their political views and behaviour. This process is apparent in most European countries but it is particularly observable in CEE.

The picture of football fandom revealed in the review indicates the strength of the right-wing sector. It is not just conservative or patriotic. The scope of behaviour includes manifestations of chauvinism/nationalism, acts of racism and homophobic behaviours. Another important feature is the culture of violence. The far-right football extremists use mostly fights and riots to manifest their beliefs. Such groups exist in almost every reviewed CEE country and are very influential in most of them.

On the other hand, there are (very) minor left-wing ultras movements (for example, Bohemians in Prague, White Angels in Zagreb, Red-White Djigits in Nalchik). Their members describe themselves as anti-fascist, anti-xenophobic and anti-homophobic. The leftists appear at the terraces but they are still on the margins. Research findings prove that in most CEE countries they do not even exist. The small scale of left-oriented fandom leads to the question about the reasons of this situation.

One side effect of this radicalisation is the absence of 'centrist voice' among the most active fans. This does not mean that there are no centrists in the terraces – they may even be the 'silent majority', but they just do not initiate performative activities. They mainly focus on different forms of civic engagement – work for the local community, NGOs, organising sports activities for the youth or governing local clubs. These forms of commitment rarely rely on riots as a form of communication.

Third, being a fan of a particular club or national team is tied to a certain political identity. This connection is particularly evident in divided societies, which are diverse in terms of ethnic or religious composition. Since fan identity requires sharp distinctions, it is defined by antagonisms and radicalisms (chauvinism, nationalism, racism, fanaticism). In this way, football political identities grow out of social cleavages rather than create new ones. They are fuelled by political conflicts. Most studies of these conflicts concern club fans. Only some of them perceive national team fans as political (for example, the Balkan states, Russia, Hungary). Surprisingly, this area is under-investigated in most of the countries.

Fourth, the existing studies provide a selective and incomplete picture of fans during transformation. Some of them analyse political activism of football supporters in the past, under the communist regime. Nevertheless, the vast majority of publications is focused only on the present, the period since the 2000s or even later, which means that most of them overlook the period of transformation. There are just a few examples of studies on the transition of fans in the early 1990s and on their role in the transformation (for example, Croatia, Romania, Bulgaria). In effect, the decisive moment for the future development of CEE countries (and their football) tends to be overlooked. More detailed examination of political commitment of fans at the time of

36 *Football fans and their political engagement*

intensive social changes provides the knowledge about less obvious aspects of transformation. Besides, studies on fans' transition – continuity and change – can provide useful 'explanatory patterns' to understand the current political activism of football supporters.

Fifthly, this review of research indicates that there are hardly any studies on the political opinions of fans in CEE available in English which would consider such issues as declared voting decisions, support for political parties or views on particular political issues (for example, EU integration, refugees). Although they probably appear in local media or in studies in native languages, the results are inaccessible for international audience. In effect, researchers are convinced that this group has particular political beliefs, even though survey results or in-depth interviews which would clearly prove this are few and far between.

In conclusion, the main findings of this literature review can be summed up as follows. On the one hand, political activism of fans in CEE countries is characterised by specific features. The stadiums appear as a 'hall of mirrors' where fans (over)react to current political developments. There are a number of studies providing examples of this mechanism (in relation to internal affairs or international tensions). Some forms of supporters' expression, like anti-establishment protests or anti-communist slogans, can be definitely considered post-transformation legacy. On the other hand, political activism of fans in Central and Eastern Europe is still under-investigated, especially in some particular areas. Many convictions are based on common knowledge or simple stereotypes. In fact, the relations between fans and politics in the examined group of countries are a more complex issue. This means that there is a potential for research and analysis. The further chapters, which investigate the case of Poland, try to fill some of these gaps.

References

Ames, N. (2017). Serbian football's eye-watering racism problem shows no sign of abating. *The Guardian* [online]. Available at: www.theguardian.com/ [accessed 5 October 2019].

Ames, N. and Ibrulj, S. (2014). Serbia vs Albania abandoned after players and fans brawl on pitch. *The Guardian* [online]. Available at: www.theguardian.com/ [accessed 5 October 2019].

Anastasovski, I., Nanev, L. and Klimper, I. (2009). *Prevention and repression for violence in the football stadiums in Republic of Macedonia.* Skopje: FFM Fleksograf-Kumanovo.

Andjelic, N. (2014). The rise and fall of Yugoslavia: Politics and football in the service of the nation(s). *Sudosteuropa. Journal of Politics and Society*, 62(2), pp. 99–125.

Armstrong, D. (2016a). Zenit – Spartak. The capital calling. *The Russian Football News* [online]. Available at: http://russianfootballnews.com/ [accessed 5 October 2019].

Armstrong, D. (2016b). The truth behind being a Russian ultra, with Spartak Moscow's Fratria. *These Football Times* [online]. Available at: https://thesefootballtimes.co/ [accessed 5 October 2019].

Armstrong, G. and Testa, A. (2008). Words and actions: Italian ultras and neo-fascism. *Social Identities. Journal for the Study of Race, Nation and Culture*, 14(4), pp. 473–490.

Armstrong, G. and Testa, A. (2010). *Football, Fascism and Fandom. The UltraS of Italian Football*. London-Oxford: Bloomsbury.

Arnason, J. (2005). East central European perspectives. *European Journal of Social Theory*, 8(4), pp. 387–400.

Arnold, R. (2015). Systematic racist violence in Russia: Between 'hate crime' and 'ethnic conflict. *Theoretical Criminology*, 19(2), pp. 239–256.

Arnold, R. (2018). Sport and official nationalism in Modern Russia. *Problems of Post-Communism*, 65(2), pp.129–141.

Arnold, R. and Veth, K.M. (2018). Racism and Russian football supporters' culture. A case for concern? *Problems of Post-Communism*, 65(2), pp. 88–100.

Azinović, V., Bassuener, K. and Weber, B. (2011). *Assessing the Potential for Renewed Ethnic Violence in Bosnia and Herzegovina: A Security Risk Analysis*. Sarajevo: University of Sarajevo.

Bairner, A. and Shirlow P. (1998). Loyalism, Linfield and the territorial politics of soccer fandom in Northern Ireland. *Space and Polity*, 2(2), pp. 163–177.

Baker, C. (2016). Football, history, and the nation in Southeastern Europe. *Nationalities Papers*, 44(6), pp. 857–859.

Bakic, J. (2013). *Right-Wing Extremism in Serbia* [pdf]. Berlin: Friedrich-Ebert-Stiftung. Available at: http://library.fes.de/ [accessed 5 October 2019].

Barcelo, J., Clinton, P. and Sero C.S. (2015). National identity, social institutions and political values. The case of FC Barcelona and Catalonia from an intergenerational comparison. *Soccer & Society*, 16(4), pp. 469–481.

Barna, I. and Hunyadi, B. (2015). Report on Xenophobia and Radical Nationalism in Hungary. *Political Capital* [online]. Available at: www.politicalcapital.hu/ [accessed 5 October 2019].

Bar-On, T. (1997). The ambiguities of football, politics, culture, and social transformation in Latin America. *Sociological Research Online*, 2(4). Available at: www.socresonline.org.uk/ [accessed 5 October 2019].

Battini, A. and Koşulu, D. (2018). When ultras defend trees. Framing politics through subcultural fandom-comparing UltrAslan and Çarşı before and during Occupy Gezi. *Soccer & Society*, 19(3), pp. 418–439.

Beiu, A. (2005). *Football Related Violence in Romania*. Dissertation [pdf]. Brussels: Université Libre de Bruxelles. Available at: www.cafyd.com/ [accessed 5 October 2019].

Beiu, A. (2006). *Football and Politics in Romania*. Dissertation [pdf]. Brussels: Université Libre de Bruxelles. Available at: https://ecpr.eu/ [accessed 5 October 2019].

Bennetts, M. (2009). *Football Dynamo. Modern Russia and the People's Game*. London: Virgin Books.

Berend, I. (2005). What is Central and Eastern Europe? *European Journal of Social Theory*, 8(4), pp. 401–416.

Bezlov, T. (2015). Football hooliganism. In: R. Dzhekova, M. Mancheva, M. Doichinova, L. Derelieva, T. Bezlov, M. Karayotova, Y. Tomov, D. Markov, M. Ilcheva, *Radicalisation in Bulgaria: Threats and Trends* [pdf]. Sofia: Center for the Study of Democracy. Available at: www.rcc.int [accessed 5 October 2019].

Blackshaw, T. (2008). Politics, theory and practice. Contemporary community theory and football. *Soccer & Society*, 9(3), pp. 325–345.

38 *Football fans and their political engagement*

Blasius, M. (2017). FC Red Star Belgrade and the multiplicity of social identifications in socialist Yugoslavia: Representative dimensions of the 'Big Four' football clubs. *The International Journal of the History of Sport*, 34(9), pp. 783–799.

Boffey, D. (2016a). Euro 2016. England and Russia fans clash before and after match. *The Guardian* [online]. Available at: www.theguardian.com/ [accessed 5 October 2019].

Boffey, D. (2016b). Whitehall fears Russian football hooligans had Kremlin links. *The Guardian* [online]. Available at: www.theguardian.com/ [accessed 5 October 2019].

Bondarenko, G. (2012). Vyrok. *Reyestr Court* [online]. Available at: www.reyestr.court. gov.ua/ [accessed 5 October 2019].

Boren, C. (2017). One Russian politician's cure for hooliganism: Turn violence into a spectator sport. *Washington Post* [online]. Available at: www.washingtonpost.com [accessed 5 October 2019].

Borisov, T. (2015). Football in Romania, Yugoslavia and Bulgaria during Stalinism 1944–1953. *Hiperboreea Journal*, 3, pp. 111–127.

Borrero, M. (2017). Beyond the unfulfilled promise of Soviet international football, 1945–1991. In: B. Elsey and S. Pugliese (eds) *Football and the Boundaries of History*. New York: Palgrave Macmillan, pp. 101–118.

Brentin, D. (2013a). The nation's most holy institution: Football and the construction of Croatian national identity. *Open Democracy* [online]. Available at: www.opendem ocracy.net/ [accessed 5 October 2019].

Brentin, D. (2013b). A lofty battle for the nation. The social roles of sport in Tudjman's Croatia. *Sport in Society*, 16(8), pp. 993–1008.

Brentin, D. (2014a). More than a game? Again? On the seemingly perpetual football-related violence in the Balkans. *The Balkanist* [online]. Available at: https://balka nist.net/ [accessed 5 October 2019].

Brentin, D. (2014b). 'Now you see who is a friend and who an enemy.' Sport as an ethnopolitical identity tool in postsocialist Croatia. *Sudosteuropa. Journal of Politics and Society*, 62(2), pp. 187–207.

Brentin, D. (2015). The 'Maksimir myth'. 25 years since the 'symbolic dissolution' of Socialist Yugoslavia. *The Balkanist* [online]. Available at: http://balkanist.net/ [accessed 5 October 2019].

Brentin, D. (2016). Ready for the homeland? Ritual, remembrance, and political extremism in Croatian football. *Nationalities Papers*, 44(6), pp. 860–876.

Brentin, D. and Tregoures, L. (2016). Entering through the sport's door? Kosovo's sport diplomatic endeavours towards international recognition. *Diplomacy & Statecraft*, 27(2), pp. 360–378.

Brentin, D. and Zec, D. (2017). From the concept of the communist 'new man' to nationalist hooliganism: Research perspectives on sport in socialist Yugoslavia. *The International Journal of the History of Sport*, 34(9), pp. 713–728.

Brimson, D. (2003). *Eurotrashed. The Rise and Rise of Europe's Football Hooligans*. London: Headline Book Publishing.

Brown, A. (ed.). (1998). *Fanatics! Power, Identity and Fandom in Football*. London: Routledge

Bylina, V. (2013a). Belarusian ultras and the regime. *The Belarus Digest* [online]. Available at: https://belarusdigest.com/ [accessed 5 October 2019].

Bylina, V. (2013b). Reviving partisan: Solidarity of Minsk football fans. *The Belarus Digest* [online]. Available at: https://belarusdigest.com/ [accessed 5 October 2019].

Bylina, V. (2015a). Football fans as an example of a community beyond the government's control in the conditions of the authoritarian regime. In: V. Bulhakau and A.

Lastouski (eds) *Civil Society in Belarus, 2000–2015. Collection of texts.* Warsaw: Wydawnictwo Tyrsa, pp. 47–59.

Bylina, V. (2015b). Belarusian authorities crack down on football fans. *The Belarus Digest* [online]. Available at: https://belarusdigest.com/ [accessed 5 October 2019].

Cashmore, E. and Cleland, J. (2012). Fans, homophobia and masculinities in association football: evidence of a more inclusive environment. *The British Journal of Sociology*, 63(2), pp. 370–387.

Cenek, J. and Smolík, J. (2015). Nationalism and its manifestations in sport: The case of football hooliganism in the Czech Republic. In: K. Cordel and K. Jajecznik (eds) *The Transformation of Nationalismin Central and Eastern Europe. Ideas and Structures*, Warsaw: University of Warsaw Press, pp. 137–154

Ceronja, P., Ivkošić, M. and Petrović, S. (2017). Football club ownership in the Republic of Croatia. A model for supporters' inclusion. In: B. García and J. Zheng (eds) *Football and Supporter Activism in Europe*, London: Palgrave Macmillan, pp. 143–163.

Charvát, J. (2017). Boots and braces don't make me racist. Antiracist skinheads in the Czech Republic. In: P. Guerrera and T. Moreira (eds) *Keep it Simple, Make it Fast! An approach to Underground Music Scenes. Volume 3*. Porto: University of Porto Press, pp. 39–48

Chládková, L. (2014). *The Far Right in Slovenia*. Master's thesis [pdf]. Brno: Masaryk University. Available at: https://is.muni.cz/ [accessed 5 October 2019].

Clark, T. (2006). 'I'm Scunthorpe til I die'. Constructing and (re)negotiating identity through the terrace chant. *Soccer & Society*, 7(4), pp. 494–507.

Cleland, J. (2015). Discussing homosexuality on association football fan message boards: A changing cultural context. *International Review for the Sociology of Sport*, 50(2), pp. 125–140.

Cleland, J. and Cashmore, E. (2016). Football fans' views of racism in British football. *International Review for the Sociology of Sport*, 51(1), pp. 27–43.

Cowley, P. and Ford, R. (2016a). How football can explain the EU referendum. *The Telegraph* [online]. Available at: www.telegraph.co.uk/ [accessed 5 October 2019].

Cowley, P. and Ford, R. (2016b). How football can explain politics: Labour dominate the Premier League while lower ranks are more Conservative. *The Telegraph* [online]. Available at: www.telegraph.co.uk/ [accessed 5 October 2019].

Crețan, R. (2018). Who owns the name? Fandom, social inequalities and the contested renaming of a football club in Timişoara, Romania. *Urban Geography*. First published online: May 8, 2018.

Cvetanovski, I. (2018). Macedonia, the dark side of football. *Osservatorio Balcani e Caucaso* [online]. Available at: www.balcanicaucaso.org/eng/ [accessed 5 October 2019].

Cvetovska, S. (2018). Russian businessman behind unrest in Macedonia. Organised Crime and Corruption Project [online]. Available at: www.occrp.org/ [accessed 5 October 2019].

Čolović, I. (2000). Football, hooligans and war. In: N. Popov (ed.) *The Road to War in Serbia*. Budapest: Central European University Press, pp. 373–396.

Čolović, I. (2002). *The Politics of Symbol in Serbia. Essays in Political Anthropology*. London: Hurst.

Daniel, P. and Kassimeris, C. (2013). The politics and culture of FC St. Pauli: From leftism, through anti-establishment, to commercialization. *Soccer & Society*, 14(2), pp. 167–182.

Dedovic, E. (2013). The Bosnian national football team: A case study in post-conflict institution building. *Open Democracy* [online]. Available at: www.opendemocracy.net/ [accessed 5 October 2019].

40 *Football fans and their political engagement*

de Menezes, J. (2016). Euro 2016: Russian official tells hooligans 'well done lads, keep it up' after Marseilles violence. *The Independent* [online]. Available at: www.indep endent.co.uk [accessed 5 October 2019].

de Waele, J.-M., Gibril, S., Gloriozova, E. and Spaaij, R. (eds) (2018). *The Palgrave International Handbook of Football and Politics*. London: Palgrave Macmillan

Djordjević, I. (2012). Twenty years later. The war did (not) begin at Maksimir an anthropological analysis of the media narratives about a never ended football game. *Glasnik Etnografskog instituta SANU*, 60(2), pp. 201–216.

Djordjević, I. (2013). 'Red Star Serbia, never Yugoslavia!' Football, politics and national identity in Serbia. *Open Democracy* [online]. Available at: www.opendem ocracy.net/ [accessed 5 October 2019].

Djordjević, I. (2014). Football and ethnic violence in the Balkans. *Open Democracy* [online]. Available at: www.opendemocracy.net/ [accessed 5 October 2019].

Djordjević, I. (2016). The role of red star football club in the construction of Serbian national identity. *Traditiones*, 45(1), pp. 117–132.

Djordjević, I. and Pekić, R. (2017). Is there space for the left? Football fans and political positioning in Serbia. *Soccer & Society*, 19(3), pp. 355–372.

Djordjević I. and Žikić, B. (2016). Normalising political relations through football: The CASE of Croatia and Serbia (1990–2013). In: A. Schwell, N. Szogs, M.Z. Kowalska and M. Buchowski (eds) *New Ethnographies of Football in Europe. Football Research in an Enlarged Europe*. London: Palgrave Macmillan, pp. 39–54.

Doidge, M. (2013). The birthplace of Italian Communism. Political identity and action amongst Livorno fans. *Soccer & Society*, 14(2), pp. 246–261.

Dorsey, J. (2012). Pitched battles: The role of ultra soccer fans in the Arab spring. *Mobilization*, 17(4), pp. 411–418.

Duke, V. and Crolley, L. (2014). *Football, Nationality and the State*. London-New York: Routledge.

Duke, V. and Slepička, P. (2002). Bohemian rhapsody: Football supporters in the Czech Republic. In: E. Dunning, P. Murphy, I. Waddington and A. Astrinakis (eds) *Fighting Fans: Football Hooliganism as a World Phenomenon*. Dublin: University College Dublin Press, pp. 49–61.

Eberhardt, A. (2011). *The Paradoxes of Moldovan Sports. An Insight into the Nature of the Transnistrian Conflict* [pdf]. Warsaw: OSW Point of View.

Edelman, R. (1993). *Serious Fun. A History of Spectator Sports in the USSR*. Oxford: Oxford University Press.

Edelman, R. (2002). A small way of saying 'no'. Moscow working men, Spartak soccer, and the Communist Party, 1900–1945. *The American Historical Review*, 107 (5), pp. 1441–1474.

Edelman, R. (2011). *Spartak Moscow. A History of the People's Team in the Workers' State*. New York: Cornel University Press.

Edelman, R. (2013). Football in the era 'changing stagnation'. The case of Spartak Moscow. In: N. Klumbyte and G. Sharafutdinova (eds) *Soviet Society in the Era of Late Socialism, 1964–1985*. Lanham: Lexington Books, pp. 143–162.

Faje, F. (2011). Football fandom in Cluj. Class, ethno-nationalism and cosmopolitanism. In: D. Kalb and G. Halmai (eds) *Headlines of Nations, Subtexts of Class. Working Class Populism and the Return of the Repressed in Neoliberal Europe*. New York: Berghahn Books, pp. 132–155.

Faje, F. (2015). Playing for and against the nation: Football in interwar Romania. *Nationalities Papers*, 43(1), pp. 160–177

Football fans and their political engagement 41

Faje, F. (2018). Romania. In: J.M. De Waele, S. Gibril, E. Gloriozova and R. Spaaij (eds) *The Palgrave International Handbook of Football and Politics.* London: Palgrave Macmillan, pp. 245–264.

Fisun, O. (2014). Ukrainian nationalism, soccer clubs, and the Euromaidan. *PONARS Eurasia* [online]. Available at: www.ponarseurasia.org/ [accessed 5 October 2019].

Forment, C.A. (2007). The democratic dribbler. Football clubs, neoliberal globalization, and Buenos Aires' municipal election of 2003. *Public Culture Winter*, 19(1), pp. 85–116.

Földesi, S.G. and Egressy, J. (2005). Post-transformational trends in Hungarian sport (1995–2004). *European Journal for Sport and Society*, 2(2), pp. 85–96.

Fridy, K. and Brobbey, V. (2009). Win the match and vote for me: The politicisation of Ghana's Accra Hearts of Oak and Kumasi Asante Kotoko football clubs. *The Journal of Modern African Studies*, 47(1), pp. 19–39.

Fshazi, F. (2013). Football matches or power struggles? The Albanian case within historical conflicts and contemporary tensions. *Sport in Society*, 16(8), pp. 1025–1037.

Galijaš, A. (2014). Football as a political passion. Football and the political life of Bosnian Serbs after the dissolution of the SFRY. *Sudosteuropa. Journal of Politics and Society*, 62(2), pp. 170–186

Gasser, P.K. and Levinsen, A. (2004). Breaking post -war ice. Open fun football schools in Bosnia and Herzegovina. *Sport in Society*, 7(3), pp. 457–472

Georgiev, G.G. (2017). Soccer hooligans, ethnic nationalism and political economy in Bulgaria. *Culminating Projects in Social Responsibility* [online], 10. Available at: http://repository.stcloudstate.edu/ [accessed 5 October 2019].

Ghosh, M. (2011). *Diversity and Tolerance in Ukraine in the Context of EURO 2012* [pdf]. Berlin: Friedrich-Ebert-Stiftung. Available at: http://library.fes.de [accessed 5 October 2019].

Gibril, S. (2015). Contentious politics and bottom-up mobilization in revolutionary Egypt: The case of Egyptian football supporters in Cairo. In: F.A. Gerges (ed.) *Contentious Politics in the Middle East. Popular Resistance and Marginalized Activism beyond the Arab Uprisings*, London: Palgrave Macmillan, pp. 305–329.

Gibson, O. (2016). Head of official Russian supporters Alexander Shprygin to be deported. *The Guardian* [online]. Available at: www.theguardian.com/ [accessed 5 October 2019].

Gibson, O. and Walker, S. (2016). Euro 2016: Notorious far-right activist at tournament with Russian FA delegation. *The Guardian* [online]. Available at: www.theguardian.com/ [accessed 5 October 2019].

Gilbert, A. (2018). Tri vjere, jedna nacija, država Tuzla! Football fans, political protest and the right to the city in postsocialist Bosnia–Herzegovina. *Soccer & Society*, 19 (3), pp. 373–399.

Glathe, J. (2016). Football fan subculture in Russia: Aggressive support, readiness to fight, and far right links. *Europe-Asia Studies*, 68(9), pp. 1506–1525

Glennon, S. (2016). A river runs through it. *Blizzard* [online]. Available at: www.theblizzard.co.uk/ [accessed 5 October 2019].

Gloriozova, E. (2018). Russia. In: J.M. De Waele, S. Gibril, E. Gloriozova and R. Spaaij (eds) *The Palgrave International Handbook of Football and Politics*. London: Palgrave Macmillan, pp. 265–285.

Gordon, D. (2014). Ultras Dinano i Metallista s pesnei o Putine proshlis' marshem po Har'kovu. *Gordonua* [online]. Available at http://gordonua.com/ [accessed 5 October 2019].

42 *Football fans and their political engagement*

Gorst, I. (2018). Russia softens prison conditions for World Cup hooligan detention. *Irish Times* [online]. Available at: www.irishtimes.com/ [accessed 5 October 2019].

Grant, S. (2014). Bolsheviks, Revolution and Physical Culture. *The International Journal of the History of Sport* 31(7), pp. 724–734.

Gurashi, R. (2017). The mutation of Albanian society during the economic transition from communism to liberalism. *Rivista Trimestrale di Scienza dell'Amministrazione*, 2. Available at: www.rtsa.eu/ [accessed 5 October 2019].

Guschwan, M. (2016). Fan politics: Dissent and control at the stadium. *Soccer & Society*, 17(3), pp. 388–402.

Guțu, D. (2017). 'Casuals' culture. Bricolage and consumerism in football supporters' culture. Case study – Dinamo Bucharest Ultras'. *Soccer & Society*, 18(7), pp. 914–946.

Guțu, D. (2018). World going one way, people another: ultras football gangs' survival networks and clientelism in post-socialist Romania. *Soccer & Society*, 19(3), pp. 337–354.

Hadas, M. (2000). Football and social identity. The case of Hungary in the twentieth century. *The Sports Historian*, 20(2), pp. 43–66.

Hamberger, J. (2008). On the causes of the tense Slovak-Hungarian relations. *Foreign Policy Review*, 1, pp. 55–65.

Harsányi, L. (2005). *Report on Hooliganism, Racism, Anti-Semitism and Intolerance in Slovak Football* [pdf]. Bratislava: Ludia proti rasizmu. Available at: http://protinena visti.sk/ [accessed 5 October 2019].

Hay, R. and Gouth, N. (2009). No single pattern: Australian migrant minorities and the round ball code in Victoria. *Soccer & Society*, 10(6), pp. 823–842.

Hayes, M. (2006). Glasgow Celtic fans, political culture and the Tiocfaidh Ar La Fanzine. Some comments and a content analysis. *Football Studies*, 9(1), pp. 5–18.

Hodges, A. (2016a). White Angels Zagreb. Combating homophobia as 'rural primitivism'. In: B. Bilić and S. Kajinić (eds) *Intersectionality and LGBT Activist Politics. Multiple Others in Croatia and Serbia*. London: Palgrave Macmillan, pp. 191–212.

Hodges, A. (2016b). Violence and masculinity amongst left-wing ultras in post-Yugoslav space. *Sport in Society*, 19(2), pp. 174–186.

Hodges, A. (2016c). The left and the rest? Fan cosmologies and relationships between Celtic's Green Brigade and Dinamo Zagreb's Bad Blue Boys. *Bulletin of Institute of Ethnography SASA/ Гласник Етнёграфскёг института САНУ*, 64(2), pp. 305–331.

Hodges, A. (2018). *Fan Activism, Protest and Politics. Ultras in Post-Socialist Croatia*. London: Routledge.

Hodges, A. and Brentin, D. (2017). Fan protest and activism: Football from below in South-Eastern Europe. *Soccer & Society*, 19(3), pp. 329–336.

Hodges, A. and Stubbs, P. (2016). The paradoxes of politicisation. Fan initiatives in Zagreb, Croatia. In: A. Schwell, N. Szogs, M.Z. Kowalska, M. Buchowski (eds) *New Ethnographies of Football in Europe. Football Research in an Enlarged Europe. Football Research in an Enlarged Europe*. London: Palgrave Macmillan, pp. 55–74.

Holme, B. (2015). Europa opponents' fans notorious for football hooliganism . *The Evening Express* [online]. Available at: www.eveningexpress.co.uk [accessed 5 October 2019].

Hughes, I. (2014). Violent clash between Hungary and Romania. *The Mirror* [online]. Available at: www.mirror.co.uk [accessed 5 October 2019].

Hughson, J. (2000). 'The boys are back in town'. Soccer support and the social reproduction of masculinity. *Journal of Sport & Social Issues*, 24(1), pp. 8–23.

Hughson, J. and Skillen, F. (eds) (2014). *Football in Southeastern Europe. From Ethnic Homogenization to Reconciliation.* London: Routledge.

Ionescu, S., Voicu, S. and Gabor, R. (2010). Sociological aspects of the Ultras phenomenon in the city of Timisoara. *Citius Altius Fortius,* 26(1), pp. 63–69.

Irak, D. (2018). 'Shoot some pepper gas at me!' football fans vs. Erdoğan. Organized politicization or reactive politics? *Soccer & Society,* 19(3), pp. 400–417.

Ishchenko, V. (2016). *The Ukrainian Left During and After the Maidan Protests* [pdf]. Kiev: GUE/NGL. Available at: www.guengl.com [accessed 5 October 2019].

Izzo, G., Munteanu, C., Langford, B., Ceobanu, C., Dumitru, I. and Nichifor, F. (2011). Sport fans' motivations. An investigation of Romanian soccer spectators. *Journal of International Business and Cultural Studies,* 1, pp. 1–13.

Jones, D.M. (2016). Is Vladimir Putin orchestrating Russian football hooligans to push Britain out of the EU? *The Telegraph* [online]. Available at: www.telegraph.co.uk/ [accessed 5 October 2019].

Jusufi, I. (2017). Albania's transformation since 1997. Successes and failure. *Croatian International Relations Review,* 23(77), pp. 81–115.

Kajtezović, A. (2015). The disintegration of Yugoslavia and football. *Electronic Theses and Dissertations* [online], 220. Available at: https://scholarworks.uni.edu/ [accessed 5 October 2019].

Kampark, B. (2018). Australian soccer rivalries. Diasporas, violence and the Balkan connection. *Soccer & Society,* 19(5–6), pp. 875–887.

Katchanovski, I. (2016). The far right in Ukraine during the 'Euromaidan' and the war in Donbas. *SSNR.com* [online]. Available at: https://ssrn.com/ [accessed 5 October 2019].

Kelly, J. (2013). Football fans in pre-referendum Scotland: folk devils, space and place. *The International Journal of the Sociology of Sport,* 3(1), pp. 207–229.

Kennedy, P. (2013). 'Left wing' supporter movements and the political economy of football. *Soccer & Society,* 14(2), pp. 277–290.

Kennedy, P. and Kennedy, D. (2014). *Fan Culture in European Football and the Influence of Left Wing Ideology.* Oxford: Routledge.

Kinder, T. (2013). Bosnia, the bridge, and the ball. *Soccer & Society,* 14(2), pp. 154–166.

Kirby, S., Francis, B. and O'Flaherty, R. (2014). Can the FIFA World Cup Football (Soccer). tournament be associated with an increase in domestic abuse? *Journal of Research in Crime and Delinquency,* 51(3), pp. 259–276.

Kirn, G. (2018). Maribor's social uprising in the European crisis. From antipolitics of people to politicisation of periphery's surplus population. In: F. Bieber and D. Brentin (eds) *Social Movements in the Balkans. Rebellion and Protest from Maribor to Taksim.* London: Routledge, pp. 38–55.

Klasić, H. (2017). How Falcons became Partizans. *The International Journal of the History of Sport,* 34(9), pp. 832–847.

Kłysiński, K. and Żochowski, P. (2016). *The End of the Myth of a Brotherly Belarus? Russian Soft Power in Belarus after 2014 – The Background and its Manifestations* [pdf]. Warsaw: Centre for Eastern Studies.

Knijnik, J. (2016). Imagining a multicultural community in an everyday football carnival: Chants, identity and social resistance on Western Sydney terraces. *International Review for the Sociology of Sport,* 53(4), pp. 471–489.

Kornievych, L. and Fedeczko, S. (2018). Romanian anti-corruption protests turn violent. *The Hromadske International* [online]. Available at: https://en.hromadske.ua/ [accessed 5 October 2019].

44 *Football fans and their political engagement*

Kortazov, D. (2012). *Football Politicized. CSKA Sofia as a tool for ideological hegemony in Socialist Bulgaria*. Master Thesis [pdf]. Helsinki: University of Helsinki. Available at: https://helda.helsinki.fi/ [accessed 5 October 2019].

Kotnik, V. (2009). Sport and nation in anthropological perspective. Slovenia as land of skiing nationhood. *Antropologija*, 7, pp. 53–66.

Krasniqi, S. and Krasniqi, B. (2018). Sport and peacebuilding in post-conflict societies: The role of Open Fun Football Schools in Kosovo. *Journal of Aggression, Conflict and Peace Research*, 1, pp. 1–14.

Krugliak, M. and Krugliak, O. (2017). The unlikely alliance of Ukrainian football ultras. In: C. Brandt, F. Hertel, and S. Huddleston (eds) *Football Fans, Rivalry and Cooperation*. London: Routledge, pp. 170–184.

Kušnierová, D. (2014). Ultras in Trnava: History, activities and ideology. *Ethnologia Actualis*, 14(2), pp. 59–96.

Lalić, D. and Wood, S. (2014). Football hooliganism in Croatia. A historical and sociological analysis. *Sudosteuropa. Journal of Politics and Society*, 62(2), pp. 145–169.

László, P. (2014). The genesis of Romanian football. Social factors and processes behind the game. *Belvedere Meridionale*, 26(4), pp. 81–94.

Lepădatu, L. (2015). The Romanian football supporter. Spectator, ultras or hooligan? Comparative analysis of the violent behaviour of the Dinamo and Steaua teams' supporters. *Romanian Journal of Sociology*, 1–2, pp. 103–120.

Lewycka, M. (2012). Don't judge a nation like Ukraine by its hooligans. *The Telegraph* [online]. Available at: www.telegraph.co.uk/ [accessed 5 October 2019].

Locals in Maribor protest against planned asylum centre. STA Official Website [online]. Available at: https://english.sta.si/ [accessed 5 October 2019].

Loginov, M. (2012). Dangerous allies: When football hooligans and politicians meet. *Open Democracy* [online]. Available at: www.opendemocracy.net/ [accessed 5 October 2019].

Manasiev, A. (2012a). Balkans' political football keeps hooligans close to heart of power. *The Guardian* [online]. Available at: www.theguardian.com/ [accessed 5 October 2019].

Manasiev, A. (2012b). Political football. The Balkans' belligerent ultras avoid penalties. *The Balkan Insight* [online]. Available at: www.balkaninsight.com/ [accessed 5 October 2019].

Mareš, M. (2012). *Right-Wing Extremism in the Czech Republic* [pdf]. Berlin: Friedrich-Ebert-Stiftung. Available at: https://library.fes.de/ [accessed 5 October 2019].

Marković, M. (2015). A culture of violence – The politics of Serbian football hooliganism. *Futbolgrad* [online]. Available at: http://futbolgrad.com/ [accessed 5 October 2019].

McArdle, D. and Veth, M. (2015). Ukrainian ultras and the unorthodox revolution. *Futbolgrad* [online]. Available at: http://futbolgrad.com/ [accessed 5 October 2019].

McDonald, M. (2014). *How Regimes Dictate Oligarchs & Their Football Clubs: Case Studies Comparison of Oligarch Football Club Ownership in Dagestan, Romania, & Transnistria from 1990–2014*. Master thesis [pdf]. Chapel Hill: University of North Carolina. Available at: https://pdfs.semanticscholar.org/ [accessed 5 October 2019].

McManus, J. (2015). Driven to distraction. Turkish diaspora football supporters, new media and the politics of place-making. *Sociological Research Online* [online] 4(2). Available at: www.socresonline.org.uk/ [accessed 5 October 2019].

Mihailović, S. (1997). The war started on May 1990. In: S. Slpašak (ed.) *The War Started at Maksimir. Hate Speech in the Media. Content Analyses of Politika and Borba newpapers, 1987–1991*. Belgrade: Media Center, pp. 97–156.

Mills, R. (2009). It all ended in an unsporting way. Serbian football and the disintegration of Yugoslavia, 1989–2006. *The International Journal of the History of Sport*, 26(9), pp. 1187–1217.

Mills, R. (2010). Velez Mostar football club and the demise of 'brotherhood and unity' in Yugoslavia, 1922–2009. *Europe-Asia Studies*, 62(7), pp. 1107–1133

Mills, R. (2012). Commemorating a disputed past. Football club and supporters' group war memorials in the Former Yugoslavia. *History*, 328(97), pp. 540–577.

Mills, R. (2013a). *Domestic Football and Nationalism in the Construction and Destruction of Socialist Yugoslavia, 1945–1995*. PhD thesis. Norwich: University of East Anglia.

Mills, R. (2013b). Fighters, footballers and nation builders. Wartime football in the Serb-held territories of the Former Yugoslavia, 1991–1996. *Sport in Society*, 16(8), pp. 945–972.

Mills, R. (2016). The pitch itself was no man's land. Siege, Željezničar Sarajevo Football Club and the Grbavica Stadium. *Nationalities Papers*, 44(6), pp. 877–903.

Mills, R. (2018a). *The Politics of Football in Yugoslavia. Sport, Nationalism and the State*. London: I. B. Tauris.

Mills, R. (2018b). Serbia. In: J.M. De Waele, S. Gibril, E. Gloriozova and R. Spaaij (eds) *The Palgrave International Handbook of Football and Politics*. London: Palgrave Macmillan, pp. 287–309.

Millward, P. (2008). Rivalries and racisms: 'Closed' and 'open' Islamophobic dispositions amongst football supporters. *Sociological Research Online* [online] 13(6). Available at: www.socresonline.org.uk/ [accessed 5 October 2019].

Molnar, G. (2007). Hungarian football: A socio-historical perspective. *Sport in History*, 27(2), pp. 293–318.

Montenegro v Russia Euro 2016 qualifier abandoned after crowd trouble. (2015). *The Guardian* [online]. Available at: www.theguardian.com/ [accessed 5 October 2019].

Nielsen, C.A. (2010). The goalposts of transition. Football as a metaphor for Serbia's long journey to the rule of law. *Nationalities Papers*, 38(1), pp. 87–103.

Nielsen, C.A. (2013). Stronger than the state? Football hooliganism, political extremism and the Gay Pride Parades in Serbia. *Sport in Society*, 16(8), pp. 1038–1053.

Nociar, T. (2012). *Right-Wing Extremism in Slovakia* [pdf]. Berlin: Friedrich-Ebert-Stiftung. Available at: http://library.fes.de/ [accessed 5 October 2019].

Numerato, D. (2010). Between small everyday practices and glorious symbolic acts: Sport-based resistance against the communist regime in Czechoslovakia. *Sport in Society*, 13(1), pp. 107–120.

Numerato, D. (2017). Between civic engagement and politics. A case study of Bohemians Prague 1905 Supporters' Trust. In: B. Garcia and J. Zheng (eds) *Football and Supporter Activism in Europe*. London: Palgrave Macmillan, pp. 211–231.

Obradovic-Wochink, J. (2012). Racism in Serbian football fan culture: The establishment fails to act. *The Guardian* [online]. Available at: www.theguardian.com/ [accessed 5 October 2019].

Obućina, V. (2012). *Right-Wing Extremism in Croatia*. Berlin: Friedrich-Ebert-Stiftung. Available at: http://library.fes.de/ [accessed 5 October 2019].

Osborne, A. (2016). Russian hooligans see themselves as Kremlin foot soldiers. *Reuters* [online]. Available at: www.reuters.com/ [accessed 5 October 2019].

Ovsepyan, K. (2017). The history of the Zenit Soccer Club as a case study in Soviet football teams. *Soccer & Society*, 18(2–3), pp. 286–295.

Özkan, Ö.D. (2013). Football fandom and formation of cultural differences in Bosnia. A comparative ethnographic study on FK Željezničar and FK Sarajevo fans in

46 Football fans and their political engagement

Sarajevo. In: *Kick It! The Anthropology of European Football, Football Research in an Enlarged Europe Conference* [online]. Vienna: University of Vienna. Available at: www.free-project.eu/ [accessed 5 October 2019].

Papoutzis L., Kyridis, A., Christodoulou, A., Fotopoulos, N. and Vamvakidou, I. (2014). Football stickers and slogans as creators of 'special' identities. The case of Aris FC Thessaloniki. *Rivista di semiotica*, 17–18, pp. 651–670.

Parkin, S. (2018). The rise of Russia's neo-Nazi football hooligans. *The Guardian* [online]. Available at: www.theguardian.com/ [accessed 5 October 2019].

Pavasovic Trost, T. and Kovacevic, N. (2013). Football, hooliganism and nationalism: the reaction to Serbia's gay parade in reader commentary online. *Sport in Society*, 16(8), pp. 1054–1076

Pearson, O. (2004). *Albania in the Twentieth Century, A History. Volume III: Albania as Dictatorship and Democracy, 1945–99*. London: I. B. Tauris.

Perasović, B. and Mustapić, M. (2013). Football supporters in the context of Croatian sociology. Research perspectives 20 years after. *Kinesiology*, 45(2), pp. 262–275

Perasović, B. and Mustapić, M. (2014). Football, politics and cultural memory. The case of HNK Hajduk Split. *Культура/Culture*, 6, pp. 51–61

Perasović, B. and Mustapić, M. (2017). Torcida and bad boys blue. From hatred to cooperation and back. In C. Brandt, F. Hertel, and S. Huddleston (eds) *Football Fans, Rivalry and Cooperation*. London: Routledge, pp. 108–124

Perasović, B. and Mustapić, M. (2018). Carnival supporters, hooligans, and the 'Against Modern Football' movement. Life within the ultras subculture in the Croatian context. *Sport in Society*, 21(6), pp. 960–976.

Petkova, M. (2018). Meet the football ultras 'all of Russia' hates. *Al-Jazeera* [online]. Available at: www.aljazeera.com/ [accessed 5 October 2019].

Petrov, A. (2017). How doing sport became a culture: producing the concept of physical cultivation of the Yugoslavs. *The International Journal of the History of Sport*, 34(9), pp. 753–766.

Podaliri, C. and Balestri, C. (1998). The ultras, racism and football culture in Italy. In: A. Brown (ed.) *Fanatics! Power, Identity and Fandom in Football*. London: Routledge, pp. 88–100.

Popović, S. and Bjelica, D. (2014). Relationship between sport and national identity in Montenegro. *Montenegrin Journal of Sports Science and Medicine*, 3(1), pp. 31–33.

Portnov, A. (2014). How 'eastern Ukraine' was lost. *Open Democracy* [online]. Available at: www.opendemocracy.net/en/ [accessed 5 October 2019].

Purs, A. (2012). *Baltic Facades: Estonia, Latvia and Lithuania since 1945*. London: Reaktion Books.

Report on Extremism in the Territory of Czech Republic in 2016. (2017) [pdf]. Prague: Ministerstvo Vnitra. Available at: www.mvcr.cz [accessed 5 October 2019].

Riach, J. (2012). Euro 2012: Poland and Russia supporters clash before match in Warsaw. *The Guardian* [online]. Available at: www.theguardian.com/ [accessed 5 October 2019].

Riordan, J. (1977). *Sport in Soviet Society*. Cambridge: Cambridge University Press.

Rothfel, E. (2016). The Kremlin, the far right and football: Just how bad is Russia's hooliganism problem? *Goal.com* [online]. Available at: www.goal.com/ [accessed 5 October 2019].

Rudic, F. (2017). Serbian football fans show support for Ratko Mladic. Balkan transitional justice [online]. Available at: https://balkaninsight.com/ [accessed 5 October 2019].

Football fans and their political engagement 47

Rudic, F., Milekic, M. and Lakic, S. (2018). How nationalism usurped anti-fascism in Balkan sports. *Balkan Transitional Justice* [online]. Available at: https://balkanin sight.com/ [accessed 5 October 2019].

Ruzhelnyk, O. (2018). Ukraine. In: J.M. De Waele, S. Gibril, E. Gloriozova and R. Spaaij (eds) *The Palgrave International Handbook of Football and Politics*. London: Palgrave Macmillan, pp. 311–326.

Sack, A. and Suster, Z. (2000). Soccer and Croatian nationalism: A prelude to war. *Journal of Sport and Social Issues*, 24(3), pp. 305–320

Saveski, Z. and Sadiku, A. (2012). *The Radical Right in Macedonia* [pdf]. Berlin: Friedrich-Ebert-Stiftung. Available at: http://library.fes.de/ [accessed 5 October 2019].

Scholz, P. (2016). Czech football hooligans' behavior. *Journal of Physical Education and Sport*, 16(2), pp. 1089–1094.

Senn, A.E. (1990). Perestroika and Lithuanian basketball. *Journal of Sport History*, 17 (1), pp. 56–61

Sergatskova, K. (2014). Ukrainian ultras. A global ceasefire. *Euromaidan Press* [online]. Available at: http://euromaidanpress.com/ [accessed 5 October 2019].

Shea, A. (2018). The troubling relationship between Serbian politics and football hooliganism. *These Football Times* [online]. Available at: https://thesefootballtimes. co/ [accessed 5 October 2019].

Simonović, B., Otašević, B. and Djurdjević Z. (2014). Criminal careers of football club fan leaders in Serbia. *Revija za kriminalistiko in kriminologijo*, 65(2), pp. 108–120

Sindbæk, T. (2013). 'A Croatian champion with a Croatian name'. National identity and uses of history in Croatian football culture – the case of Dinamo Zagreb. *Sport in Society*, 16(8), pp. 1009–1024.

Smolík, J. (2004). Football hooliganism from the standpoint of extremism. *Středoevropské politické studie*, 6(4).

Smolík, J. (2012). Football hooligans in the Czech Republic. Selected topics. *Kultuta – Społeczeństwo – Edukacja* [Culture – Society – Education], 2, pp. 75–95.

Spaaij, R. and Viñas, C. (2013). Political ideology and activism in football fan culture in Spain: A view from the far left. *Soccer & Society*, 14(2), pp. 183–200.

Stankovic, P. (2005). Sport and nationalism: The shifting meanings of soccer in Slovenia. *The Landscapes of Cultural Studies*, 7(2), pp. 1–14.

Sterchele, D. (2007). The limits of inter-religious dialogue and the form of football rituals: The CASE of Bosnia-Herzegovina. *Social Compass*, 54(2), pp. 211–224.

Sterchele, D. (2013). Fertile land or mined field? Peace-building and ethnic tensions in post-war Bosnian Football. *Sport in Society*, 16(8), pp. 973–992.

Stewart, C. (2008). *Hunting the Tiger. The Fast Life and Violent Death of the Balkans' Most Dangerous Man*. New York: Thomas Dunne Books.

Straton, J. (2015). Playing the Jew: Anti-Semitism and football in the twenty-first century. *Jewish Culture and History*, 16(3), pp. 293–311

Stylianou, S. and Theodoropoulou, V. (2013). Performing fan identities. The role of politics in the antagonistic communication of football fans in Cyprus. In: *Kick It! The Anthropology of European Football, Football Research in an Enlarged Europe Conference* [online]. Vienna: University of Vienna. Available at: www.free-project. eu/ [accessed 5 October 2019].

Sugden, J. and Tomlinson, A. (2000). Football, ressentiment and resistance in the break-up of the former Soviet Union. *Culture, Sport, Society*, 3(2), pp. 89–108.

Thaçi, R. (2016). 'Furia Albanica'. The last myth for the preservation of Albanian National identity. *Mediterranean Journal of Social Sciences*, 7(4), pp. 533–539.

48 *Football fans and their political engagement*

Todorov, A. (2013). *The Extreme Right Wing in Bulgaria* [pdf]. Berlin: Friedrich-Ebert-Stiftung. Available at: http://library.fes.de/ [accessed 5 October 2019].

Tomić, D. (2013). On the 'right' side? The radical right in the post-Yugoslav area and the Serbian case. *Fascism. Journal of Comparative Fascist Studies*, 2, pp. 94–114.

Toplak, C. and Haček, H. (2012). *Slovenia. Political Insight* [pdf]. Warsaw: European School of Law and Administration. Available at: www.fdv.uni-lj.si [accessed 5 October 2019].

Tregoures, L. (2017). Beyond the pattern. Corruption, hooligans, and football governance in Croatia. In: B. Garcia and J. Zheng (eds) *Football and Supporter Activism in Europe*. London: Palgrave Macmillan, pp. 165–186.

Tregoures, L. (2018). Croatia. In: J.M. De Waele, S. Gibril, E. Gloriozova and R. Spaaij (eds) *The Palgrave International Handbook of Football and Politics*. London: Palgrave Macmillan, pp. 205–222.

Tregoures, L. and Šantek, G. (2017). A comparison of two fan initiatives in Croatia: Zajedno za Dinamo (Together for Dinamo) and Naš Hajduk (Our Hajduk). *Soccer & Society*, 19(3), pp. 453–464.

Tsoukala, A. (2009). *Football Hooliganism in Europe. Security and Civil Liberties in the Balance*. London: Palgrave Macmillan.

Tuastad, D. (2014). From football riot to revolution. The political role of football in the Arab world. *Soccer & Society*, 15(3), pp. 376–388.

Turan, Ö. and Özçetin, B. (2017). Football fans and contentious politics. The role of Çarşı in the Gezi Park protests. *International Review for the Sociology of Sport*.

Uthoff, J. (2013). Partizan Minsk. Die Fußball-Freiheitskämpfer aus Weißrussland. *Die Zeit* [online]. Available at: www.zeit.de/ [accessed 5 October 2019].

Valantinė, I., Grigaliūnaitė, I. and Danilevičienė, L. (2017). Impact of basketball fan behaviour on the organization's brand. *Baltic Journal of Sport& Health Sciences*, 104(1), pp. 47–54.

Vangelovski, T. (2017). *Macedonia. Ethno-Religious Conflict (1991–2016)*. Canberra: Australian National University – Centre for Arab and Islamic Studies.

Vest, E.K. (2014). *The War of Positions. The Football in Post-Conflict Bosnia- Herzegovina*. Doctoral Thesis. London: Brunel University.

Veth, M. (2013). Ukrainian ultras – Where two wings collide. *Futbolgrad* [online]. Available at: http://futbolgrad.com/ [accessed 5 October 2019].

Veth, M. (2015). The empire that is Shakhtar Donetsk FC. *Open Democracy* [online]. Available at: www.opendemocracy.net/ [accessed 5 October 2019].

Vickers, M. (2001). *The Albanians. A Modern History*. London: I. B. Tauris.

Volkava, E. and Bartkowski, M. (2014). The Ukrainian soccer ultras: Allies of the resistance. *Open Democracy* [online]. Available at: www.opendemocracy.net/ [accessed 5 October 2019].

Vrcan, S. (2002). The curious drama of the president of a republic versus a football fan tribe. A symptomatic case in the post-communist transition in Croatia. *International Review for the Sociology of Sport*, 37(1), pp. 59–77.

Vrcan, S. and Lalić, D. (1999). From ends to trenches, and back. Football in the former Yugoslavia. In: G. Armstrong and R. Giulianotti (eds) *Football Cultures and Identities*. London: Palgrave Macmillan, pp. 176–185.

Vukušić, D. and Miošić, L. (2017). Reinventing and reclaiming football through radical fan practices? NK Zagreb 041 and Futsal Dinamo. *Soccer & Society*, 19(3), pp. 440–452.

Walker, S. (2018). Football in Crimea: The club split in two by Russia's invasion. *The Guardian* [online]. Available at: www.theguardian.com/ [accessed 5 October 2019].

Wilson, J. (2007). How the Montenegrin title race got nasty. *The Guardian* [online]. Available at: www.theguardian.com/ [accessed 5 October 2019].

Wood, M.R. (2010). *'Football is War'. Nationalism, National Identity and Football* [pdf]. Available at: https://yabastamedia.wordpress.com/ [accessed 5 October 2019].

Wood, S. (2013). Football after Yugoslavia: Conflict, reconciliation and the regional football league debate. *Sport in Society*, 16(8), pp. 1077–1090.

Zaimakis, Y. (2018). Football fan culture and politics in modern Greece: The process of fandom radicalization during the austerity era. *Soccer & Society*, 19(2), pp. 252–270.

Zec, D. (2010). The origin of soccer in Serbia. Serbian Studies. *Journal of the North American Society for Serbian Studies*, 24(1–2), pp. 137–159.

Zec, D. and Paunović, M. (2014). Football's positive influence on integration in diverse societies: The case study of Yugoslavia. *Soccer & Society*, 16(2–3), pp. 232–244.

Zeller, M. (2011). 'Our own internationale', 1966 Dynamo Kiev fans between local identity and transnational imagination. *Kritika: Explorations in Russian and Eurasian History*, 12(1), pp. 53–82.

Zenit St. Petersburg fans petition club to sack black players and demand all-white heterosexual team. (2012). *The Telegraph* [online]. Available at: www.telegraph.co.uk/ [accessed 5 October 2019].

Zivanovic, M. (2018). Red Star Belgrade face punishment for anti-Muslim banner. *Balkan Insight* [online]. Available at: https://balkaninsight.com/ [accessed 5 October 2019].

Zwicker, S. (2013). Prague and Czechoslovak football in the Cold War Period. In: *Kick It! The Anthropology of European Football, Football Research in an Enlarged Europe Conference* [online]. Vienna: University of Vienna. Available at: www.free-project.eu/ [accessed 5 October 2019].

3 Socio-economic and political transformation of Poland since the collapse of communism

Introduction

After 1989 Poland underwent transformation from a country with centrally planned economy and authoritarian system, member of the Soviet bloc with limited sovereignty, to a democratic state embracing rules of free market economy and pursuing independent internal and foreign policies. This chapter highlights key processes occurring in the course of post-socialist transformation. The aim is to provide the readers who are not familiar with recent Polish history with an overview of the state of affairs in crucial spheres: economic and social policy on the one hand, and social divisions, political discourse and party politics on the other. Particular attention is paid to the issues which will be discussed in the following parts in reference to the main theme of this book.

The 1980s and the beginning of the end of communism in Poland

The People's Republic of Poland (PRL) emerged from the post-war turmoil in 1948, but it was the Yalta Conference of 1945 that decided the fate of the country, leaving it in the sphere of military and political influence of the Soviet Union. The three superpowers compensated Poland's significant territorial losses in the east with the so-called 'recovered territories' in the west, the land formerly belonging to Germany. While the political system imposed in Poland after 1945 is generally referred to as communism, the economic reality was more ambiguous than the classical understanding of the term. Although the majority of assets and property was nationalised, private property was legal and – unlike in other countries in the sphere of Soviet influence – there was no full collectivisation of the agricultural sector: most farms belonged to private owners. Nonetheless, the communist Polish United Workers' Party (*Polska Zjednoczona Partia Robotnicza*, herafter PZPR) entirely controlled the functioning of the state. Largely dependent on the decisions made in the Kremlin, the PZPR had full control over public affairs in Poland for forty years. In the highly centralised system of administration, the party controlled various institutions and their regional and local branches, and thus had a complete authority over decision-making in all matters relating to sport and football.

Socio-economic and political transformation of Poland   51

There have been various proposals concerning the periodisation of the communist era, but detailed historical analysis is beyond the scope of this study. From the perspective of the main topic of this book, the most crucial period was the 1980s. In many respects, the shape of modern Polish politics (both in terms of discourse and institutional setting) is a legacy of the events and processes from the 1980s. Martial law, which was introduced in 1981, marked the end of the so-called 'carnival of Solidarity', 16 months of relative liberalisation of the communist regime, sparked by the PZPR's decision to register the Solidarity [*Solidarność*] trade union as the first independent organisation in the Soviet bloc. The mass-scale mobilisation, about ten million people joined, came to an abrupt end – on 13 December 1981 the new union was banned. The following decade was marked by growing repressions, decreasing political engagement of Poles and a severe economic crisis. More than ten thousand Solidarity activists were imprisoned; ninety people were killed in the clashes with the *Milicja* (communist police) and the army. About 700,000 people, many of whom were former anti-communist activists, emigrated in the course of the 1980s. Periodical shortage of supplies, typical of the centrally planned socialist economy, turned into permanent shortage of even basic goods, accompanied with the growth of inflation causing the phenomenon of *shortageflation* (Kornai, 1980; Kolodko and McMahon, 1987). Everyday practice of rationing resources (and the system of coupons used for the purpose) was coupled with the significant decrease of legitimation both for the communist party and anti-communist opposition (Kolodko, 2002).

Initiated in 1988, the Round Table talks between the communist party and the representatives of anti-communist opposition (some of whom had only recently been released from prisons) were supposed to give a new impulse to Polish politics (Friszke et al., 2019; Kowalik, 2012). For the first time in the history of the Soviet bloc, the Round Table Agreements (1989) allowed the anti-communist opposition to form an official electoral committee and take part in parliamentary elections. The communist party secured themselves at least two-thirds of seats in the Sejm (the lower chamber of parliament), but the elections to the newly formed Senate (the upper chamber) were entirely free. The ban on Solidarity was lifted, and the organisation united the whole pluralist anti-communist opposition under its banner.

To the dismay and surprise of the communist circles, and contrary to their expectations based on opinion polls, the elections held on 4 June 1989 brought a landslide victory for the opposition, which won 99 out of 100 seats in the Senate, and all one-third of seats in the Sejm that were available. Symbolically, this result is sometimes considered one of the events that contributed to or enhanced the political processes which consequently led to the collapse of the Soviet Union and the dismantling of bipolar global political order set out in the Yalta Agreement. The first non-communist government, led by Tadeusz Mazowiecki, was appointed three months later. What followed was the implementation of fundamental changes in the Polish economic and legal system,

52 *Socio-economic and political transformation of Poland*

including the restitution of civil and economic liberties, which effectively introduced Poland to the group of countries embracing principles of democracy. In less than four months the Polish United Workers Party dissolved – the communist party, which had been in power for over forty years, and which since 1976 had been hailed in the Polish constitution as 'the leading force of the nation', ceased to exist.

Economic and social policy: from central planning to market economy

The reforms undertaken since the beginning of transformation were in line with the then dominating neoliberal creed. Although the anti-communist movement was pluralist, most leading politicians with the Solidarity background found neo-liberal ideas attractive regardless of their previous ideological stance. Tadeusz Kowalik, a former advisor to the Solidarity trade union, was one of the few economists who not only criticised the pathway and the consequences of neoliberal reforms, but publicly questioned the dogma of TINA (There Is No Alternative). He claimed that the choice of Leszek Balcerowicz as the main founder of the economic policy at the beginning of transformation was somewhat accidental; other candidates approached with the proposal had refused. Although Tadeusz Mazowiecki famously declared that as the prime minister he was looking for 'a Polish Ludwig Erhard', Balcerowicz's economic views, particularly on the role of the state, were much more in line with the most dogmatic versions of neoclassical economics proposed by Milton Friedman and Friedrich Hayek, and the practical neoliberal applications of Thatcherism and Reaganomics (Kowalik 2012, p. 55).

Polish policymakers implemented new ideas far more eagerly than their counterparts in the West would dare. Poland quickly earned the reputation of 'a stellar neo-liberal reformer' (Orenstein, 2013, p. 389). The main economic advisors to the first non-communist government affiliated with the International Monetary Fund, David Lipton and Jeffrey Sachs, proposed three pathways of economic reforms. To their surprise, the government, largely consisting of members of Solidarity, opted for the most radical and socially costly one (Kowalik, 2012). This involved rapid privatisation of state-owned enterprises, state retrenchment from many of the obligations towards worse-off citizens, gradual dismantling of the pay-as-you-go pension system and decentralisation of state administration.

The overarching belief in the free market ideology and self-regulating capitalism may be exemplified by the statement made by Tadeusz Syryjczyk, one of the most prominent politicians in the field of economic policy and the minister of industry in the first non-communist government, who famously and completely seriously quipped that 'the best industrial policy is no industrial policy' (Karpiński et al., 2013, p. 10). Consequently, the privatisation processes were spontaneous and not designed in any strategic way.

From socialist welfare state to the retrenchment of the state

The socialist welfare state was founded on the principle of full employment. All social provisions were allocated through state-owned companies, but the generosity and quality of the services were never fully adequate and never actually approached the standards of the Western welfare state during its post-war 'golden age' (see Golinowska, 2013; Księżopolski, 2013; Ferge, 2008). The very first and crucial consequence of the shock therapy was mass-scale unemployment caused by rapid deindustrialisation.

In the early 1990s, the institutions of social and labour policy were either non-existent or completely unprepared to the challenges posed by the massive loss of jobs, with registered unemployment growing from none in 1989 to 6.5 per cent in 1990, and to 16.4 per cent three years later. This meant that at the end of 1993 there were almost three million unemployed, which went contrary to official predictions made by Balcerowicz, estimating that unemployment would not exceed 400 thousand (Kolodko and Nuti, 1997). These figures would have been significantly higher if it had not been for the opportunities of early retirement for workers over 55 years of age, and quite flexible scheme for receiving disability benefits (Kowalik, 2012). In the following years the unemployment rate stabilised at around 10 per cent; it began rising again in 1999, reaching the level of 20 per cent (regionally 30+ per cent) in 2002 and 2003. For almost two decades, then, younger generations of Poles, particularly with lower educational background, entered the labour market facing a permanent threat of falling into unemployment trap, and suffered from low wages and precarious working conditions. As in the case of the United Kingdom a decade earlier, the increase of hooliganism and football-related violence in the 1990s has been frequently attributed to the situation on the labour market, with precarisation and pauperisation largely affecting also young male working-class population. This theme will be further elaborated in the following chapters.

The pay-as-you-go pension system was effectively dismantled in 1999 with the introduction of capital-based elements, a move taken under the influence of lobbyists from multinational corporations (Orenstein, 2008). Replacement of the system based on intergenerational solidarity with capital-based system of commercial Open Pension Funds and Individual Pension Accounts was very much in line with the dominating pro-market narrative, which viewed it necessary to support private entrepreneurship, even if it means transferring part of the pensions to multinational financial corporations, and individual responsibility for one's own fate and future well-being (the reform was partially reversed in 2015).

Even before the final decline of the socialist and officially classless People's Republic of Poland, the level of income inequalities measured by the Gini coefficient exceeded those recorded in many capitalist states (1988). Since then, it was growing steadily until 2005, when it reached 0.4 according to the data from surveys (Domański 2007, p. 312). This was coupled with the

54 *Socio-economic and political transformation of Poland*

increase of poverty rates and income inequality. In fact, towards the end of communist Poland, in 1988–1989, the latter was higher than in many capitalist states embracing the Nordic or corporatist model of welfare state (e.g. Nordic states or West Germany), and was growing until 2005, with the level of education becoming the crucial factor of stratification.

Poland remained a 'green island' in the course of the post-2008 global economic downturn, to use a phrase coined by the Polish government on the grounds that the country was the only member of the European Union which did not suffer recession at the time. Since 2009, the map of Europe with Poland painted green was the key element of promotional materials of the ruling parties. Nevertheless, the GDP growth dropped significantly, from 6.7 per cent in 2007 and 5 per cent in the following year to 1.8 per cent in 2009. The key socio-economic indicators had started improving since Poland's accession to the European Union (2004). In 2008, the level of registered unemployment fell to a one-digit figure (9.5 per cent) for the first time since the beginning of the transformation.

The reasons behind the improving statistics are both directly and indirectly linked with the consequences of the accession. Although the inflow of EU structural funds accelerated investments and had an impact on the growth of GDP, it seems that the key factor at play was the massive wave of emigration in the post-accession period. The governments of the United Kingdom, Ireland and Sweden opened their labour markets to the citizens of new member states immediately after the accession. Consequently, between two and two and a half million Poles emigrated (either temporarily or permanently).

The Polish model of social policy has been described as a hybrid, characterised by family-centred approach in terms of family and care policies on the one hand, and very liberal in terms of the organisation of labour policies on the other, particularly when it comes to the level of state support for the unemployed, with no more than 15 per cent of them entitled to any form of direct financial benefits (Jasiecki, 2013, pp. 175–176). Throughout the transition period, Polish economy relied on low wages of relatively well-educated and skilled workforce as the major competitive advantage: the adjusted wage share as a percentage of GDP is among the lowest in Europe. Thus, the relative economic success visible in statistics and international comparisons does not necessarily translate into the improvement of economic well-being and quality of life in different echelons of society (Rek-Woźniak and Woźniak, 2017).

Democracy without engaged citizens

Although Poland quickly achieved the formal markings of a democracy, international rankings and indexes of political culture indicate that it has flaws in the spheres of working out consensus, perception of democracy and separation between the Church and state (Jasiecki, 2013, p. 179). According to some foreign scholars (Ackerman, 1992; Dahrendorf, 1990), one of the 'original sins' of the Third Polish Republic concerned the lack of a serious

Socio-economic and political transformation of Poland 55

debate about the way the state would be organised. With such a debate largely neglected in the early days of the transformation, the institutional setting was mostly emerging spontaneously in response to the most urgent challenges and pressures. The necessity of adaptation of the Polish legal system and institutional frameworks to EU standards became a great challenge when Poland officially opened membership negotiations

Indeed, the organisation of the state as described in the constitution adopted only in 1997 was a bricolage or a hybrid of various systemic elements which were not necessarily coherent. Kamiński (2010) writes retrospectively about the 'missed constitutional moment' in the 1990s. He elaborates on a missed opportunity for a debate on the state and for a clear decision about the institutional setting and the distribution of powers, obligations and supervisory tasks in various policy fields, as well as about a system of checks and balances which would prevent the public sphere from becoming a political spoil after every election.

After the decades of a highly centralised communist state, the new ideology of self-governance was winning the minds of key policy makers. This led to almost unquestioning support for the development of civil society and decentralisation of administration. In practical terms, the development of civil society meant the development of the so-called third sector, non-governmental organisations, which – in accordance with the constitutional principle of subsidiarity – were supposed to take over many functions previously performed by the state. The whole process, then, can be viewed as top-down, driven by lawmakers, rather than as officially praised grass-roots activity of engaged citizens. On the other hand, the decentralisation of administration and the introduction of a three-level self-government (communes [*gminy*]; districts [*powiaty*]; and provinces [*województwa*]) was not accompanied by the adequate redistribution of resources for the allocated tasks. Jadwiga Staniszkis, a leading scholar of the post-communist transition, claims that effectively it was yet another way to dismantle what was left of the welfare state (Staniszkis, 2001, p. 93).

Although many of the reforms mentioned above were positively evaluated by experts, it is difficult to overlook that the level of social trust in state institutions is low in Poland, which is usually attributed to the legacy of communism (Ziółkowski, Drozdowski and Pawłowska, 1994). Less than half of Poles 'definitely trust' or 'rather trust' courts and local government institutions, one quarter trust the parliament, and 27.1 per cent – the government (Statistics Poland, 2015). At least to some extent, it is probably low trust that contributes to low voting turnout in Poland. Presidential elections attracted more than 60 per cent of voters, but only in the first three campaigns: in 1990, 1995 and 2000; in the twenty-first century the highest turnout was 55 per cent (in 2010). No more than 63 per cent casted their vote in the symbolic election of 1989. In the parliamentary elections of 2007, the turnover was 53.88 per cent, and in 2015–50.92 per cent. In all other national elections less than a half of eligible voters bothered to visit polling stations (Cześnik, 2018). The lack of trust and the lack of citizens' engagement are important components

56 *Socio-economic and political transformation of Poland*

of the mindset that to some extent may be connected with questioning the significance of democratic values or a lacking sense of allegiance to the Third Polish Republic, quite frequently observed in the football terraces in contemporary Poland.

Intelligentsia and the restoration of the capitalist order

Whereas in Russia or Ukraine the post-1989 transformation saw massive takeover of the state-owned capital by members of the former communist *nomenklatura*, which was the backbone of the field of political power, this was not the case in Poland. The process known as nomenclature enfranchisement occurred on a significantly smaller scale than to the east of Polish borders (Staniszkis, 2001). At the same time, the communist elites effectively escaped any form of either individual or collective responsibility. Unlike in some other post-communist countries, membership in the highest echelons of communist power has not ruled out membership in the political elite of a newly restored democratic state. This kind of forgiveness on the part of the new elites was used in the following decades as proof of a deal made during the Round Table talks between the former communist elite and a significant part of the anti-communist opposition. This narrative, prevalent in the discourse of many right-wing political entities throughout the transformation period, is frequently echoed in the anti-communist 'memory policy', which is still visible in the terraces of Polish football stadiums today, almost three decades after the collapse of the Iron Curtain.

Nevertheless, relative economic weakness of the communist elites and their political weakness in comparison with the opposition circles prevented them from forming an oligarchy in Polish post-1989 economy. The anti-communist opposition was too strong politically to leave the space for a full-scale post-communist 'political capitalism' scenario, and united in support of the radical pathway of neoliberal transformation. The reforms of the first non-communist government delivered under the umbrella term of 'the Balcerowicz Plan' allowed Western capital a quick and easy access to the Polish markets via the rapid process of privatisation of state-owned assets. The economic field is thus dominated by Western players, Polish private entrepreneurs operate mainly in the area of small and medium-sized business, while practically all the largest Polish-owned companies in the strategic fields of energy or natural resources are controlled by the state (Jasiecki, 2013). As Zarycki and others (Zarycki, Smoczyński and Warczok, 2017) conclude, this was possible without serious protests owing to the discursive domination of the intelligentsia, a group which came back to the position of dominance in the field of culture once again, like in 1918, when it effectively formed a modern political field in the re-established Polish state. The intelligentsia emerged in the nineteenth century as a specific Eastern European social group with a unique ethos, characterised by a concern about the unity within society and alleged responsibility for the weak; the group played an important role in preserving

Socio-economic and political transformation of Poland 57

and fostering Polish patriotism and national values during the years of partition (Zarycki, 2003).

Members of intelligentsia had a prestigious position in top-level circles of both post-communist and former opposition elites. They legitimised the neoliberal pathway of economic transformation, thus shifting the public and political discourse from economic topics to historical and cultural themes. Economic topics were considered a matter of technocratic and a-political consensus among the elites, and even if they were debated during election campaigns, the reality of policy making followed the neoliberal principles. As Zarycki puts it:

> This process seems to be a key moment for the strengthening of the dominant position of Polish intelligentsia, as it prevented the consolidation of national economic elites and of post-communist political elites. Western capital and Western institutions proved to be an ideal partner for the Polish intelligentsia. The latter group was granted total freedom in the cultural sphere, along with considerable autonomy in politics; at the same time, the intellectual elite was provided by Western companies with a steady source of income. Some intellectuals were employed on a full-time basis, others provided advisory services to commercial and foreign entities, public institutions, and engaged in a wide range of activities financed from the EU funds.
>
> (2014, pp. 70–72)

During the communist period, the branch of the economy and membership in the *nomenklatura* circles were the main stratifiers. Very quickly after accession to the EU the level of education became a decisive factor for location in the social structure. This was very much in line with the dominating ideology of the newly emerging middle class as the crucial stratum in the social structure, responsible for the future of the country. Well educated, entrepreneurial and ambitious people were supposed to be forerunners of the modernisation of Poland, which would enable it to catch up with the West. Some scholars claim that both in Polish academic and public discourse the middle class became the new 'leading force of the nation', replacing the working class, which was officially declared as such in the communist constitution (Pluciński, 2010). This was very much in line with widely promoted discourse of individualism and self-fulfilment, which – in accordance with the neoliberal, consumerist and pro-market creed – was directly related to satisfying material needs in the realities of newly established market economy.

On the other hand, the industrial working class, the backbone of the Solidarity movement, very quickly came to pay the price of the transformation. Those who were laid off in the process of mass-scale, rapid de-industrialisation were neglected in political terms: not only did they have no political representation for many years, but they also suffered from the 'blame the victim strategy', applied to legitimate the economic processes leading to their impoverishment. This could be

58 *Socio-economic and political transformation of Poland*

exemplified by academic works and public statements of a prominent sociologist and intellectual Piotr Sztompka (e.g. 2000, 2001, 2008). He conceptualised and popularised the term *homo sovieticus*, coined by the Russian writer and dissident Alexander Zinoviev, as the description of those who are the 'victims' of economic transformation not due to the structural processes but due to their personal deficiencies and deficits. Sztompka portrayed them as 'civilizationally incompetent', 'anti-intellectual' and 'anti-elitist', characterised by the 'support of egalitarianism' and 'disinterested envy'. Although the data showed that the support for egalitarianism and state paternalism was equally high or even higher in Western democracies, and that former manual workers were the group most frequently starting up their own business (ten times more frequently than members of the intelligentsia), Sztompka claimed that this syndrome was shaped by the indoctrination under the communist regime (Sztompka, 2008, p. 137).

Although Sztompka's position and similar takes on the transformation period provided by prominent members of the intelligentsia were sometimes criticised in scholarly works (Buchowski, 2006; Aronoff and Kubik, 2013), they had a significant impact on the market of ideas and dominated mainstream public discourse about the consequences of socio-economic processes. Associating the impoverishment of certain echelons of society with personal traits of those suffering corresponded to the dominating mood and contributed to the increasing support of 'the winners of transformation' for further state retrenchment and austerity policies. In this respect, the observed pattern was similar to the processes observed in Britain or the United States a decade or two earlier: the discursive usage of the term *homo sovieticus* could be compared to how 'the underclass' was portrayed in the Anglo-Saxon world, and to how this discursive tool paved the way for the neoliberal reforms (Woźniak, 2012). This is just one example of the fundamental, class-based axiological split between the intelligentsia and the working class, which no more than a decade before had been allies in the process of forming the Solidarity movement, as described in the fundamental book by David Ost: *The Defeat of Solidarity: Anger and Fear in Postcommunist Europe* (2006; see also: Dunn, 2004).

The anti-elitist or anti-establishment threads which are present in the discourse of die-hard Polish football supporters may be at least partly interpreted as the backlash against these discursive stigmatisation and victim-blaming narratives, which dominated the political discourse and the mass media for a better part of the transformation period.

Social divisions and party politics

The 'post-communist cleavage', which was the axis of political divisions in Poland for the first 16 years of the transformation period, was a conflict over the communist past, over the place of religion and the Roman Catholic Church in the socio-political life, over the need of reckoning and retribution against former members of the communist party, and over attitudes towards

Socio-economic and political transformation of Poland 59

the neighbours and the multicultural legacy of the pre-war Poland (Grabowska, 2004). In this way, then, the major political divisions shaping the Polish political scene for well over a decade after the breakthrough of 1989 stemmed from the times of communist *ancien régime*.

Political parties which originated from the anti-communist opposition became bitterly conflicted from the very beginning of transformation, mainly based on personal struggles between various groups within the Solidarity and other opposition movements. In 1990, the first non-communist Prime Minister, Tadeusz Mazowiecki, lost the very first free presidential election to Lech Wałęsa, the legendary leader of Solidarity. A year later, as many as 29 political parties and electoral committees won seats in the first fully democratic parliamentary elections. In 1993, the heavily fragmented parliament was unable to form a stable majority government, which lead to snap elections and the unquestioned victory of the post-communist Democratic Left Alliance (*Sojusz Lewicy Demokratycznej*, hereafter SLD), whose leadership was exclusively recruited from the power circles of the communist Polish United Workers' Party (which had ceased to exist in 1990). The triumph of post-communists only four years after the beginning of transformation was confirmed just two years later, when Lech Wałęsa was defeated in the second ballot of presidential election by Aleksander Kwaśniewski, former prominent politician of the communist party.

The neoliberal pathway of economic transformation and the major goals of foreign policy were an area of general consensus among the main political actors. Accession to NATO and the European Union were universally viewed as the key tasks to achieve and unanimously supported by all the parties. Their respective fulfilment (in 1999 and 2004) became a milestone – the political elites and the majority of Polish general public perceived them as the ultimate confirmation of Poland's allegiance to Western values and culture, and a sign that the country was in the Western sphere of influence.

The post-communist party, which was in power twice (1993–1997 and 2001–2005), sought recognition and acceptance on the national and international political scene by pursuing an alliance with Western European countries and the United States. From 2001, Poland was actively involved in the Afghanistan War against the Taliban as a member of International Security Assistance Force. In 2003, the Polish government of the post-communist Democratic Left Alliance supported the decision of George W. Bush administration which effectively started the Iraq War. In contrast to large-scale anti-war protests all over the world, this was not a matter of nationwide debate, and the deployment of Polish troops to Iraq caused neither political controversy in the parliament, nor any significant protests of the public opinion.

Although in 2001 the populist party called Self-defence [*Samoobrona*], which openly contested the pathway of economic reforms, won over 10 per cent of votes and entered the parliament, it was not until 2005 that economic issues became a major topic in election campaigns. Symbolically, that year may be viewed as the end of 'the post-communist cleavage'.

60   *Socio-economic and political transformation of Poland*

Previously, economically motivated voting had rarely been the case during elections. A series of corruption scandals came as a severe blow to the post-communist parties, particularly the SLD, which has not recovered its position on the political scene to this day. The clash between two parties with roots in the anti-communist opposition (Law and Justice [*Prawo i Sprawiedliwość*] hereafter PiS, versus Civic Platform [*Platforma Obywatelska*] hereafter PO) shaped the political scene in Poland in a new way. The former presented itself as a conservative, right-wing party declaring allegiance to Roman Catholic values and a tough stance on fighting crime, corruption and eliminating the lingering post-communist influences in state institutions. The latter was economically neoliberal, but relatively conservative in other spheres. The triumph of Law and Justice in the general elections of 2005 was strengthened with the victory of their leader, Lech Kaczyński, in the presidential race later the same year.

Law and Justice won the double elections of 2005 with the promise of a fairer redistribution of wealth and taking more care of those who may be described as the 'victims of transformation', previously left on their own by the triumphant liberal elites. Regardless of those promises, the neoliberal pathway of economic policy continued. The ideological and axiological chaos in Polish political discourse may be exemplified with the interview of Kazimierz Marcinkiewicz, the nominee of the Kaczyński twins for the function of the prime minister in the government whose electoral platform was built on anti-liberal rhetorics. In one of his first interviews, given to the mainstream liberal weekly *Polityka* [Politics], he mentioned the legacy of Margaret Thatcher in the UK as his main inspiration, and Francis Fukuyama and Milton Friedman as the key thinkers for his approach (Żakowski and Marcinkiewicz, 2005; Woźniak, 2012). The policy-making that followed was quite in line with these ideas. The allegedly pro-social government abolished the inheritance tax regardless of the level of assets involved, lowered personal taxation in favour of high earners (by introducing two income brackets, taxed at 18 and 32 per cent, instead of three, taxed at 19, 30 and 40 per cent), and reduced social insurance contributions. The decade that followed has been marked by the growing political conflict between these two right-wing parties (PO and PiS), accompanied by the weakening of other political actors and the demise of the political left in Poland.

2007–2015: the policy of 'hot water in the tap' in the shadow of the tragedy

After two years, the right-wing government of Law and Justice and two minor coalition partners collapsed. The snap elections of 2007, as well as the subsequent ones four years later, brought the victory of the Civic Platform, which won more than 200 seats in the 460-seat Sejm. The Civic Platform formed a coalition government with the Polish People's Party [*Polskie Stronnictwo Ludowe*] (hereafter PSL), an agrarian party with about 30 seats. This was a period of relative stability. The government benefited from economic growth,

Socio-economic and political transformation of Poland 61

largely dependent on the lasting effects of the EU accession. Euro 2012, the largest ever sports event held in Poland, was effectively used to showcase the modernisation and economic success of the transformation. This event was also an important factor concerning the relationships between the political circles and football fans, the topic which will be elaborated on in the following parts of this book.

The rule of the Civic Platform was sometimes described as the policy of 'hot water in the tap', both by the followers and the critics. The phrase was used by Donald Tusk, who served as Prime Minister between 2007 and 2014, and stepped down to take over the function of the President of the European Council. In an interview he gave in September 2010, after the Civic Platform candidate Bronisław Komorowski won the presidential election, he said:

> As long as I am present in the public life, I will always prefer the politics that guarantees, as some sarcastically say, hot water in the tap. And many people welcome this with appreciation, that there finally is a strong political party which is self-restrained and modest when it comes to formulating great goals for the people and provides great stability instead.
> (Machała and Tusk, 2010)

The party indeed attempted to avoid serious conflicts, controversial decisions and far-reaching reforms for most of its two terms in power. What proved the most costly in political terms was probably the decision to increase the retirement age to 67 years both for men and women, which went contrary to the expectations of the majority of the population. The hosting of the UEFA Euro 2012 tournament became a trademark achievement of the government, widely used in country-branding campaigns. Considering that the coalition had a comfortable majority, the critics ridiculed a lack of ambition on its part.

The conflict between Civic Platform and Law and Justice lasted for the entire two terms and was fuelled by the political aftermath of the Smolensk disaster of 10 April 2010. On that day, a plane carrying a high-ranking Polish delegation to the ceremony commemorating the 70th anniversary of the Katyń massacre crashed in the forest near Smolensk North Airport. The death of President Lech Kaczyński, his wife Maria and 94 other passengers (including the chief of Polish General Staff and many senior military officers, 18 members of parliament, head of the National Bank of Poland, many government officials, senior representatives of the clergy, families of the victims of the Katyń massacre) became another reason for the radical criticism of the government. Although official reports ruled that the crash had been an accident caused by a combination of different factors (pilot error, inadequate training of the crew, inadequate technical equipment at the airport and adverse weather conditions), PiS voiced serious accusations against the Polish government. These ranged from negligence and misconduct to deliberately exposing the passengers to the risk of disaster. Some PiS politicians openly claimed that the crash was in fact a result of a clandestine operation of the

62 *Socio-economic and political transformation of Poland*

Russian secret services aimed at the assassination of the Polish president, and that the PO government was an accessory in orchestrating it and covering it up. Such accusations were voiced by Jarosław Kaczyński, the leader of PiS and the late president's twin brother, and led to a further escalation of the conflict between the two parties. Nevertheless, for the first time in post-1989 Poland, the government coalition survived for two full terms (Stanley and Cześnik, 2018; Cześnik, 2014; Szczerbiak, 2013).

2015 – the triumph of right-wing politics, the demise of the left

In 2015 – contrary to the expectations of the pundits and the opinion polls which just a week before presidential election had suggested his victory in the first round of the ballot – Bronisław Komorowski, the president in the office and PO candidate for the next term, lost the election to Andrzej Duda, a relatively unknown PiS politician, former member of the Sejm and European Parliament (Janicki and Władyka, 2015). This gave a further momentum to the PiS party and ultimately led to its landslide victory (38 per cent vs 24 per cent for the PO) in parliamentary elections held few months later. One of the crucial factors behind this domination is the system of proportional representation. The situation where 16 per cent of active voters 'wasted' their votes by supporting parties and coalitions which did not make it to the parliament effectively resulted in a majority government formed by a single party (PiS) for the first time since 1989 (Markowski, 2016). Although the lists of PiS candidates also included members of two small right-wing political formations, which in fact amounts to a three-party coalition, the domination of the largest player, the party led by Jarosław Kaczyński is unquestionable.

PiS capitalised on the political scandals surrounding the twilight of the two-term rule of the PO and several unpopular decisions taken by the government in the second term (mainly the increase of retirement age to 67). Additionally, the PiS promised the largest and the most generous scheme for direct support to families with children in Poland. The programme called '500 plus' (a monthly cash benefit of 500 PLN, about 110 euros, for all children under 18 except the first one in the family) became the trademark of the party in the election campaign, attracting voters who had not benefited from the economic growth under the PO and PSL governments as the adjusted wage share as a percentage of the GDP remained at the level of about 55 per cent, the lowest in the European Union.

For the first time since the collapse of the communist system, the term 2015–2019 was also marked with the total absence of left-wing parties in the parliament. The post-communist Democratic Left Alliance missed the threshold of 8 per cent for party coalitions, and the new left political formation called *Razem* [Together] failed to reach the 5 per cent threshold for parties (Szczerbiak, 2016).

Since the 2015 elections, Poland – along with Hungary – has been perceived as the European stronghold of right-wing ideology and conservative orthodoxy. Even though Law and Justice does not have a majority that would enable it to pursue constitutional reforms, the systemic reforms it has undertaken have been aiming at a deep reconstruction of the political and legal order of the state (Stanley and Cześnik, 2018). The context of the Polish political landscape – which is crucial for this book – including the memory policy, the use of xenophobia as a political tool and the general ideological turn in politics and in the discourse in Poland, will be approached in subsequent chapters with reference to the topic of Polish football fandom.

The social and cultural context of contemporary Polish politics: discursive and cultural dominance of the right

One crucial consequence of political cleavages described above concerns the domination of right-wing and conservative narratives in Polish public discourse and politics.

Although, as in 2020, Poland is widely viewed as a stronghold of conservatism and right-wing orthodoxy in Europe, the cultural dominance of conservative values and right-wing narratives does not result directly from the PiS getting full control over the state in 2015. This process could be exemplified by the role of the Roman Catholic Church in both cultural and discursive sphere, as well as in policy-making.

In 1990, religious education was reintroduced in the Polish education system. The concordat between the Vatican and the Republic of Poland guarantees that the lessons are held at schools and the teachers are paid by the state or local councils, but the curricula are developed and teaching is supervised by the Church. In this form, then, religious education effectively serves as instruction in the Roman Catholic doctrine. Students who opt out should be offered courses in ethics instead, but, as in 2017, these were only available in 11 per cent of schools (Szpunar, 2017). The way the Roman Catholic Church is acculturated in Polish reality makes it the major institution influencing not only spiritual, but also political and cultural, life in Poland (Nijakowski, 2008, pp. 242–244).

The very beginning of the transformation period brought the radical tightening of abortion laws. Since 1993, abortion is legal only in three cases: when the pregnancy is a result of rape or incest, when the foetus is seriously and irreversibly damaged, or when the pregnancy poses a serious risk to the life and health of the mother. As reported by opinion polls, the worldview of the majority of Poles was shifting towards a more conservative stance throughout this period. In the early 1990s, the majority accepted 'abortion on request', and almost a half of the respondents declared that 'difficult living conditions' are a legitimate reason to perform an abortion. In 2016 the right to terminate early pregnancy 'on request' was supported by 42 per cent, and only one in five of the respondents viewed it as morally acceptable (CBOS, 2016a, p. 2); in 2016, only 11 per cent stated that abortion on the grounds of 'difficult living conditions' should be allowed (CBOS, 2016b, p. 9). Since the PiS

64 *Socio-economic and political transformation of Poland*

government took over in 2015, several attempts have been made to introduce a total ban on abortion. This was done under the influence of the ultra-conservative non-governmental organisations which, partially due to direct support from the Roman Catholic Church, managed to collect hundreds of thousands of signatures in favour of the ban. The proposed bill ignited the so-called 'black protest', which, owing to its unprecedented scale, made the ruling party discontinue legislative work on the issue altogether in spring 2019. According to Geneviève Zubrzycki, Polish Roman Catholicism is at the core of national mythology, which is disseminated in homes, circulated in the public sphere, as well as reproduced in various academic circles in Poland and abroad [and] paradigmatically goes as follows: essentially and eternally Catholic, Poland is the bulwark of Christendom defending Europe against the infidel (however defined). A nation assailed by dangerous neighbours, its identity is conserved and guarded by its defender, the Roman Catholic Church, and shielded by its Queen, the miraculous Black Madonna, Our Lady of Częstochowa. (Zubrzycki, 2011, p. 25)

The position of conservatism, closely associated with the Roman Catholic Church, seems to be in line with the socio-political attitudes prevalent among the population as a whole. Nonetheless, these attitudes intensified throughout the period of post-communist transformation. The only ruling party associated with the left was the post-communist Democratic Left Alliance (SLD). Composed mainly of former members of the communist party, the SLD sought legitimisation by avoiding controversies over historical topics and cultural conflicts with the Church, and by accepting the pathway of pro-market reforms. Progressive language was virtually absent in the public discourse, with notions from the leftist vocabulary disgraced trough association with the *ancien régime*. None of the newly formed left-wing political entities (e.g. the Polish 'Greens') have ever made it to the parliament, and their impact on the public debate is very limited (see Woźniak, 2012; Sowa, 2010; Ost, 2006, 2010; Hardy, 2009). At the same time, Polish school textbooks also present very conservative narratives, both on Polish history and cultural issues (e.g. family models, gender relations, LGBT issues; see Chmura-Rutkowska et al., 2015).

Since the end of the Second World War, several generations of Poles have been living in the most homogenous society in Europe, with approximately 95 per cent of the population belonging to the white, ethnically Polish, Roman Catholic majority, and with the lowest proportion of migrants on the continent. Consequently, the topic of minority rights was virtually absent in political discourse and ethnic homogeneity is perceived as beneficial by the ruling right-wing party, and the lack of intercultural contacts correlates with negative attitudes towards multiculturalism (Krzyżanowski, 2017).

The aim of this chapter was to highlight crucial socio-economic processes occurring in Polish reality in the course of the transformation period. It provides a background for better understanding of the phenomena taking place in those aspects of the social life in Poland which constitute the main theme of this book.

References

Ackerman, B. (1992) *The Future of Liberal Revolution*. New Haven: Yale University Press.

Aronoff, M. J. and Kubik J. (2013). *Anthropology and Political Science. Convergent Approach*. New York–Oxford: Berghan Books.

Buchowski, M. (2006). The spectre of orientalism in Europe: From exotic other to stigmatized brother. *Anthropological Quarterly*, 3(79), pp. 463–482.

Bukowski, P. and Novokmet, F. (2017). *Top Incomes during Wars, Communism and Capitalism: Poland 1892–2015*. Working paper 17. London: The London School of Economics.

CBOS (2016a). *Opinie o Dopuszczalności Aborcji* [Opinions on the Acceptability of Abortion]. Research report 51. Warszawa: Centrum Badania Opinii Społecznej. Available at: https://www.cbos.pl/SPISKOM.POL/2016/K_051_16.PDF [accessed 10 October 2019].

CBOS (2016b). *Komunikat z Badań. Dopuszczalność Aborcji w Różnych Sytuacjach* [Acceptability of Abortion in Various Circumstances]. Research report 71. Warszawa: Centrum Badania Opinii Społecznej. Available at: https://www.cbos.pl/SPIS KOM.POL/2016/K_071_16.PDF [accessed 20 October 2018].

Chmura-Rutkowska, I., Duda, M., Mazurek, M. and Sołtysiak-Łucza, A. (eds) (2015). *Gender w podręcznikach. Projekt badawczy. Raport* [Gender in textbooks. Report]. Warszawa: FundacjaFeminoteka. Available at: http://feminoteka.pl/raport-gender-w-p odrecznikach-tom-1-3-publikacja-do-pobrania/ [accessed 10 October 2019].

Cześnik, M. (2014). In the shadow of the Smolensk catastrophe – The 2010 Presidential election in Poland. *East European Politics and Societies*, 28(3), pp. 518–539.

Cześnik M. (2018). Political activity of the citizens. In: J. Szymanek (ed.) *Polish Political System. An Introduction*. Warszawa: Wydawnictwo Sejmowe, pp. 160–177.

Cześnik, M., Żerkowska-Balas M. and Kotnarowski M. (2013). Voting as a habit in new democracies – Evidence from Poland. *Communist and Post-Communist Studies*, 46, pp. 95–107,

Dahrendorf, R. (1990). *Reflections on the Revolution in Europe: In a Letter Intended to Have Been Sent to a Gentleman in Warsaw*. New York: Random House.

Domański, H. (2007). *Struktura Społeczna* [Social Structure]. Warszawa: Scholar.

Dunn, E. (2004). *Privatizing Poland: Baby Food, Big Business, and the Remaking of Labor*. Ithaca: Cornell University Press.

Ferge, Z. (2008). Is there a specific East-Central European welfare culture? In: W. Oorschot, M. Opielka and B. Pfau-Effinger (eds), *Culture and Welfare State: Values and Social Policy in Comparative Perspective*. Cheltenham: Edward Elgar.

Friszke, A., Grzelak, J., Kofta, M., Osiatyński, W. and Reykowski, J. (2019). *Psychologia Okrągłego Stołu* [Psychology of a Round Table]. Sopot: Smak Słowa.

Golinowska, S. (2013), The Polish welfare state birth and twilight? In: P. Michoń, J. Orczyk and M. Żukowski (eds) *Facing the Challenges. Social Policy in Poland after 1990*. Poznań: Poznań University of Economics Press, pp. 7–36.

Grabowska, M. (2004). *Podział Postkomunistyczny. Społeczne Podstawy Polityki w Polsce po 1989 roku* [Post-communist Cleavage. Social Bases of Politics in Poland after 1989]. Warszawa: Scholar.

Hardy, J. (2009). *Poland's New Capitalism*. London-New York: Pluto Press.

Janicki, M. and Władyka, W. (2015). Dziesięciu na jednego [Ten against one]. *Polityka*, (3018), pp. 10–11.

66 Socio-economic and political transformation of Poland

Jasiecki, K. (2013). *Kapitalizm po Polsku. Między Modernizacją a Peryferiami Unii Europejskiej* [Capitalism Polish Style. Between Modernisation and Peripheries of European Union]. Warszawa: IFiS PAN.

Jasiecki, K. (2014). Institutional transformation and business leaders of the new foreign-led capitalism in Poland. In: K. Bluhm, B. Martens and V. Trappmann (eds) *Business Leaders and New Varieties of Capitalism in Post-Communist Europe*. New York-London: Routledge, pp. 23–57.

Jasiewicz, K. (2008). The new populism in Poland: The usual suspects? *Problems of Post-Communism*, 55(3), pp. 7–25.

Jasiewicz, K. (2009). The party is never dead: Identity, class and voting behavior in contemporary Poland. *East European Politics and Societies*, 23(4), pp. 491–508.

Kamiński A.Z. (2010). Stracony moment konstytucyjny w pokomunistycznej Polsce: skutki dla jakości rządzenia dwadzieścia lat później [Lost constitutional moment in post-communist Poland: effects on the quality of governance twenty years later]. In: W. Morawski (ed.) *Modernizacja Polski* [Modernization of Poland]. Warszawa: Wydawnictwa Akademickie i Profesjonalne.

Karpiński, A., Paradysz, S., Soroka, P. and Żółtkowski, W. (2013). *Jak Powstawały i Upadały Zakłady Przemysłowe w Polsce* [How Industrial Plants Were Established and How They Have Collapsed in Poland]. Warszawa: MUZA.

Kelley, J. and Zagórski, K. (2004). Economic change and the legitimation of inequality: The transition from socialism to the free market in central and east Europe. *Research in Social Stratification and Mobility*, 22, pp. 319–364.

Kolodko, G. (2002). *Globalization and Catching-up in Transition Economies*. Rochester, NY: University of Rochester Press.

Kolodko, G.W. and McMahon, W.W. (1987). Stagflation and shortageflation: A comparative approach. *Kyklos*, 40(2), pp. 176–197.

Kolodko, G.W. and Nuti, D.M. (1997). The Polish alternative. Old myths, hard facts and new strategies in the successful transformation of the Polish economy. *Research for Action*, 33, Helsinki: WIDER.

Kornai, J. (1980). *Economics of Shortage*. Amsterdam: North Holland Press.

Kowalik, T. (2012). *From Solidarity to Sellout. The Restoration of Capitalism in Poland*. New York, NY: Monthly Review Press.

Krzyżanowski, M. (2017). Discursive shifts in ethno-nationalist politics: On politicization and mediatization of the 'refugee crisis' in Poland. *Journal of Immigrant & Refugee Studies*, doi:10.1080/15562948.2017.1317897

Księżopolski, M. (2013). Between guarantees of communism and a paternalistic market hybrid. Polish social policy at the turn of the 20th century. *Poznań University of Economics Review*, 13(3): pp. 23–41.

Letki, N., Brzeziński, M. and Jancewicz, B. (2014). The rise of inequalities in Poland and their impacts: When politicians don't care but citizens do. In: B. Nolan, W. Salverda and D. Checchi (eds) *Changing Inequalities and Societal Impacts in Rich Countries: Thirty Countries' Experiences*. Oxford: Oxford University Press, pp. 488–513.

Markowski, R. (2016). The Polish parliamentary election of 2015: A free and fair election that results in unfair political consequences. *West European Politics*, 39(6), pp. 1311–1322.

Matthes, C-Y. (2016). The state of democracy in Poland after 2007. *Problems of Post-Communism*, 63(5–6), pp. 288–299.

Nijakowski, L. (2008). *Polska polityka pamięci. Esej socjologiczny* [Polish memory policy. Sociological essay]. Warszawa: Wydawnictwa Akademickie i Profesjonalne.

Socio-economic and political transformation of Poland   67

OECD (2011). *Divided We Stand: Why Inequality Keeps Rising*. Paris: OECD Publishing.

Orenstein, M.A. (2008). *Privatizing Pensions: The Transnational Campaign for Social Security Reform*. Oxford and Princeton: Princeton University Press.

Orenstein, M.A. (2013). Reassessing the neo-liberal development model in Central and Eastern Europe. In: V.A. Schmidt and M. Thatcher (eds) *Resilient Liberalism in Europe's Political Economy*. Cambridge: Cambridge University Press, pp. 374–402.

Ost, D. (2006). *Defeat of Solidarity. Anger and Politics in Postcommunist Europe*. Ithaca, London: Cornell University Press.

Ost, D. (2010). Obrachunek z kategorią 'klasy' w dyskursie politycznym post-komunistycznej Polski. [Assesing the category of 'class' in Polish post-communist political discourse]. In: M. Czyżewski, S. Kowalski and T. Tabako (eds) *Retoryka i Polityka. Dwudziestolecie Polskiej Transformacji* [Rhetorics and Politics. Twenty Years of Polish Transformation]. Warszawa: Wydawnictwa Akademickie i Profesjonalne.

Pluciński, P. (2010). Dyskurs klasowy polskiej socjologii potransformacyjnej: niedyskretny urok klasy średniej [Class discourse of Polish post-transition sociology: indiscreet charm of the middle class]. In: P. Żuk (ed.) *Podziały Klasowe i Nierówności Społeczne. Refleksje Socjologiczne po Dwóch Dekadach Realnego Kapitalizmu w Polsce* [Class Divisions and Social Inequalities. Sociological Reflections after Two Decades of Restored Capitalism in Poland]. Warszawa: Oficyna Naukowa, pp. 101–116.

Rek-Woźniak M. and Woźniak W. (2017). From the cradle of 'Solidarity' to the land of cheap labour and the home of precarious. Strategic discourse on labour arrangements in post-socialist Poland. *Social Policy and Administration*, 51(2), pp. 348–366.

Sowa, J. (2010). Mitologie III RP. Ideologiczne podstawy polskiej transformacji. [Mythologies of Third Republic of Poland. Ideological foundations of Polish transformations]. In: P. Żuk (ed.) *Podziały klasowe i Nierówności Społeczne. Refleksje Socjologiczne po Dwóch Dekadach Realnego Kapitalizmu w Polsce* [Class Divisions and Social Inequalities. Sociological Reflections after Two Decades of Restored Capitalism in Poland]. Warszawa: Oficyna Naukowa, pp. 23–39.

Staniszkis J. (2001). *Postkomunizm. Próba opisu* [Postcommunism. An attempt at portrayal]. Gdańsk: Słowo/obraz terytoria.

Stanley, B. and Cześnik M. (2018). Populism in Poland. In: D. Stockemer (ed.) *Populism Around the World. A Comparative Perspective*. Cham: Springer, pp. 67–87.

Statistics Poland (2015). Values and social trust in Poland. Available at: https://stat. gov.pl/download/gfx/portalinformacyjny/en/defaultaktualnosci/3305/8/1/1/zaufa nie_ang.pdf [accessed 8 October 2019].

Szczerbiak, A. (2013). Poland (mainly) chooses stability and continuity: The October 2011 Polish Parliamentary Election. *Perspectives on European Politics and Society*, 14(4), pp. 480–504.

Szczerbiak, A. (2016). An anti-establishment backlash that shook up the party system? The October 2015 Polish parliamentary election. *European Politics and Society*, 18 (4), pp. 404–427.

Szpunar, O. (2017). Rząd etyki nie tyka: było źle i będzie [The government does not touch ethics: it was and will be bad]. *wyborcza.pl*. Available at: http://wyborcza.pl/ 7,75398,22319927,rzad-etyki-nie-tyka-bylo-zle-i-bedzie-jakie-prawa-maja-rodzice. html [accessed 8 August 2018].

Sztompka, P. (2000). *Civilisational Competence: A Prerequisite for Post-Communist Transition*. Cracow: Centre for European Studies. Jagiellonian University in Cracow.

68 *Socio-economic and political transformation of Poland*

Sztompka, P. (2001). *The Ambivalence of Social Change: Triumph or Trauma?*Berlin: Wissenschaftszentrum Berlin für Sozialforschung GmbH.

Sztompka, P. (2008). The ambivalence of social change in post-communist societies. In: A. Śliż and M.S. Szczepański (eds) *Czy koniec socjalizmu? Polska transformacja w teoriach socjologicznych* [Whither the End of Socialism? Polish Transformation in Sociological Theories]. Warszawa: Scholar, pp. 36–57.

Machała, T. and Tusk, D. (2010). Tusk: jestem u władzy, żeby innym było lepiej [I am ruling so that the others are better off]. *Wprost*. Available at: https://www.wprost.pl/210022/Tusk-jestem-u-wladzy-zeby-innym-bylo-lepiej [accessed 8 October 2019].

Woźniak, W. (2012). *Nierówności Społeczne w Polskim Dyskursie Politycznym* [Social Inequalities in Polish Political Discourse]. Warszawa: Scholar.

Zarycki, T., Smoczyński, R. and Warczok, T. (2017). The roots of Polish culture-centered politics: Toward a non–purely cultural model of cultural domination in Central and Eastern Europe. *East European Politics and Societies*, 31(2), pp. 360–381.

Zarycki, T. (2003). Cultural capital and the political role of the intelligentsia in Poland. *Journal of Communist Studies and Transition Politics*, 19(4), pp. 91–108.

Zarycki, T. (2009). The power of intelligentsia: The Rywin Affair and the challenge of applying the concept of cultural capital to analyze Poland's elites. *Theory and Society*, 6(38), pp. 613–648.

Zarycki, T. (2014). Social dialogue under the supremacy of the intelligentsia. *Warsaw Forum of Economic Sociology*, 5(2), pp. 69–79.

Zarycki, T. (2015). Class analysis in conditions of a dual-stratification order. *East European Politics and Societies: And Cultures*, 29(3), pp. 711–718.

Ziółkowski, M., Pawłowska, B. and Drozdowski, R. (1994). *Jednostka wobec władzy*. Poznań: Nakom

Zubrzycki, G. (2011). History and the national sensorium: Making sense of Polish mythology. *Qualitative Sociology*, 34, pp. 21–57.

Żakowski, J. and Marcinkiewicz, K. (2005). Mój gabinet: Wywiad z Kazimierzem Marcinkiewiczem. *Polityka*, 45(2529), pp. 22–26.

4 Football fandom in Poland in a historical perspective

Introduction

The aim of this chapter is to provide an overview of the historical context and a processual perspective on the institutionalisation of football in Poland and the formation of football fandom in the country. Special attention is paid to the social context and political circumstances which had an impact on this particular pathway and on the shape of the football world and the fan scene.

Institutionalisation of football in Poland: the emergence of the football association and the national team (1903–1921)

From 1795, the Polish territory was divided among three neighbouring powers: the Habsburg Monarchy, the Kingdom of Prussia and the Russian Empire. As a result, in the second half of the nineteenth and the early twentieth centuries, when football was becoming institutionalised, with clubs and football associations mushrooming all over Europe, Poland did not exist on the political map. Although this process also occurred on the territory of future Poland, it was only after regaining independence in 1918 that the circumstances allowed for the formation of the Polish Football Association [*Polski Związek Piłki Nożnej*, PZPN], an institution responsible for the organisation and supervision of all football-related issues in the newly unified country. Previously – during what Seweryn Dmowski refers to as 'the period of partitions' in his periodisation of the political history of football in Poland – the development of the game was characterised by significant differences between the three territories (Dmowski, 2013a, p. 99). Despite notable distinctions in terms of the economic, political and social situation, processes similar to those occurring elsewhere in Europe can be traced in all parts of the partitioned country. In order to trace the uneasy beginnings of football in what is now the Polish Republic, these traits need to be followed separately.

70 *Football fandom in Poland in a historical perspective*

The beginnings of football in Poland under the partitions

The Prussian Partition

In the period of partitions, the western part of contemporary Poland belonged to the Prussian state. Consequently, two major regions of the country – Greater Poland and Upper Silesia – were influenced by the nineteenth-century industrialisation, just as with many areas of Western Europe. With one of the world's largest bituminous coalfields, Upper Silesia was crucial for the economy of the rapidly modernising Prussia and Germany, and soon became one of the most urbanised areas on the continent. This was quickly followed by the development of modern bureaucracy and efficient administration, proverbial in German-governed territories. We can notice the heritage of this period even today. Looking at the contemporary map of urbanisation or the railway network in Poland, we can easily trace the borders of the partitions. Like in other parts of Europe experiencing industrial modernisation, football clubs were 'born out of the industry', flourishing in rapidly developing urban centres (Woźniak, 2015; 2018).

Considering the multi-ethnic social structure of the population in Upper Silesia, the clubs usually defined their distinct identity by reference to the ethnic origins of the founders. In 1903 German Sportverein Ratibor 03 was established in the city known today as Racibórz. The clubs called VfR Königshütte and Ruch were founded in Bismarckhütte in 1910 and 1920, respectively; both locations are now districts of the city of Chorzów. The latter was formed in the immediate aftermath of the First World War, becoming a centre of the movement (in Polish *Ruch* means movement) for Polish culture in Upper Silesia. One of the two most decorated clubs in the history of Polish football, Ruch was established by veterans of Silesian Uprisings against German rule (1919–1921), which aimed to support the Second Polish Republic in a diplomatic struggle with the Weimar Republic over the border dividing the region between the neighbours. When Chorzów was finally declared a Polish city, VfR remained in the structures of the German Football Association [*Deutscher Fußball-Bund*, DFB] and played in the German league until 1923, when it was renamed Amateur Football Club [*Amatorski Klub Sportowy*, AKS] and accepted into the Polish league. Ethnic tensions remained an important source of conflicts within Upper Silesia bitterly divided teams, although local animosities also played a role (Łęcki, 2009).

In the region of Greater Poland, in turn, there was the Greater Poland's Association of Sports' Associations, founded within the DFB in 1913. In 1907, the club Normania was founded in Poznań, the regional capital, the team was established by Poles, but officially affiliated with German Football Association. Therefore, it is Venetia Ostrów Wielkopolski, founded a year later, which is universally considered as the first Polish club of the region. Both these teams were Polish rivals of the dominant German clubs in the period of ongoing cultural Germanisation. In the world of football, this was marked by a ban on speaking Polish during the games. Normania was renamed as Posnania following its liquidation as a result of an incident during one of the games, when footballer Marian Sroka was sent off for speaking Polish. This led to the boycott of the game by other Normania players, and the club was punished by the football association. The newly re-established Posnania officially declared itself the First Polish Sports Club (Hałys, 1986). Following the successful Greater Poland Uprising of 1918–1919, which secured Polish dominance over this territory, the regional association joined the PZPN, becoming its regional branch (Owsiański and Siwiński, 2013; Owsiański, 2016).

The Kingdom of Galicia and Lodomeria

The Kingdom of Galicia and Lodomeria, commonly known as Galicia, covered the territory which after the partitions became part of the Habsburg (Austrian) Monarchy (later Austro-Hungarian Empire). The population of the Austrian partition of Poland enjoyed relatively more liberal conditions than the other two parts of the country. Poles were represented in the National Parliament in Vienna and formed the regional Diet of Galicia and Lodomeria. It was a predominantly agricultural region with two large cities – Lviv and Cracow – vibrant economic, cultural and intellectual centres in an otherwise very poor province. Both of them had a growing bourgeoisie and intelligentsia. Practitioners in the two cities included football in the curriculum of physical education as early as in the 1890s; the first matches were played in 1891, and the description of the game in the textbook by Edmund Cenar entitled: 'Gymnastic games for school youth' is probably the first description of football in the Polish language. The increase in physical recreation of kids and youth was enabled by a massive action of creating the so-called 'Jordan park' playgrounds [*ogródki jordanowskie*], modern children's playgrounds equipped with facilities for physical activity, named after Henryk Jordan, a physician and pioneer of physical education in Poland, who was behind the idea (Gawkowski and Braciszewski, 2012, pp. 22–23). Nevertheless, in its early days football was treated only as a supplementary form of recreation and not as a separate game. As Józef Hałys puts it, the pathway from these recreational facilities to gyms in schools and universities was open (Hałys, 1986, p. 14).

Educational institutions, high schools and particularly two major universities – Lviv University (the John Casimir University in the interwar period, currently the Ivan Franko University) and Jagiellonian University in Cracow – became a fertile ground for mushrooming sport organisations at the very beginning of the twentieth century. Sława (renamed as Czarni) and Pogoń, established in 1903, were the first clubs in Lviv. The latter turned out to be a leading force in Polish football, winning the championships in the pre-Second World War era four times. Czarni and Pogoń, along with Hasmonea (formed by the local Jewish community) and Sparta were major teams from the city of Lviv (Beniuk, 2018). In Cracow, two teams with the longest history

72 *Football fandom in Poland in a historical perspective*

of derby rivalry in Poland were established in 1906 by people connected to the Jagiellonian University (Cracovia) and by high school teachers (Wisła Cracow). Slightly later Jutrzenka and Makkabi were formed by the local Jewish circles; both of them belonged to the Maccabi World Union. These clubs were instrumental in developing the institutionalised football scene in Poland. Established in 1911, the Association of Polish Football [*Związek Polskiej Piłki Nożnej*, ZPPN] was part of the *Österreichischer Fußball-Verband*, which organised the regional championships until the outbreak of the First World War. The association was joined by the Jewish clubs, while those established by the Ukrainians remained outside (Woźniak, 2018).

The Kingdom of Poland

The Congress Poland, or The Kingdom of Poland [*Królestwo Polskie*], formed as a result of the Congress of Vienna, was effectively a puppet state within the Russian Empire. Most of the territory of the former Polish-Lithuanian Commonwealth belonged to this partition, including the capital city of Warsaw and the city of Łódź, which recorded the fastest growth in population among European industrial cities in the second half of the nineteenth century (Marzec and Zysiak, 2011, pp. 67–78). The process of Russification and repressions against Poles led to several unsuccessful uprisings against the tsar, resulting in the further suppression of liberties. Both Warsaw and Łódź were islands of modernity in otherwise rural society, where serfdom was abolished only in 1864 by Tsar Alexander II.

The beginnings of football in Warsaw largely followed the story of Cracow and Lviv, and were mainly dependent on educational institutions. English expats served as coaches and referees. The first club, named Korona, was established in 1909. Some clubs emerged from unofficial teams affiliated with primary and secondary schools. After the merger of four such teams, Polonia Warsaw was established in 1911. The Jewish club Makabi appeared in 1915, and *Akademicki Związek Sportowy* [Academic Sports Association] in 1916 (Hałys, 1986, pp. 16–17). In 1920, two years after regaining independence, officers of the Warsaw garrison established a club called *Wojskowy Klub Sportowy* [Military Football Club]. In 1922, after the merger with Korona, it was renamed as 'Legia', a sign of allegiance to the Polish Legions, military troops led in the First World War by Józef Piłsudski, the Provisional Chief of State and Commander in Chief after the rebirth of independent Poland.

In the 1920s, the largest Polish city witnessed the establishment of numerous clubs. Warszawianka and Skra were founded by socialist cooperatives, Świt by one of the largest labour unions, Varsovia by the scouting organisation, PKS by the Warsaw police force, Marymont by the Polish Socialist Party, Sarmata by Warsaw Trams (a municipal company), to name just a few (Hałys, 1986, pp. 24, 38). Every one of these clubs had a strong identity and the political allegiances of the members and fans were clear. Support for a football club was yet another way to express the support for a

Football fandom in Poland in a historical perspective   73

political idea that was behind the organisation. Ethnic, religious and political contexts frequently overlapped in the reality of multicultural pre-war Poland. The terraces were constantly the arena of political agitation and political tensions during the games.

Contrary to Warsaw, Łódź followed a pattern of the institutionalisation of football observed in large industrial centres elsewhere. The city established in an agricultural settlement was supposed to become the largest centre of textile industry at the westernmost frontier of the Russian Empire. Know-how and capital from the west of Europe was encouraged to invest in Łódź through a system of tax exemptions and by cheap labour force recruited from the neighbouring rural regions. The majority of foreign entrepreneurs came from Prussia, but when COATS Corporation took over one of the local factories in 1906, British engineers and workers arrived in the city bringing their favourite pastime. They quickly started to teach the locals how to play and the first football tournaments were organised from 1909. At the time, Łódź was a multi-ethnic city. The majority of the working class was Polish with a significant share of Jewish people, who were working in the local trade and some became wealthy entrepreneurs. German factory owners dominated in the upper echelons of the class structure, while the city was administered by Russian officials (Woźniak, 2018; Glica, 2013).

In 1912 the *Lodzer Fusball Verband* was formed and official Łódź Championships were held since. The first trophy, allegedly funded by Robert Smith and Alexander Gilchrist, two Englishmen working in Łódź, was won by German TV Kraft. The second tournament was also won by a team formed by German workers, but named Newcastle to honour the city of origin of the coach (Bogusz, 2007). Two most decorated clubs from Łódź – ŁKS and Widzew – were formed in 1908 and 1910, respectively, and the former managed to win two championships of Łódź before the tournament was suspended due to the outbreak of the Great War. When Poland regained independence, some of the clubs were Polonised, but the city remained multi-ethnic. In the interwar period at least five Jewish and five German teams remained in the city, preserving their cultural and religious identity while participating in local and national competitions (Chomicki and Śledziona, 2014).

One story is symbolic, though probably apocryphal. In November 1918, on the eve of regaining independence, during the game between ŁKS and German team Sturm, a controversial situation on the pitch escalated to the riot during which German soldiers were disarmed by the crowd of Polish football fans. This, according to what may be simply an urban legend, started the process of disarming German troops across the whole city. The disarmament of German soldiers all over the territory of Poland in this period is universally perceived as a symbol of regaining sovereignty after 123 years of absence from the political map of Europe (Gawkowski and Braciszewski, 2012, p. 89).

74 *Football fandom in Poland in a historical perspective*

Political and ethnic divisions within football fandom in pre-Second World War Poland (1918–1939)

The establishment of the PZPN and the league

Soon after the First World War, in the spring of 1919, the Galicia-based ZPPN (Association of Polish Football) was re-established. Towards the end of the same year, the PZPN (Polish Football Association) was formed during the inauguration meeting of the delegates of 31 football clubs from the whole territory of re-united Polish Republic (Dmowski, 2013a). Most members of the first board were former officials of ZPPN, which was disbanded the following year. Regional branches of the PZPN were formed either from scratch or on the basis of regional associations formerly subordinated to the national associations of the three partitioning powers. Recognition of the particular role of Galicia was confirmed with the selection of Cracow as the home of the headquarters of the new organisation. The first congress also appointed a managerial staff tasked with the forming of the male national team. The first aim was to take part in the 1920 Summer Olympic Games in Antwerp, but the Polish-Soviet War interrupted. Until the ceasefire proclaimed in October, in 1920 war was raging again on the territory of Poland, and the Polish Olympic Committee had to cancel participation of Polish sportsmen. Consequently, the very first official international football game of Poland's national team was played on 18 December 1921 in Budapest. The next year saw the first victory (2–1 against Sweden in Stockholm), while the first home games were hosted in 1923 in Lviv and Cracow. The football tournament of the Summer Olympic Games held in 1924 in Paris was the first large event with the participation of the Polish national team. No sporting success was achieved this time, as the team lost 0–5 to Hungary in the first round of the tournament (Woźniak, 2018).

The first tournaments of Polish Championships held between 1921 and 1926 were based on a two-stage system. The regional tournaments in five districts decided which five teams made it to the final group, where they competed playing two games against each other. In 1927 a new body within PZPN was formed: *Polska Liga Piłki Nożnej* (Polish Football League), which gathered 57 clubs from all over Poland. The PZPN's headquarters was moved to Warsaw, and the new era started with regular football championships played by fourteen teams in the top division of the national league, and regional leagues played at the lower levels of competition.

Football fans of the inter-war period

Interestingly, the two monumental volumes on the history of Polish football hardly mention the question of fandom at all. In a huge 1,000-page book on the history of Polish football, published in many editions during the communist period (latest edition: Hałys 1986), not a single chapter is devoted

Football fandom in Poland in a historical perspective   75

exclusively to the topic of football fans. A more recent monograph contains one such chapter, symptomatically entitled: 'Fans: The eternal problem' (Gawkowski and Braciszewski, 2012, pp. 87).

The title refers to the first operationalisation of football fandom in official documents of the football governing bodies in Poland. In 1933 the Monthly Bulletin of the Association of Polish referees defined a particular kind of a football supporter using the word 'fanatic' (an exact equivalent to the English term) and in a surprisingly modern way. According to the unnamed author:

> A football fanatic is a person who attends the match and who attaches far greater importance even to the most minor events on the pitch than a regular supporter. Every incident on the pitch is experienced through the whole nervous system, totally subjectively. (...) Wherever we go to the game, be it the capital city or the provinces, large cities or small villages, wherever football has arrived, we can find such typical fanatics.
> (Gawkowski and Braciszewski, 2012, p. 87)

The author also stressed that the idyllic image of peaceful and polite football fans, which was frequently presented by the media, was very far from the truth. Indeed, violent disorder was frequent, and the police were often helpless in the face of massive riots, which left fans wounded or sometimeseven dead. Violence occurred not only during the games. In 1930 alone, three stadiums in Lviv (of Ukraina, Czarni and Hasmonea) were set on fire by unknown perpetrators. The regulations on how to deal with troublemakers were in force since 1926, and the PZPN specified the number of security guards which the host club was required to employ to prevent disorder (Gawkowski and Braciszewski, 2012, p. 91).

Anti-Semitism in Polish football in the pre-war period: fandom and politics

In the inter-war period, when football was gaining mass following, Poland was a multi-ethnic state. According to census data from 1931, the population of Poland was composed of 68.9 per cent ethnic Poles, 13.9 per cent Ukrainians, 8.7 per cent Jews, 3.1 per cent Belarusians and 2.3 percent Germans (Jałowiecki and Szczepański, 2007, p. 70). During what Dmowski calls 'the period of autonomy' in the history of Polish football (1919–1939), regional and ethnic conflicts stirred political and economic tensions within society at large. These were quickly transferred also to the world of football, resulting in prolonged conflicts between cities, clubs and certainly supporters (Dmowski, 2013a, p. 99). As elsewhere in Europe, anti-Semitic tension was growing in Poland during the 1920s and 1930s, which also affected the social world of football.

In many places in Poland, Jewish communities formed their own teams, many of them under the umbrella of the Maccabi World Union. This was also the case in Cracow. In the twenty-first century, anyone interested in Polish football associates the term 'Holy War' with the fiercest derby rivalry in Poland: between Wisła and Cracovia in Cracow. The brutal conflict between the fans of these two teams resulted in a dozen or so fatal victims of violent confrontations with the use of deadly weapons (knives, machetes, axes, even guns; see: Kossakowski, 2017a). Few people know that this expression originated in the first decades of the twentieth century and used to refer to the conflict between fans of two Jewish clubs: Makkabi and Jutrzenka. The former was connected to the Zionist movement, while the latter originated among members of the Bund, socialist party of Jewish working class. Their derby games usually ended with violent clashes in the terraces, which stemmed not only from football-related issues, but also ideological and class-based tensions between the fans (Wilczyńska, 2015).

The context of ethnic relations added another layer to conflicts between other teams as well. The divisions were well reflected in the differences between two largest Polish clubs in the city of Cracow. Wisła Cracow declared its allegiance to the Roman Catholic faith and the Church, and followed the *numerus nullus* principle: non-Polish and non-Catholic players were not allowed to play or train at the club. Anti-Semitic incidents sometimes happened in the terraces or football pitches, although it was not always possible to attribute them to racially motivated animosity.

Figure 4.1 Many derby rivalries were political in pre-war period, but only in case of Wisła–Cracovia derby of Cracow, the ethnic, religious, political and class tensions were overlapping so profoundly. The photo taken during the derby match on 07 May 1939 at the Wisła stadium.

Source: National Digital Archive, Poland

Political and class divisions were frequently more crucial than national or ethnic identities. Being a Polish worker with socialist sympathies could mean supporting a Jewish working-class team against a Polish club associated with ultra-right-wing National Democracy, while for instance Jewish socialists from Gwiazda supported Polish working-class team Skra against Zionist Makabi (Kulesza, 2014, pp. 141–150). In the summer of 1924, Warsaw witnessed unprecedented riots stemming from ethnic tensions among fans, occasioned by the game between Polonia Warsaw, supported mainly by followers of the openly anti-Semitic National Democracy party, and Hakoah Vienna, supported by the local Jewry of Warsaw. A few days later, the game of Hakoah against the Best of Warsaw team, composed of the players from all Warsaw clubs, was played under heavy control, with military units and mounted police present (Gawkowski, 2013, pp. 91–93). Anti-Semitism was an important political problem in those days. With incidents occurring in university lecture rooms and in the streets, football terraces were not immune from the disease either. Although such incidents were significant, they did not seem to be prevalent.

One of the incidents which could be described as the *signum temporis* of those years, and as proof of the dominant mood in the terraces, occurred when the star player of Poland and Wisła Cracow Henryk Reyman was sent off from the pitch by a referee named Rosenfeld. Reyman, a captain of the Polish Army and decorated war veteran, refused to leave, declaring that no Polish officer shall obey Jewish orders (Vogler, 1994). Today Wisła's stadium bears the name of Reyman. On the other hand, Wisła's local rival, Cracovia, was a truly multicultural team, accepting players of various ethnic backgrounds and denominations. Like almost everywhere in Europe, in the course of the 1930s anti-Semitism was becoming more politically fuelled. The growth of chauvinism and xenophobia was apparent with the rise of increasingly more radical right-wing parties. Their agenda was visible also in the world of football. In 1938, the Greater Poland regional football association (interestingly, the region with the lowest share of the Jewish population) demanded that Jewish clubs should be excluded from PZPN, and Jewish players – banned from official competitions. The motion was blocked by the group of Polish teams lead by Cracovia (Rympel, 1964, p. 584). Only a year later the Second World War brought the end to multicultural Poland.

The national football team in the multi-ethnic state

Many footballers of non-Polish ethnic background living in multi-ethnic regions of the country decided to play in the national team of Poland in the interwar period. This was particularly the case in the former Prussian partition. 1938 saw a symbolic situation: during the first ever game of Poland in the World Cup finals, the very first goal was scored by Fryderyk Eugeniusz Scherfke, born Fritz Egon Scherfke in the city of Poznań (then German Posen). Although listed as underdogs, Poland played a surprisingly close

78 *Football fandom in Poland in a historical perspective*

game against favoured Brazil, losing 5–6 only in extra time. The four remaining goals for Poland (the best result in World Cup finals until Oleg Salenko scored five goals in Russia's win over Cameroon in 1994) were scored by Ernest Wilimowski. Both Scherfke and Wilimowski were born German under Prussian administration. They received Polish citizenship and decided to play for Polish teams. Scherfke became a legendary player for Warta Poznań, scoring 131 goals. Wilimowski's story was even more complex, yet not unusual for the region of Upper Silesia. Born Prandella, he received his Polish surname after his stepfather, who married his German mother. He spoke German at home, and he used the Silesian dialect on the pitch and at school. To the dismay of the local German population, he chose to play for Ruch Chorzów, a Polish team, and his great football skills were revealed early. Playing in the top Polish division, he quickly became a star. With 112 goals scored in 86 games during his five seasons (1934–1939), he remains one of the top scorers in the history of Polish club football. He was also a regular player of the national team throughout this period (Urban, 2011).

The years 1938 and 1939 saw Wilimowski at his best, and the latter year was crucial for him and for the whole generation. In May, he became the all-time leader in the number of goals scored during a single match – Ruch won against German team from Łódź, Union Touring, 12–1, with Wilimowski scoring 10 goals. A few months later, he became a folk hero in the whole country. Hungary, the runner-up in the previous year's World Cup final, came to Poland to play a prestigious friendly game. Unsurprisingly, after 33 minutes Poland was losing 0–2. In the remaining hour Wilimowski scored three goals and earned a penalty kick allowing a 4–2 win. Four days later, the German army invaded Poland, bringing an end to Wilimowski's career as a Polish footballer, with a record of 22 goals scored in 21 games of the national team.

Residents of territories annexed to the Third Reich were offered an opportunity to sign the *Deutsche Volksliste*, a declaration of allegiance to Germany and Nazi ideals. A German by birth, Wilimowski was automatically awarded German citizenship of the highest category. Sepp Herberger, the future coach of the 1954 World Cup winners, quickly called him up to the national team of the Third Reich. Due to suspension of international competitions, the team only played friendly games with the allied Axis countries. Nevertheless, Wilimowski managed to score 13 goals in eight games within the next two years. He also pursued a successful club career with TSV 1860 Munich: he won the 1942 German Cup, and his record of fourteen goals in one edition of the *Deutsche Pokal* is still unsurpassed. He gained immense popularity and soon became a poster boy for the Nazi propaganda (Smolorz, Czado and Waloszek, 2012). The assertion of British author Jonathan Wilson that Wilimowski's choice to play for Germany was motivated by sporting considerations ('Evidently recognizing he was much too good for Polish football, Wilimowski defected and later played for Germany' (Wilson, 2006, p. 44)) is a clear misinterpretation.

Figure 4.2 The unprecedented triumph against vice-World Champion Hungary came on 27 August 1939, just 4 days before German invasion of Poland. The joyful crowd in the photo carries the heroes of the day: Władysław Szczepaniak and Ernest Wilimowski. The former will spend the occupation playing in clandestine tournaments in occupied Warsaw and will play his next international game for Poland only in 1947. Meanwhile, Wilimowski, the best Polish footballer of this era, will play eight games and score 13 goals for the National team of the Third Reich.

Source: National Digital Archive, Poland

Although the details of his wartime years remain unclear, it seems that his choices were to some extent dependent on the leverage that the German authorities had over him: his mother was imprisoned for the crime of racial defilement (maintaining sexual relationships with a Jewish person). After 1943, even prominent and successful German sportsmen were conscripted. There were rumours that Wilimowski fought at the Ukrainian front, but these stories have never been confirmed (Urban, 2011, pp. 58–59).

He survived the war and played in the Bundesliga until 1955. The scale of his talent is confirmed by the fact that according to the rankings compiled by Rec.Sport.Soccer Statistics Foundation, until 2016 he still remained in the top ten of the all-time list of the best scorers in football history. In the last four decades he was surpassed only by Romario, Cristiano Ronaldo and Leo Messi (RSSSF, 2016).

In Poland, the photo of Wilimowski on the cover of sports magazines with a swastika that replaced the white eagle on his football shirt is probably the

80 *Football fandom in Poland in a historical perspective*

most popular image of him, along with the photo of him making a Nazi salute before one of the games. These images were used by the Polish media in the post-war period to portray Wilimowski as a traitor. His surname became synonymous with treason, and the Polish star turned Nazi collaborator was to be erased from the annals of Polish football history. This was in line with official communist propaganda of the post-war period, with its fearmongering about German revanchist sentiments, particularly over Upper Silesia and the so-called Recovered Territories (which Germany lost to Poland in 1945). Wilimowski remained *persona non grata* in Polish football until the end of his life. When officials of Ruch Chorzów declared their intention to invite one of the Ruch's most famous players to the 75th anniversary of the club, the media reacted furiously and the idea was quickly abandoned (Woźniak, 2015).

The Second World War: football as a forbidden pastime (1939–1945)

The German invasion on 1 September 1939, followed by the Red Army attack from the east on 17 September, brought an end to barely over two decades of Poland's independence. The country was yet again divided between neighbouring powers. The Second World War changed forever the future of the state and all its people.

Germany occupied a territory of 188 thousand square kilometres inhabited by 22 million people. Approximately half of it, with the population of 10 million, was directly annexed to the Third Reich, while the remaining part was organised as the General Governorate (Czubiński, 2011), established already in October 1939. The rules imposed by the Nazi administration were significantly harsher than anywhere else in the occupied Europe. Imprisonment in concentration camp or death penalty was a punishment for a large number of offences, such as walking streets during the curfew, playing Chopin's music in public or owning a radio.

All facilities and financial resources owned by Polish clubs and sports organisations were confiscated, and organised sport was banned. In July 1940 General Governor Hans Frank issued an official regulation forbidding Poles to hold any sports events. This move was justified explicitly: 'Gymnastic and sports organisations which would enhance fitness of the [Polish] population are not in our interest' (Szarota, 1988, quoted after Kulesza, 2014, p. 37). The highest official in charge was Sports Commissioner Georg Niffka, an SS officer. Before the war he had been editor-in-chief of the *Kattowitzer Zeitung*, a German newspaper issued in the Polish part of Upper Silesia, and thus had a good orientation in sporting life in Poland. His position was firm: despite numerous requests he fully enforced the ban on participation of Poles in any form of sport-related activity (Chemicz, 1982, p. 35).

Thus, practising organised sport became illegal, along with dozens of other activities which were available to people living in other occupied European territories. Police roundups in the streets were everyday experience under the German occupation in Poland. Getting caught in any of them

Football fandom in Poland in a historical perspective   81

could lead to imprisonment or deportation to Germany as a forced labourer. Any suspicion of misdemeanour carried the same threat. Regardless of the repressions and surveillance, the resistance movement and the structures of the Polish Underground State (see: Karski, 2014) began to form almost immediately. The underground world of sport also institutionalised, particularly in large cities like Cracow and Warsaw. Within months since the beginning of the occupation, the new clandestine Regional Football Committees emerged in both cities with the task to organise the games. The challenges they faced were huge, but so was the demand of the general public. The new teams were formed out of the footballers who survived the invasion of Poland.

One of the main obstacles was the fact that major Warsaw stadiums were used exclusively for the purpose of military exercises, propaganda gatherings or games organised by and for the Germans. The signs reading *Nur für Deutsche*, displayed in order to impose almost total separation between the occupant and the occupied, were to be seen not only in cinemas, theatres, means of public transport, parks and cafes, but also many sports facilities. Nevertheless, the first football games were played within the first weeks of the occupation. The initial venue was the Mokotów Field, a large park complex in the central part of Warsaw. Information about the planned matches spread by the word of mouth, and thousands of fans gathered to watch them. To avoid allegations of premeditation, the players did not wear the same colour shirts and often did not wear sports shoes. The growing presence of the police and military patrols, together with the growing attendance, made it difficult to stage the games and pretend that they were spontaneously initiated by a random group of people. To minimise the risk, the venue was soon moved to a football pitch at Poskarbińska street in the working-class district of Praga. Distant from the city centre, it became the main venue of the underground football due to the lower presence of *Schutzpolizei* and Wehrmacht patrols. Importantly, the pitch was surrounded by tenement houses, which offered some protection from surveillance and made it easy for the crowd to disperse in the case of problems. Sometimes even four matches were played daily, and the number of teams was constantly growing: in 1944, on the eve of the Warsaw Uprising, the number of officially registered teams from Warsaw and nearby towns was fifty (Kulesza, 2014, p. 49). What is even more surprising, although statistics both from the war and pre-war period are not precise, it seems that the level of match attendance was similar. According to Andrzej Gowarzewski, a leading historian of football competitions in Poland, the attendance rarely exceeded ten thousand, and at most of the games ranged between four and eight thousand (Gowarzewski, 1995).

The level of control and surveillance in Cracow was not as harsh as in the former capital city. According to some sources, the first game was played there in the presence of approximately four thousand fans already on 22 October 1939 (Chemicz, 1982, pp. 25–26). Unlike in Warsaw, the clubs from Cracow managed to preserve their identities and they played under their

82 *Football fandom in Poland in a historical perspective*

original names. Most clubs from Cracow and the neighbouring towns took part in the competitions throughout the whole period of occupation. This was certainly impossible for the Jewish clubs, as the beginning of the occupation marked the beginning of racial cleansing. The Jewish minority was separated; some Jews were deported while the remaining population was forced to live in the ghetto.

The local conditions in Cracow made it possible to organise well-planned tournaments attracting thousands of fans. In September 1941, the tournament celebrating the 35th anniversary of Wisła and the 20th anniversary of Zwierzyniecki included a ceremonial mass in one of the churches. Despite travel restrictions and strict checks, some of the tournaments were attended by teams from Warsaw, and sometimes Cracow teams returned those visits (Chemicz, 1982, p. 57, pp. 77–81). Interestingly, due to the relatively low level of police surveillance and the lack of security provided by the organisers, many games occasioned violent confrontations between fans. For instance, in 1943 both the match for the third place and the final of the Cracow Championships were abandoned because of the growing tension on the pitch and among fans. The final game between Wisła and Cracovia was followed by a full-scale riot which spread to the streets of the Podgórze district. The German police did not react – according to some stories the local commander named Mitschke, himself a former player of the First Vienna football club, commented that football fans are always the same everywhere (Chemicz, 1982, pp. 92–94).

All those incidents were reported in official documents of the local football association. A historian writing on the events from 1943, comments: 'These reports illuminate this strange, feverish atmosphere of the games. It seems that nobody remembered about the general political and wartime situation of the Poles, that local chauvinism and fanaticism prevailed over cautiousness, hampering the proper assessment of these events' (Chemicz, 1982, pp. 102–103).

There are no reports of such misbehaviour among fans in Warsaw. The reason behind this may be stricter surveillance, as well as the fact that Warsaw teams were formed from scratch at the beginning of the occupation, and thus identity-based local conflicts were no longer the case. This does not mean that the world of football in Cracow did not suffer. One of the worst tragedies came just a few days before Wehrmacht left the city. On 15 January 1945 in the Dąbie district German troops executed 79 residents, including almost all the players and staff of the local team Dąbski (Chemicz 1982, p. 153).

In the shadow of this atrocity, the Soviet Army entered the city just three days later. Unlike most Polish cities, Cracow did not suffer much damage and most residents remained in their homes. The very first sports event, an ice hockey game, was organised just three days later. The first football matches were held a week later as part of events celebrating the liberation of the city from the German occupation. The sign *Nur für Deutsche* was torn down from the entrance to the Wisła stadium and although the temperature was minus 15 degrees Celsius ten thousand people came to watch two charity games: Juvenia vs Zwierzyniecki and Wisła vs Cracovia. The event began with the Polish national anthem being sung by the fans and players alike (Chemicz, 1982, pp. 153–156). One of the Wisła players recalled this as one of the most touching and memorable experiences of their lifetime:

> I remember I was once again wearing my black sweater and I was in the goal on this pitch where I had no chance to play for six years. It's not strange that I was emotional. Like in the past, I was looking at the old stands, the Kościuszko Mound, familiar poplars on 3 May avenue. It felt like a new life beginning from scratch.
>
> (Chemicz, 1982, p. 159)

Another player commented three decades later on his wartime years as a footballer taking part in illegal competitions:

> Today, after 34 years, I still wonder why we were taking such a risk to play football in spite of a strict ban. Usually, we, players and fans, we did not give in to fear; even in the most tragic periods we were convinced that sport can be a remedy for the mood of despair and gloom.
>
> (Chemicz, 1982, p. 160)

The region of Greater Poland along with the Western part of the pre-war Polish territory (including Łódź) was annexed to Germany and in early 1940 renamed as *Reichsgau Wartheland* (District of the Warta Land; Warta is the name of the river flowing through the region) under NSDAP Gauleiter Arthur Greiser. Like elsewhere, the Polish population was forbidden from involvement in sports activities. Although the level of surveillance and repressions was not as harsh as in the General Governorate, as proved by several documented instances, footballers, officials, referees and supporters risked arrest and severe beating. Nevertheless, thousands of fans came to watch the games. Sometimes, when the German authorities learned about illegal matches, they intervened by destroying the football pitch, thus making it impossible to play (Jurek, 2001, pp. 104–107). Similar examples can be found in historical studies on different large Polish cities which were annexed to the Third Reich (Rukowiecki, 2012).

The situation on the territories conquered by the Red Army and governed by the Soviet Union was different: the sporting life existed and participation in organised sport was available to Poles, even though some traditionally Polish clubs were liquidated. This refers in the first place to the case of Lviv, where decorated Pogoń and Czarni ceased to exist and were replaced by Spartak and Dinamo, which emerged at the very beginning of the Soviet rule in the region.

People's game in the People's Republic of Poland: football under communism (1945–1989)

The end of the Second World War saw Poland as a different country. The population had diminished substantially: almost six million Polish citizens lost their lives, including 90 per cent of the Jewish population, and even more remained on the territories which were incorporated into the Soviet Union. Poland had lost its historic, yet multicultural city of Lviv, which surrendered to the invading Soviet forces on 22 September 1939. As a result, its rich football world vanished from the sporting map of the country. The post-war treaties compensated the loss of the eastern territories with the so-called Recovered Territories in the west.

As it is today, Poland is the most homogenous European country, with more than 95 per cent of the population sharing the same language, ethnicity and religion. Owing to various historical processes – mainly mass-scale migration resulting from wars, partitions and the occupation – regional identities in twentieth-century Poland were not very strong, except Upper Silesia.

The flourishing world of organised Jewish sport ceased to exist with the beginning of the occupation. There were some attempts to revive this movement in the post-war reality, although the topic seems under-researched. Nevertheless, between 1945 and 1948 fifteen Jewish sport clubs were established in Lower Silesia alone; the region was part of the so-called Recovered Territories, where many Holocaust survivors settled after the war. Three factors contributed to the fact that this process did not last long. First, the growing centralisation of the communist state had an impact on all independent organisations, including sports teams. Second, in 1949 the communist government liquidated the limited autonomy of the Jewry and all Jewish organisations were nationalised. Finally, the proclamation of the independent state of Israel in 1948 brought the first wave of migration of Polish Jews (Włodarczyk, 2014, pp. 114–115; see also Olejnik, 1997). Historical research into Jewish sport in the following years concentrates on documenting the role of Jewish sportsmen, coaches and officials in the formation of new, fully centralised structures of sports institutions in the People's Republic of Poland (e.g. Włodarczyk, 2014; Einhorn, 2014).

For forty-five years when Poland remained on the eastern side of the Iron Curtain, football in the country was destined to serve the ideological purposes of the dominating ideology; Dmowski calls it 'the period of subordination' (2013a, p. 99). The official policy of the communist state was aimed at centralisation and full control over any domain of social life, including football. The Russian term *uravnilovka*, enforced uniformity, adequately describes the socio-political atmosphere in the stands.

All clubs were owned by state-controlled entities, and the rivalry between them was a proxy for a power struggle between various branches of socialist economy and security forces. Top clubs were affiliated and financed by the army (Legia Warsaw, Śląsk Wrocław), the police (Wisła Cracow) or various

Football fandom in Poland in a historical perspective 85

branches of industry: textile industry (ŁKS Łódź, Widzew Łódź), railway (Lech Poznań), shipbuilding and maritime transport (Pogoń Szczecin, Arka Gdynia, Lechia Gdańsk), mining (all major clubs from Upper Silesia, which won 25 of 42 championships during the communist period: Górnik Zabrze, Ruch Chorzów, Polonia Bytom). Although these industrial affiliations provided a sense of identity, they did not necessarily contribute to the long-lasting attachment to a particular factory or branch of economy. As will be shown later, in some cases the uneasy affiliation with the 'power ministries' of the communist state activated the processes of forgetting or erasing this particular part of club legacy from popular narratives (Fryc and Ponczek, 2009). The games played by Polish national team occasionally became an opportunity to express political discontent, which will be presented in the chapter devoted to the Polish national team and its fandom.

Nevertheless, most of the factors which Dmowski (2013b, pp. 334–335) enumerates as traditional elements of club rivalries (ethnic/national identity, religion, territory and place of origin) were almost non-existent in communist Poland. The rivalries were formed on the basis of hostility against the local or regional neighbour, but their political undertones were absent. The strongest animosity was aimed at the clubs affiliated with the army, at Legia Warsaw in particular. This, however, mainly stemmed from the practice of conscripting the most talented youngsters from all over the country and making them play for Legia, thus stripping other football clubs of promising players.

Like national teams from the eastern side of the Iron Curtain, in some seasons clubs from the East played remarkably well against their rivals from the West in the European competitions, which from the late 1950s became one of the few platforms of regular contacts between the West and the East. Legia Warsaw and Widzew Łódź made it to the semi-finals of the European Champion Clubs' Cup (in 1969/1970 and 1982/1983, respectively), and Górnik Zabrze appeared in the final of the European Cup Winners' Cup (1969/1970).

There were some restrictions concerning top players – they were not allowed to sign for foreign teams. Top players of the 1970s, Kazimierz Deyna and Włodzimierz Lubański, were not even informed at the time that Real Madrid approached their respective clubs, Legia Warsaw and Górnik Zabrze, with an offer. Transferring players to the country ruled by General Franco, whose regime was perceived as an enemy of the socialist bloc, was seen as unacceptable. When Poland enjoyed international successes in the 1970s, particularly after the bronze medal at the FIFA World Cup in 1974, the rules began to change. At first, only decorated players over thirty years of age were allowed to sign for Western clubs. Hard currency received by the Ministry of Sport for such contracts (and subsequently redistributed to the clubs) was an important factor, but many transfers also involved political considerations. It was not accidental that Zbigniew Boniek, the star of Polish national team and Widzew Łódź, was sold to Juventus Turin at only 27 years of age in 1982. The Fiat Automobiles company owned the club and was engaged in close cooperation with Polish industry, licensing the production of its cars in factories in Poland (Woźniak, 2018).

86 *Football fandom in Poland in a historical perspective*

Some informal, but organised, fan groups emerged only in the 1970s. They adopted patterns of organised support for their teams which they observed during the games with foreign clubs in European competitions. Radosław Kossakowski views fans of Polonia Bytom as the forerunners of organised fandom (Kossakowski, 2017a, pp. 84–86). Contacts with the Western world were limited and the local fandom culture transformed at its own pace and in its own way. According to some older football fans interviewed by Kossakowski, in the same decade the football stands witnessed the growing presence of the 'git-people' subculture (*gitowcy, git-ludzie* [right guys]), whose members brought to the stadiums rules typical of the prison code of conduct (violence, loyalty restricted to members of the group only, hatred of the police). To young members of the football crowd, these behaviours appealed far more than the officially established 'fan-clubs', which were an attempt to shape the fanbase in accordance with central planning and socialist ideas about the formation of youth, successfully achieved through communist scouting organisations and numerous other initiatives. At the end of the 1970s, there were about 30 informal, but organised, fan crews. Scarce research into the collective memory of members of this subculture shows no traces of their political engagement. Their trips to away games served the purpose of enhancing in-group cohesion, partying with friends, testing their masculinity in fights with fans of rival teams, feeling the vibe of even limited independence through engaging in uncontrolled and informal activities. Clashes with the police force were scarce. Particularly since the declaration of the martial law, the Citizens' Militia (the communist police) had a notoriously bad reputation for its brutality, which actually fostered respect and limited inclination for violent confrontation with the troops (Kossakowski, 2017a).

Many respondents recalling that period, despite their awareness of living under an unfavourable system, emphasised that the Militia was much worse prepared to deal with fan incidents than modern security forces. In cases that required intervention, the Militia arranged everything in the simplest ways, and benefited from the fact that the police force commanded a great respect: 'These were different times; after all, only fifteen policemen were enough to appease everyone because of respect they had' (Arka Gdynia supporter). Also the media, controlled by communist authorities, noticed only positive aspects of supporting. Although one reason for this was the ideology of 'law and social order', the fact was that except for some occasional incidents, fans were not a 'problem' in the 1970s, and they could be seen as a significant part of the whole propaganda project related to social 'massification' of sport. Also, the level of sensitivity to violence was different, and what today is assessed as unacceptable could be regarded as 'normal' at the time (see Kossakowski, 2017b).

Communist authorities tried to channel the movement by setting up official fan clubs which received state sponsorship for their activity, including organisation of social events and trips to away matches. According to the logic of the communist regime, the authorities tried to make fandom a 'planned' process, as was the case of centrally planned economy. 'Planning' was an

Football fandom in Poland in a historical perspective 87

inherent feature of the communist system: 'In the communist countries, the view of history as a structured change of society in a specific direction remains alive. But with it, there survives at the same time the idea that this change is leading inevitably to the realization of communist ideals' (Elias, 2009, p. 18).

Although there are examples of fans' (and footballers') engagement in anti-communist opposition, these were rare. Most supporters had a working-class background and were not involved in any political activism (Woźniak, 2013). Surveillance of football fans and repressions against them were limited in comparison with, for instance, East Germany (Grix, 2012; Wojtaszyn, 2012), and expression of political views in the stands was rare during this period. This is also confirmed by the records of the communist secret police. Historians studying these records have written on the surveillance of journalists and football players, and open or secret cooperation of some football officials with secret services. In some cases, the expertise of historians from the Institute of National Remembrance provided excuse for former footballers who had been on the payroll of communist secret services, and intended to become members of parliament in the democratic era (Majchrzak, 2017).

These historical studies reveal hardly any information about politically motivated surveillance or repressions against football fandom. The only notable exception is the case of Lechia Gdańsk and the terraces of this football club. Gdańsk was the cradle of the Solidarity movement, established in 1980 as a trade union in the Gdańsk shipyard, the first organisation independent from communist authorities in the Soviet bloc. Numerous shipyard workers, as well as top activists of the Solidarity and other local anti-communist initiatives were regulars at Lechia games (Wąsowicz, 2012). Only 16 months after the Solidarity was founded, communist authorities imposed martial law in the whole country. The union was officially banned and most of its top figures imprisoned, while some went to operate in the underground structures. The repressions and surveillance increased and remained in force for the next two years. 28 September 1983, just a weeks after the suspension of martial law, saw the most memorable political demonstration involving football fans. This year, while playing in the Third Division, Lechia sensationally won the Polish Cup. For its first ever appearance in European competitions, Lechia was drawn to play Juventus Turin. During the second leg of the first round of the Cup Winners' Cup, Solidarity activists outmanoeuvred agents of the security forces, and Lech Wałęsa – the leader of Solidarity, recently released from prison – managed to sneak into the stadium. As a result of his presence in the terraces, the event turned into a major anti-communist manifestation (Nawrocki, 2012). Anti-communist resentment is very strong among Lechia fans until today, but this story remains exceptional, regardless of the current 'memory policies' involving anti-communist overtones, pursued among the fanbases of every significant football club in Poland (see Kossakowski, 2017a, p. 125).

88 *Football fandom in Poland in a historical perspective*

In the 1980s, news of the activity of English 'hooligans' reached Poland and the level of football-related violence increased. Owing to the official 'success propaganda', the scale of the phenomenon was never publicly acknowledged. For example, as unofficially reported, in the riots during the 1980 Polish Cup final between Legia Warsaw and Lech Poznań there was at least one dead and several hundred injured. On the other hand, the same period saw the stands become a scene of anti-communist activity. Slogans such as 'Solidarity' [*Solidarność*] and 'Down with the commies' [*Precz z komuną*] were often to be heard in Lechia Gdańsk stadium (Wąsowicz, 2012). Rioting against the authorities and fights with the police have remained a distinctive feature of Polish fans ever since. Official 'fan clubs' organised by the authorities perished, and fans organised themselves in their own way, which was usually manifested in mass trips to away matches. Taken on regular trains, the trips were spontaneous and involved binge drinking and fights with opposing fans. Law enforcement officers acted reactively, there was no special law regulating football matches. The most common 'strategy' of the Citizens' Militia was to punish the most hot-headed supporters by beating them and to release them home. The chaos of the fall of the state system was matched by the lack of any serious structures of the fan movement. The fatalistic mood of the end of an era was dominated by violence between fans, and between the police and fans.

The year 1989 was a turning point for Polish society, football and fandom. The process of systemic transformation brought the opportunity to modernise and 'civilise' all domains of social life, and all processes emerging during the post-1989 period have had a significant impact on the field of fandom. At the same time, as presented in this chapter, transformation of the fan world has been largely connected with the legacy of historical processes outlined above. To a considerable extent, contemporary Polish fandom, whether consciously or by making omissions, permanently performs memory work on the history of Polish society and the world of Polish football since its difficult beginnings. As will be shown, this memory work is one of the crucial processes shaping football fandom here and now. Therefore, it is not possible to fully trace and interpret contemporary events and processes without making constant references to the past.

References

Beniuk, S. (2018). O piłkarskich trybunach Lwowa lat 30. XX wieku na łamach pracy sportowej [Football terraces of Lviv in the 1930s in the sports press. Selected issues]. *Kultura Fizyczna*, 17(1), pp. 23–56.

Bergmann, O. (2012). Patriotyczne i obywatelskie aspekty działalności wielkopolskich klubów piłkarskich, ich zawodników i działaczy w pierwszej połowie XX wieku [Patriotic and civic aspects of functioning of football teams in Wielkopolska region]. *Kronika Wielkopolska*, 4, pp. 15–28.

Bogusz, A. (2007). *Dawna Łódź sportowa 1824–1945* [Old-time sporting Łódź 1824–1945]. Łódź: Muzeum Historii Miasta Łodzi.

Football fandom in Poland in a historical perspective   89

Chemicz, S. (1982). *Piłka Nożna w Okupowanym Krakowie* [Football in Cracow under Occupation]. Kraków: Wydawnictwo Literackie.

Chomicki, P. and Śledziona, L. (2014). *Rozgrywki Piłkarskie w Łodzi 1910–1919* [Football Competitions in Lodz 1910–1919]. Mielec: NADA.

Czubiński, A. (2011). *Historia Powszechna XX Wieku* [History of XX Century]. Poznań: Wydawnictwo Poznańskie.

Dmowski, S. (2013a). Polityczna historia polskiej piłki nożnej – wprowadzenie do tematyki badawczej [Political history of Polish football: introducing the field of research]. *e-Politikon*, 8, pp. 89–108.

Dmowski, S. (2013b). Geographical typology of European football rivalries. *Soccer & Society*, 14(3), pp. 331–343.

Einhorn, I. (2014). Żydzi w tenisie stołowym na Śląsku i Pomorzu Zachodnim [Jews in table tennis in regions of Silesia and West Pomerania]. In: J. Maliniak, P. Sroka and G. Strauchold (eds), *Z dziejów Sportu na Ziemiach Zachodnich i Północnych Polski po II wojnie światowej* [History of Sport in Western and Northern Poland]. Wrocław: Ośrodek Pamięć i Przyszłość, pp. 97–118.

Elias, N. (2009). Towards a theory of social processes. In: N. Elias. *Essays III. On Sociology and the Humanities*. Dublin: University College Dublin Press, pp. 9–39.

Fryc, A. and Ponczek, M. (2009). The communist rule in Polish sport history. *The International Journal of the History of Sport*, 26(4), pp. 501–514

Gawkowski, R. (2007). *Encyklopedia Klubów Sportowych Warszawy i jej Najbliższych Okolic w Latach 1918–1939* [Encyclopedia of Football Teams based in Warsaw and its Surroundings]. Warszawa: Wydawnictwo Uniwersytetu Warszawskiego.

Gawkowski, R. (2013) *Futbol Dawnej Warszawy* [Football of Old Warsaw]. Warszawa: Wydawnictwo Uniwersytetu Warszawskiego.

Gawkowski, R. and Braciszewski, J. (2012). *Historia Polskiej piłki Nożnej*. Warszawa: Wydawnictwo SBM.

Glica, S. (2013). *Od 1824. Opowieść o Łódzkim Sporcie* [Since 1824. Story of Sport in Łódź]. Łódź: Muzeum Miasta Łodzi.

Gowarzewski, A. (1995). *80 lat 'Zielonych' – Księga Jubileuszowa* [80 Years of the 'Greens' – History of the Legia – The Jubilee Book]. Katowice: Wydawnictwo GiA.

Grix, J. (2012). *Sport under Communism – Behind the East German 'Miracle'*. Basingstoke: Palgrave Macmillan.

Hałys, J. (1986). *Piłka Nożna w Polsce* [Football in Poland]. Kraków: KAW.

Jurek, T. (2001). Piłka nożna w latach okupacji. In: Woltmann, B. (ed.) *Piłka Nożna w Wielkopolsce 1921–2001* [Football in Greater Poland 1921–2001]. Poznań: PTNKF, pp. 104–108.

Karski, J. (2014). *Story of a Secret State*. Washington: Georgetown University Press.

Kijonka-Niezabitowska, J. (2009). Z problemów narodowości i tożsamości śląskiej - dylematy i wybory [From the problems of nationality and Silesian identity: dilemmas and choices]. *Studia Socjologiczne*, 195(4), pp. 85–111.

Kossakowski, R. (2017a) *Od Chuliganów do Aktywistów. Polscy Kibice i Zmiana Społeczna* [From Hooligans to Activists. Polish Fans and the Social Change]. Kraków: Universitas.

Kossakowski, R. (2017b). From communist fan clubs to professional hooligans: A history of Polish fandom as a social process. *Sociology of Sport Journal*, 34(3), pp. 281–292.

Kulesza, J. (2014). *Zakazane Gole. Futbol w Okupowanej Warszawie* [Forbidden Goals. Football in Warsaw under Occupation]. Warszawa: Wydawnictwo ERICA i Muzeum Powstania Warszawskiego.

90 Football fandom in Poland in a historical perspective

Łęcki, K. (2009). Śląski 'Ruch' – ponowoczesne meandry regionalnej tożsamości (na przykładzie klubu piłkarskiego i jego społecznego otoczenia) [Silesian 'Ruch' – Postmodern meanders of regional identity (case of a football club and its social surroundings)]. *Studia Socjologiczne*, 195(4), pp. 129–147.

Majchrzak, G. (2017). *Tajna Historia Futbolu* [Secret History of Football]. Warszawa: Fronda.

Marzec, W. and Zysiak, A. (2011). Młyn biopolityki. Topografie władzy peryferyjnego kapitalizmu na łódzkim [Biopolitical mills. Topographies of power in early peripheral capitalism]. *Praktyka Teoretyczna*, 2(3), pp. 65–86.

Nawrocki, K. (2012). Więcej niż mecz. Lechia Gdańsk-Juventus Turyn. [More than a match. Lechia Gdańsk-Juventus Turin]' In: S. Ligarski and G. Majchrzak (eds), *Nieczysta gra. Tajne Służby a Piłka Nożna* [Dirty Play. Secret Services and Football]. Chorzów: Videogaf, pp. 151–159.

Olejnik L. (1997). Społeczność żydowska w Łodzi w latach 1945–1950. Zarys Problemu [Jewish community in Łódź between 1945 and 1950. Outline of a problem]. *Acta Universitatis Lodziensis. Folia Historica*, 60, pp. 125–147.

Owsiański, J. (2016). *Rozgrywki Piłkarskie w Wielkopolsce do roku 1919* [Football Competitions in Wielkopolska after 1919]. Mielec: Nada Sp. z o.o.

Owsiański, J. (2017). *Lech Poznań. Przemilczana prawda* [Lech Poznań. Hidden Truth]. Self-publishing.

Owsiański, J. and Siwiński, T. (2013). *Historia Futbolu Wielkopolskiego* [History of Football in Wielkopolska]. Poznań: Zibigrafia.

Rec.Sport.Soccer Statistics Foundation (RSSSF). (2016). *Prolific Scorers Data*. Available at: www.rsssf.com/players/prolific.html [accessed 10 October 2019].

Rukowiecki, A. (2012). *Łódź 1939–1945. Kronika Okupacji* [Łódź 1939–1945. The Diary of the Occupation]. Łódź: Księży Młyn.

Rympel, M. (1964). Słowo o Żydach krakowskich w okresie międzywojennym (1918–1939) [The word on Jews in the interwar period (1918–1939)]. In: W. Bodnicki (ed.), *Kopiec Wspomnień* [The Mound of Memories]. Cracow: Wydawnictwo Literackie, pp. 555–589.

Smolorz, D., Czado, P. and Waloszek, J. (2012). *Górnoślązacy w Polskiej i Niemieckiej Reprezentacji Narodowej w Piłce Nożnej – Wczoraj i Dziś. Sport i Polityka na Górnym Śląsku* [Upper Silesians in Polish and German National Teams in Football – Yesterday and Today]. Gliwice, Opole: Dom Współpracy Polsko-Niemieckiej.

Szarota, T. (2008). *Okupowanej Warszawy Dzień Powszedni* [Daily Life in Occupied Europe]. Warszawa: Czytelnik.

Urban, T. (2011). *Schwarze Adler, Weiße Adler. Deutsche und polnische Fußballer im Räderwerk der Politik*. Göttingen: Die Werkstatt.

Vogler, H. (1994). *Wyznanie Mojżeszowe. Wspomnienia z Utraconego Czasu* [Mosaic Faith. Memories from the Lost Time]. Cracow: Austeria.

Wąsowicz, J. (2012). *Futbol i polityka. Przypadek kibiców Lechii Gdańsk* [*Football and politics. The case of Lechia Gdańsk fans*]. In: S. Ligarski and G. Majchrzak (eds), *Nieczysta Gra. Tajne Służby a Piłka Nożna* [Dirty Play. Secret Services and Football]. Chorzów: Videogaf, pp. 130–150.

Wilczyńska, B. (2015). Żydzi i Polacy na boiskach międzywojennego Krakowa, czyli co piłka nożna może powiedzieć o społeczeństwie [Jews and Poles at the football pitches of pre-war Cracow or what football tells about society]. *Studia Judaica*, 2 (36), pp. 293–319

Football fandom in Poland in a historical perspective   91

Wilson, J. (2006). *Behind the Curtain: Travels in Eastern European Football*. London: Orion Publishing.

Włodarczyk, T. (2014). *Sport Żydowski na Dolnym Śląsku w latach 1945–1959* [*Jewish sport in Lower Silesia between 1945 and 1959*]. In: J. Maliniak, P. Sroka and G. Strauchold (eds), *Z Dziejów Sportu na Ziemiach Zachodnich i Północnych Polski po II Wojnie Światowej* [History of sport in Western and Northern Poland]. Wrocław: Ościodek Pamięć i Przyszłość, pp. 97–118.

Wojtaszyn, D. (2012). *Kibice w Socjalizmie. Trybuny Piłkarskie w NRD. Studium Historyczno-Społeczne* [Fans in Socialism. The Football Terraces in DDR. The Historical-Social Study]. Wrocław: ATUT.

Woźniak, W. (2013). Zawodowe amatorstwo? Futbol w okresie PRL w relacjach polskich piłkarzy [Professional amateurship? Football under communism in an account of Polish footballers]. In: M. Kazimierczak and J. Kosiewicz (eds), *Sport i Turystyka. Uwarunkowania Historyczne i Wyzwania Współczesności* [Sport and Tourism. Historical Considerations and Contemporary Challenges]. Poznań: Akademia Wychowania Fizycznego im. Eugeniusza Piaseckiego w Poznaniu, pp. 537–550.

Woźniak, W. (2015). Industrial heritage and football in the imagined identity of Upper Silesians. In: S. G. Roberts (ed.), *Sport, Media and Regional Identity*, Newcastle upon Tyne: Cambridge Scholars Publishing, pp. 29–48.

Woźniak, W. (2018). Poland. In: J-M. De Waele, S. Gibril, E. Gloriozova and R. Spaaij (eds), *Palgrave International Handbook of Football and Politics*. Basingstoke: Palgrave Macmillan, pp. 223–244.

5 The pathological 1990s

Violence, anomie and political extremism among fans

Introduction

This chapter concerns the first years after the fall of communism in Poland in 1989. The 1990s can be viewed as one of the most difficult periods in modern Polish history, the times of economic 'shock therapy', transformation, political chaos, social austerity and uncertainty (Kowalik, 2009; see Chapter 3 for more details). In those challenging times, the Polish government and elites struggled to achieve economic and political stability. As a result, many different aspects of social life were considered 'less important' and remained underdeveloped.

One such domain was certainly the entire sphere of sport, which experienced severe problems owing to systemic negligence – clubs were left on their own and lost their financial and organisational stability. Before 1989 most of them had operated as entities exclusively financed by the socialist state (industrial enterprises, such as coal mines, shipyards, railways, or state institutions, like the militia (police) or the army). Following the transformation, both the structural and human resources of sports clubs were insufficient to face the needs of management in the new, free market reality. In the 1990s, financial problems of the state and severe crises in many sectors of industry led to the economic collapse of many clubs all over the country. After the decentralisation of the state, in some cases financial responsibility for the clubs was taken over by municipalities, which radically reduced the level of spending. Additionally, the lack of government control in the field of sport resulted in many scandals, such as large-scale corruption in football. Sports infrastructure was falling into disrepair, and stadiums and halls became places only frequented by the most ardent fans.

In sport, the anomic spirit of the 1990s – a Durkheimian breakdown of crucial standards necessary for regulating behaviour – had an impact on the structure of fandom. Since most hardcore fans had a working-class background, the first stage of the post-transformation period was difficult for their families and social environment. Many young people searched for group bonds and a sense of belonging. As result, subcultures like punks, metal fans, Goths, as well as skinheads and football fans developed on an unprecedented scale. Each of them involved a meaningful set of values which were absent in broader social space.

The pathological 1990s 93

Polish football and fandom dealing with post-transformation anomie

Poland – as a state, nation and society – stepped into a new era completely unprepared for democratic government, both in socio-cultural and institutional terms. There were no civic communities, associations or grass-roots initiatives resembling the Western culture of social movements. The elements of social fabric enhancing the development of functional differentiation in the space of community and citizenship had not formed, as the circumstances of communist times forced people to act in different ways. Human activity was confined to the private sphere; in other words, individuals 'withdrew' to their small groups. This resulted from the fact that, at the level of the system, communist institutional instruments of terror and coercion – at least theoretically – tamed 'uncivilised' behaviour of individuals, while ideological censorship blocked the possibility of manifestation of alternative ways of thinking in order to 'integrate' people in the communist spirit. As a result, even after the first few years of capitalism, some mental and habitual residues could be traced in different dimensions of social life (trade, media, state-owned enterprises, etc., see Lipiński and Matys, 2018). Still, all these drawbacks and systemic obstacles did not prevent some people from engaging in social activism: 'For instance, it has been argued that social movement organizations in postsocialist Europe may be less able to mobilize people into traditional forms of participatory activism; however, they have been quite effective in so-called transactional activism' (Jacobson and Korolczuk, 2017, p. 9).

As presented in the chapter on the socio-political transformation, the first period of the post-1989 era saw the new democratically elected authorities, without stable structures, having to face the necessity of suppressing enormous inflation, high unemployment and supporting the collapsing economy, which was not able to compete in a free market environment. The situation of the labour market brought instability and a decline in the quality of life for many people. It also significantly limited the scope of opportunities for the younger generation, particularly those with working class background and those living outside large cities (where, mostly thanks to foreign investments, opportunities were significantly better). That situation illustrates Robert K. Merton's claim on anomie as the circumstances where people lack an acceptable means of achieving their personal goals.

Old rules versus new order

Apart from these problems, there was also anachronistic law and disputes about the impact of the old communist apparatus on public life. All this meant that the field of football was left to itself. A Lechia Gdańsk supporter recalls that period as follows:

> Shortly after the transformation of the political system, it was necessary to sort out the state from the scratch and deal with completely different,

94 *The pathological 1990s*

more important matters, and there wasn't enough time for such things like football. Nobody had time to deal with FIFA procedures, fandom procedures, not even safety in the streets, let alone in the stadiums. The law enforcement agencies were completely unprepared; we based on the model of supporting from the times of the People's Republic of Poland, so supporting meant a constant struggle with the old system.

Consequently, the first years of the democratic system in the discipline were characterised by large-scale disintegration, nepotism and corruption. Corruption scandals were not at all conducive to laying sound foundations for the football world in Poland. The problem was serious as it did not only concern particular clubs, their coaches or fraudulent players. The practice would not have been possible without 'networking' and without the interdependence between corrupt 'players' and the structures of the Polish Football Association (PZPN). It is hardly surprising that such scandals, coupled with the very poor level of the Polish football league, did not foster good relations between fans and the football authorities. Indeed, these relations were antagonistic; for many fans PZPN was 'the greatest enemy'. In the last decade of the twentieth century, the situation deteriorated owing to the very poor level of the national team, which from 1986 until 2002 failed to qualify for any championship event (see the chapter on the national team). With informal networks and corruption on the one hand, and no proper stadium infrastructure or youth training system on the other, the scale of the failure was evident.

However, those taking part in match-fixing schemes did not seem to be ostracised. Convicted or suspended players and coaches were back in business, signing new contracts immediately after their suspension periods were over. They were rarely shamed for what they had done, and if they were, it was usually fans of rival teams who expressed their contempt. This phenomenon could be partially explained by the features of the Polish general public inherited from the communist period (see Woźniak, 2018), when most citizens had to resort to wangling, manipulation and cheating the system, as many goods and services were only available thanks to corruption.

Wild capitalism in football

Polish football clubs entered the capitalist reality with no experience, which sometimes led to bizarre situations when 'new' entrepreneurs tried to establish 'professional' football clubs. A Polish national team player from the 1990s describes what the transfer market looked like in those days: 'I remember one time, the boss from [one of the best clubs in Poland] invited me for a drive. He stopped the car in a remote place. He opened the boot, showed me a big plastic bag and asked: "Do you want to play in [the name of the club]?" The bag was full of banknotes' (personal interview).

One example of unprecedented changes in the first half of the 1990s is Sokół Pniewy, a local football club from a small town in central-western

The pathological 1990s 95

Poland. Following investments made by a 'new' Polish entrepreneur, it gained promotion to the top league. Between the 1990/1991 season and its organisational collapse in 1996/1997, the club was renamed five times and even changed its location from Pniewy to Tychy (in the south of the country). Owing to financial problems, it was withdrawn from competition in 1997. Kornelia Sobczak writes that 'the story of Sokół Pniewy could be a metonymic story about the adventures of Polish clubs in the times of capitalism and chimeric owners-presidents, about ownership changes, mergers, title sponsors, buying licences, changing names, relocation, abandoning fans' (2017, p. 92).

Interestingly, however, in most cases fans did not protest against mergers or renaming of their clubs. One of the very few exceptions to the rule was the case of Lechia Gdańsk (see Kossakowski, 2011), where some supporters voiced their opposition against two mergers, with Olimpia Poznań ('Lechia/ Olimpia' Gdańsk) and Polonia Gdańsk ('Lechia/Polonia' Gdańsk). The fact that most fans did not perceive transformation of clubs as a problem is difficult to explain, especially in the context of similar examples in the twenty-first century (protests by fans of Legia Warsaw, Zawisza Bydgoszcz, Chrobry Głogów and many more; see Chwedoruk, 2015; Kossakowski, 2017a). One possible explanation could be that in the early days of the transformation period the level of identity awareness and sense of attachment was still low due to the communist past. Before 1989 it was impossible for fans to feel that they were 'part of the club', as clubs were managed by people strictly related to the communist order. Although clubs provided a platform of identity, especially in the context of local rivalries (see Ćwikła, 2017), fans did not have a say in their running due to structural reasons. In the new, democratic era they slowly developed the 'we are the club' attitude. However, this complex issue requires more in-depth study.

Violent times

What is crucial to note at this point, however, is that the absence of identity bonds with the clubs and the overwhelming atmosphere of crisis and anomie led to pathological and destructive behaviours in the fan world. One case in point was violence – in the early years of the post-1989 transformation the culture of violence in Polish football stadiums developed on an unprecedented scale. The police data indicated an increasing number of hooligan incidents: 190 cases in 1991, 220 in 1992, 440 in 1993, 584 in 1994, 906 in 1995, 917 in 1996 and 1,075 in 1997 (Gorący, 2009). A 'hardcore' supporter of ŁKS Łódź describes the atmosphere of those times in his two-volume diary (Ruban 2014; 2015). He recalls travelling across Poland in a most 'uncivilized' manner: free-riding on trains (endless conflicts with the conductors), vandalising public property, heavy drinking (sometimes for several days), 'hunting' for supporters of rival teams, shoplifting, conflicts with the police. A Miedź Legnica supporter recalls:

96 *The pathological 1990s*

> Each trip meant a scrap, literally, every single trip. We travelled with the gear, wooden planks and stones; we ran away from the police; the police escorted us across Poland. (…) the 1990s, it was like … bricks flying in the stadium, people threw just about anything. It was often a miracle that no one was killed every week. When you ripped out all those bricks from the stadium over and over again, the stadiums were already falling apart and there was no stuff left to fight with, just planks, bits of wood, fencing; [there was] no CCTV. (…) Back then, you ran around the city and fought because no one could do anything. How could they? And now you just go out and you're getting recorded.

An Arka Gdynia supporter admits that using weapons was something common in those days:

> Yes, we used equipment [dangerous objects, ed. authors] in the fights; nothing sharp, unlike Lechia guys [Lechia Gdańsk, Arka's local rival, ed. authors], but it happened that people were beaten with metal rods. (…) We took metal rods, nunchakus, brass knuckles for our actions. It was, let's say, something that was normal. No one even mentioned honour; the thing was to get the enemy and beat them, and that's it. Sometimes we got them, and sometimes they got us.
>
> (Arce w pewnym okresie… 2017, p. 67–68)

Indeed, the scale of violence and vandalism was incomparable with the pre-1989 era. The communist system, even if economically inefficient, had procedures and power to implement them using uniformed services. They commanded respect even among hooligans, who had a good reason to be afraid of physical force being used against them by the police. The level of liberties varied in different phases of the communist period in Poland, but a high level of control over citizens justifies calling it a 'police state' (see Łoś and Zybertowicz, 2000). After the fall of the system, however, the cultural, moral, political and legal order was in chaos, which means that fans acted in very difficult social contexts. Although the scale of their 'savagery' seemed to surpass all limits, both moral and legal, anyone who wants to understand the roots and the level of disorder of those days has to consider the spirit of the period.

It is unreasonable to say that during communist times Polish society functioned on a higher level of the 'civilizing process' but restrictive and oppressive system forced citizens to be obedient. After the collapse of the system the fiction of public order fell apart. This phenomenon exemplifies 'decivilizing spurts' related to the fact that 'rising levels of danger and incalculability in social life quite quickly render people more susceptible to fears and fantasies' (Mennell, 1996, p. 113). Stephen Mennell argues that in the case of the 'decivilizing process' one can put two kinds of questions:

The first group of questions are 'structural': in what circumstances do the chains of interdependence in society begin to break, and thus why do levels of complexity, differentiation, and integration start to decline? The second group concerns the outcome of such processes of structural unravelling for people's experience: what are the cultural and psychological consequences and the impact on people's day-to-day conduct?

(1996, p. 113–114)

In the Polish context, it seems that 1989 brought an unprecedented structural break that pushed the levels of complexity, differentiation and integration into decline (or revealed the superficial nature of pre-1989 social 'integration').

Fan culture in transformation

Following this approach, it is reasonable to ask the questions: How did structural changes and Polish post-1989 transformation influence fan culture? What was their impact on the everyday life of individual supporters? In this context, it is worth quoting Norbert Elias:

The armour of civilized conduct would crumble very rapidly if, through a change in society, the degree of insecurity that existed earlier were to break in upon us again, and if danger became as incalculable as it once was. Corresponding fears would soon burst the limits set to them today.

(2012, p. 576)

Without any doubt, the first years of the new system in Poland brought a change involving a high 'degree of insecurity' in different aspects of life, especially economic ones (Antonowicz and Grodecki, 2016). Perhaps involvement in groups of football supporters compensated young people for the 'vacuum' of the initial period of the new reality, when the structures of civil governance were not yet developed and a meaningful agenda of identity formation outside the family was difficult to find. Lack of control on the one hand, and the patterns of fan behaviour on the other, favoured spontaneous decisions which were often quite inexplicable from a rational point of view:

There was this guy among Górnik Zabrze fans, a kind of leader. One day he travelled on his own across the whole country to a match with Pogoń Szczecin. And he arrived in the stand ... all alone, so that everyone could see that he was there. And he left it, all alone. (...) And then they chased him all the way to the station, so he jumped on the first train going wherever; not so much jumped, he just hung on to the handle at the back and went to the next station to escape them.

(Górnik Zabrze supporter)

98 *The pathological 1990s*

The democratic structures of the state did not have any tools to react to hooligan incidents at their disposal. In the first years of the 1990s, football matches had a similar scenario: fights between fans (at railway stations, streets, around the stadiums, in the stands), sometimes leading to invading the pitch (interruption of the sporting event), followed by police intervention and escorting supporters to their stand or train (Miedź Legnica supporter: 'The rules were like this: the police beat us, we beat the police, no one went to court. Today, when the police beat us, you go to court'). One perfect example comes from the 1998 winter indoor tournament (played between eight clubs from the top Polish league). An eyewitness of the events recalls them as follows:

> At some point during the third match in the tournament something started higher up from where we were sitting. A dozen or so metres away from us a fight broke out between GKS Katowice and Górnik Zabrze fans. They used belts, wooden backs of the seats and the whole seats, as it was relatively easy to rip them up. They hurled these weapons at each other. When Górnik guys began to withdraw, Wisła folks attacked them from the other side. It's impossible to describe what was going on. Someone falls a few meters down, a few people get him and kick the shit out of him using whatever they have at hand; a moment later they become the victims of other aggressors. 'Heysel. Fuck it; it's the Polish Heysel' – strange thoughts passed through my mind as I witnessed the bloody events from such a close distance.
>
> (Spodek 1998 – Katowice 2018, p. 80)

The above description reads a bit like a report from the battlefield, and yet this was not the only case of riots and acts of violence at the time. What is significant about the development of state structures understood as a monopolist in the use of violence is a kind of 'helplessness' of the police. It must be noted, however, that neither adequate legal regulations nor professional training in the field of crowd management strategies were there at the time. It is also worth remembering that countries such as England developed appropriate tools (both legal and practical) over a long time.

It should be stressed that, in most cases, confrontation between fans was not planned or arranged. 1997 marked an important turning point: in view of the situation in the stadiums (e.g. in the riots during Polonia Warsaw vs Legia Warsaw match a club building was set on fire and thirty-seven police officers were injured), the government decided to introduce the *Law on the Safety of Mass Events* (*Ustawa z dnia 22 sierpnia 1997 roku o bezpieczeństwie imprez masowych*; in 1995 Poland ratified the European Convention on Spectator Violence and Misbehaviour at Sports Events and in particular at Football Matches). The new legislation was an important step in the fight against stadium violence in Poland. The act regulated a number of issues related to football matches, such as the use of pyrotechnics, and introduced stadium bans. For a long time, however, its implementation was merely symbolic, as its internal coherence was questioned. As will be shown in further parts of this study, subsequent amendments to this law have affected fan culture.

The first years of the new era were characterised not only by football-related violence. Some fans, especially those who had the highest position in the group hierarchy, became engaged in criminal activity. A fan from Gdynia (where two clubs operate – Arka and Bałtyk) recalls this phenomenon as follows:

> The 90s in Poland was a time of complete chaos, where the state was the largest mafia organisation. (…) Unfortunately, among young people – as they didn't have prospects for a decent life doing honest work – there was this myth of the gangster. (…) The myth of a gangster who drives at least a Volkswagen, who has cash for a pizza, a beer on the beach, a gym, clothes, sports supplements, prostitutes … and who is a well-known guy in the city. (…) In Gdynia, there were car thefts, there were drugs, brothels, minor and larger extortions, protection rackets. Some 'good guys' couldn't separate their work from their fan passion and used gangsta methods to settle their scores with other fans.
>
> (Goły, 2017, p. 59)

As the history of fandom after 1989 shows (Grodecki, 2018; Kossakowski, 2017b), the connections between some fans (particularly hooligans) and the criminal world had not been over by the end of the decade and continued in the new century as well. It is legitimate to say that at least two lines of activity developed in the structure of fandom: one of them has been related to legal, civic engagement (e.g. involvement in supporters' associations and rescuing football clubs; see Grodecki, 2018; Kossakowski, 2017a), and the other to criminal activity and mafia-like style of operation.

The rise of the far right in the terraces

The first years of the new era were marked by a paradox. On the one hand, the old political and structural forces had gone, on the other – most people were not prepared for the new rules. While communism was a system which suppressed individualism, capitalism is individualistic by definition and requires taking responsibility for one's own fate. It would be naïve to assume that young people would be able to step from an oppressive system to freedom and democracy in a matter-of-fact way. For most of them, the collapse of the old system and the advent of a new one meant an urgent need of identity constructions and a sense of belonging and meaning. That is why so many young people became members of various subcultures in those days (see Pęczak, 1992), and that is why football hooligans were so vulnerable to ideological extremism.

Although many different subcultures remained in conflict with one another at the time, it was clashes between members of punk and skinhead groups that became a regular occurrence. Their animosity was related to different sets of values to which they were attached. The skinhead subculture represented

100 *The pathological 1990s*

mainly extreme right-wing attitude, with the ideology of 'racial purity' and 'white power' clearly visible (it is very important to stress that during the 1990s Polish skinheads related to football were only inclined to right-wing ideology and not to anti-fascist ones, like skinheads from the SHARP movement (Skinheads Against Racial Prejudice)). Skinheads cut their hair very short; they wore high army boots with white shoelaces, jeans and flyer jackets with orange linings, which became characteristic of football fans engaged in skinhead subculture. During many matches in the 1990s right-wing fans attending the games wore their jackets inside out, so the stands were full of people in orange. One of the fans explained this in terms of unification and anonymity: 'When the vast majority is dressed almost the same, it is hellishly difficult to find the guilty one even in a small group. Uniformity helps. It helped some people avoid getting into serious trouble' (Zieliński, 1993, p. 11).

On the other hand, punks represented anti-racist and rebellious styles and values – they also stressed their different approach by their appearance (for example, they wore a tuned-down Mohawk hairstyle, and the shoelaces of their heavy boots were red or red and black). Since Poland did not have practically any ethnic minorities at the time, skinheads identified punks (who represented 'dirtiness' and life style unworthy to follow) as their 'natural' enemies and a 'problem' to destroy.

As one fan of Glinik Gorlice states, confrontation between skinheads and punks was sometimes related to football. Surprisingly, however, for some time they shared the same terrace in the local stadium, which was a unique situation for Poland:

> There were such paradoxical situations that punks and skinheads stood side by side in the stands during a match. (...) The breakthrough ... came in 1992–1995. (...) We spent a lot of time eliminating punks not only from our stadium, but also from the town. (...) At that time there was a lot of fighting between subcultures. It was very dangerous in the town. I personally had problems walking around my own town wearing a flyer jacket or a red and white Poland scarf.
>
> ('Fixi' Glinik Gorlice, 2019, p. 46)

In many pictures from those times, available both in fanzines and on Internet forums, one cannot fail to notice right-wing symbols. The most popular was the Celtic cross, but some symbols related to Nazism (e.g. swastika) also appeared among fans. In the early 1990s old members of fan groups began to lose ground to young members who belonged to the skinhead subculture. This was the case of, for example, Ruch Chorzów fandom, where the new 'fashion' for right-wing extremism came with generational change. One chant used there at the time was 'Adolf Hitler KS Ruch' ('KS' stands for 'sports club').

A considerable proportion of the fan figuration consisted of individuals loyal to ultra-right-wing ideology; racist chants could often be heard in the stadiums, and symbols of skinhead culture were a familiar sight. A supporter of Victoria Jaworzno recalls the local skinhead group as follows:

> In this group there were ideological national socialists, who showed their sympathies during matches by waving flags with a skull, shouting 'SS SA Victoria', displaying the symbols of the KKK [Ku Klux Klan]. (...) The beating of a black player of Garbarnia [a club from Cracow], which received wide coverage in the media, was associated with Victoria skinhead fans.
>
> (Simon. Victoria Jaworzno, 2014, p. 44)

One of the fans interprets this as a result of the absence of the 'former' enemy (the communist system before 1989) and the prevailing post-transformation anomie:

> In general, at the beginning of the 90s, there was a crisis of values. (...) I'm convinced that it also affected fans. The enemy had disappeared. (...) When I travelled [to matches, ed. authors], it struck me that some factions of fans, or some fans who were my friends or acquaintances, used slogans which can be described as Nazi, for example 'Our role model is Rudolf Hess' [*Naszym wzorem jest Rudolf Hess*], 'Barack 6, Zyklon B ...' [*Barak 6, cyklon B ...*] and so on. There were also Celtic crosses at that time. I think that this was a moment of some kind of ideological chaos, there was no clear form, no ideology that could attract them. And this ideology would have to meet several criteria, first of all it would have to be clear, to appeal to people who are steadfast, to go against the mainstream of the surrounding reality.
>
> (Lechia Gdańsk supporter)

At that time, there in fact was no ideological proposal for fans. Most of them were young adults and males from the cities in which industry and clubs were crumbling (most of them were managed by state-run agencies). They were students (mostly at primary and secondary schools) or poorly educated people who either were victims of transformation (unemployed themselves or with unemployed parents), or experienced environmental and sports degeneration (a collapse of their clubs). A 'strong', radical right-wing proposal offered a new and attractive group identity. In the 1990s, skinheads were a strong subculture and were able to recruit new members at the stadiums. Sometimes, however, the extreme ideological perspective was taken with no deeper understanding, and symbols and clothes were useful as a sign of identity and belonging to a community. As history shows, no serious political movement was born from the skinhead subculture of the 1990s. One of the old fans engaged in fandom in first decade after 1989 explains that many fans who belonged to skinhead groups were not politically aware:

102　*The pathological 1990s*

> Is a flyer jacket and a Celtic cross a sign of political attitude in the case of a seventeen-year-old? If someone had asked me at that time who is leftist or rightist, I wouldn't have been able to say. Yes, it's true – there were flyers and Celtic crosses around, but we didn't give a shit about what they meant. We never discussed political issues. One thing united us from a young age – hatred of communism and an awareness how bad and how destructive that system was.
>
> (Rafał 'Uszol' Dąbrowski, 2019, p. 31)

The subcultures filled the normative vacuum, as during the 1990s football and fandom were not the object of massive commodification. It means that, in marketing terms, fans were not offered merchandise or attractive commercial packages. The market of fan paraphernalia practically did not exist: all scarves, flags and banners were produced by fans at their own expense, e.g. using home materials. Adding the dilapidated stadium infrastructure and hooligan aggression filled with extremist political content, the field of football of the 1990s in Poland was a repulsive environment.

The end of the decade had not only a symbolic meaning, as football fandom culture started to undergo some important changes. As mentioned above, in 1997 the Polish government implemented a new law on sports events. Although the new regulations did not eradicate violence from the stadiums, acts of aggression became considerably less frequent. The turn of the century brought substantial changes in the fan movement at many levels. The eclectic culture of the 1990s – in which there was no division into ultras and hooligans, and any kind of activism was virtually non-existent – was slowly changing. The consolidation of the state apparatus was an important factor at play – in the new century the authorities began to react to stadium violence more energetically and more effectively. Step by step, the pressure of system imperatives became stronger, which had an impact on Polish football as it forced the reactions of fans and their adaptation.

Conclusions

Without any doubt, the 1990s brought a new order for the whole Polish society; state-governed industries and enterprises, the political system and the habitus of citizens faced new requirements. It was a difficult time for most people, as the communist system had not provided significant resources which could serve as a starting point. The consequences were dramatic. The collapse of industry, mass-scale unemployment, political crisis, inflation and many other problems influenced people's attitudes, moods and perspectives. Sport reflects socio-political changes and it was clearly the case in the Polish context. The field of football experienced – on an unprecedented scale – great problems related to the transformation. Many clubs faced bankruptcy as state-owned enterprises were not able to finance them after 1989. The post-transformation period exposed the whole fiction that communism had been

Figure 5.1 Pathology was a buzzword used to describe football fandom in the late 1990s in media reports portraying fans as dangerous folk devils. The stigma was semantically reclaimed by supporters of ŁKS Łódź who proclaimed their yard in the impoverished district of the city as 'The Stronghold of Pathology'.
Source: Wojciech Woźniak

based on. Most clubs were poorly managed entities with too many sports sections, excessive bureaucracy and archaic training systems. In new times, many football agents tried to operate the old-style way, also by using corruption. The scale of this practice seemed to be immense. Additionally, the 1990s were a period of unsuccessful attempts for the national team. All dysfunctions of those times also had an impact on fandom structure, with some pathologies – 'barbaric' violence, crime, extreme right-wing tendencies – flourishing in the fan community as a result. It is not an exaggeration to say that the first decade of 'new Poland' was a period of catharsis, 'cleansing the balance sheets' and preparation for the twenty-first century, when Poland has become a 'normal', modern European country with a rapidly growing economy, a country that became a member of the European Union and witnessed the successes of the 'Lewandowski generation'.

References

Antonowicz, D. and Grodecki, M. (2018). Missing the goal: Policy evolution towards football-related violence in Poland (1989–2012). *International Review for the Sociology of Sport*, 53(4), pp. 490–511.

104 The pathological 1990s

Arce w pewnym okresie poświęciłem wszystko [I devoted everything to Arka in certain time]. (2017) *To My Kibice*, 7(190), pp. 64–79.

Chwedoruk, R. (2015). Protesty kibiców piłkarskich w Polsce w XXI wieku. Analiza ruchu społecznego [Football fans protest in Poland in XXI century. Social movement analysis]. *Przegląd Socjologii Jakościowej*, 11(2), pp. 84–114.

Ćwikła, P. (2017). Odradzanie się regionalnej tożsamości. Na przykładzie społecznego otoczenia klubu piłkarskiego "Zagłębie" Sosnowiec [Rebirth of regional identity. On the example of the social environment of the 'Zagłębie' Sosnowiec football club]. *Studia Socjologiczne*, 2(225), pp. 109–135.

Elias, N. (2012). *On the Process of Civilisation: Sociogenetic and Psychogenetic Investigations*. Dublin: University College Dublin Press.

'Fixi' Glinik Gorlice (2019). *To My Kibice*, 4(211), pp. 44–58.

Goły. Polemika Gdyńska (2017). *To My Kibice*, 9(192), p. 59.

Gorący, A. (2009). *Widowisko Sportowe – Studium Agresji. Uwarunkowania Zachowań Agresywnych Kibiców piłki Nożnej* [Sports Event – The Study of Aggression. determinants of Aggressive Behavior of Football Fans]. Pruszków: WSKFiT.

Grodecki, M. (2018). *Życie po Meczu. Formy Wykorzystania Kapitału Społecznego Kibiców Piłkarskich w Polsce* [Life after Match. Forms of Using Social Capital by Football Fans in Poland]. Warszawa: UW.

Jacobson, K. and Korolczuk, E. (2017). Introduction: Rethinking Polish civil society. In: K. Jacobsson and E. Korolczuk (eds) *Civil Society Revisited. Lessons from Poland*. New York, Oxford: Berghahn, pp. 1–35.

Kossakowski, R. (2011). Solidarność na zielonej murawie [Solidarity on the green pitch]. In: K. Ciechorska-Kulesz, R. Kossakowski and P. Łuczeczko (eds) *Kultura Solidarności. Socjologiczno-antropologiczne Analizy Kulturowego Dziedzictwa „Solidarności"* [The Culture of Solidarity. Sociological-anthropological Analyses of Cultural Heritage of 'Solidarity' Movement]. Pszczółki: Orbis Exterior, pp. 343–358.

Kossakowski, R. (2017a). From the bottom to the premiership: The significance of the supporters' movement in the governance of football clubs in Poland. In: B. García and J. Zheng (eds) *Football and Supporter Activism in Europe: Whose Game Is It?* Basingstoke: Palgrave Macmillan, pp. 233–255.

Kossakowski, R. (2017b). *Od Chuliganów do Aktywistów. Polscy Kibice i Zmiana Społeczna* [From Hooligans to Activists. Polish Fans and the Social Change]. Kraków: Universitas.

Kowalik, T. (2009). www.polskatransformacja.pl. Warszawa: Muza.

Lipiński, P. and Matys, M. (2018). *Niepowtarzalny Urok Liwidacji* [The Unique Charm of Liquidation]. Wołowiec: Wydawnictwo Czarne.

Łoś, M. and Zybertowicz, A. (2000). *Privatizing the Police-State. The Case of Poland*. Basingstoke: Palgrave Macmillan.

Mennell, S. (1996). Civilizing and decivilizing process. In: J. Goudsblom, D. M. Jones and S. Mennell, *The Course of Human History: Economic Growth, Social Process and Civilization*. Abingdon, New York: Routledge, pp. 101–116.

Pęczak, M. (1992). *Mały Słownik Subkultur Młodzieżowych* [A Small Dictionary of Youth Subcultures]. Warszawa: Semper.

Rafał 'Uszol' Dąbrowski (2019). *To My Kibice*, 2(209), pp. 14–43.

Ruban, A. (2014). *Z pamiętnika Galernika. Magia lat 90-tych* [From Diary of the Fanatic. The Magic of the 90s]. Łódź: Sprint Studio.

Ruban, A. (2015). *Z pamiętnika Galernika. Magia lat 90-tych* [From Diary of the Fanatic. The Magic of the 90s], vol. 2. Łódź: Sprint Studio.

Simon. Victoria Jaworzno (2014). *To My Kibice*, 44.

Sobczak, K. (2017). W składzie węgla i papy. Cudowne lata dziewięćdziesiąte polskiej piłki nożnej [In the storehouse of coal and roofing felt. The wonderful 90s of Polish football]. *Kultura Współczesna*, 94(1), pp. 89–103.

Spodek 1998 – Chcieli krwi (1998). Available at: http://gzg64.pl/spodek-98/ (accessed 15. 01. 2020)

Woźniak, W. (2018). Match-fixing in Polish football: Historical perspectives and sociological interpretations. *The International Journal of the History of Sport*, 35(2–3), pp. 247–263.

Zieliński, R. (1993). *Pamiętnik Kibica* [The Diary of the Fan]. Wrocław: CROMA.

6 Polish political elites versus football fandom

Introduction

In 2019, the fourth year of its rule, the Law and Justice party (PiS) still enjoyed strong support in the opinion polls despite its firm condemnation by Polish and European liberal media and political elites. The victory of the right in the elections of 2015 can be viewed as a culmination of various processes. One of them concerned the shift to conservative values and right-wing sympathies which was observed among the younger generation – first suggested by opinion polls, it was confirmed by the results of the 2015 parliamentary and presidential elections. The stability of this trend was further confirmed by the outcome of elections to the European Parliament in 2019 (Messyasz, 2015; CBOS, 2017). Contrary to some other European contexts, the anti-establishment sentiment of young people in Poland finds its expression in the rejection of liberal, democratic values, which is confirmed by the fact that they most frequently chose even more radical political options than Law and Justice.

A closer scrutiny of the relations between the Polish political elite and the part of the younger generation which forms a significant proportion of football fandom in Poland may enable some interpretations of the growth of support for anti-establishment movements and their rejection of liberal values. Processes occurring in football stands in the last decade may be interpreted as a proxy of relations and processes on the societal level, at least partially predicting this right-wing mobilisation among the youth. We claim that the grass-roots activity, political mobilisation of fandom and its anti-leftist single-mindedness have been largely reactive – they came in response to discourse and policy-making pursued by political elites. Devoted to this issue, this chapter differs from others in this book as it applies a top-down approach. The analysis offered here considers how the world of football fandom and football as such were the object of political decisions and policy-making – legislative solutions and narratives designed and implemented by the top power circles in Poland. Their actions sparked many of the events and processes that had an impact on both of these social worlds.

At the beginning of the period of post-socialist transformation, the only contact point between the world of football fandom and institutions of the

Polish political elites versus football fandom 107

state was violent confrontations between hooligans and the police. In the course of time, football supporters increasingly came under political scrutiny and became a subject of media debates, political actions and policy initiatives. This chapter aims to present these processes and their contextualisation.

Football policy, football policing

1990s: the advent of football hooliganism and the weak response of the state

As shown in the chapter on the history of Polish football fandom, the starting point for analysing the political response of the state and pluralist party politics to the problem of football-related violence may be no other than the beginning of the period of transformation. Polish fans had not been the focus of any particular policies or political actions before. As described in Chapter 5, the 1990s are frequently referred to as the golden era of football hooliganism in the stadiums. The lack of proper response to the growing problem can be explained by the ongoing transformation of the post-socialist state in general, and its weak institutional structure and security apparatus in particular. Permanently reformed and busy dealing with other challenges, the state did not have any particular strategy of how to deal with hooliganism.

The hated and feared Citizens' Militia [*Milicja Obywatelska*] – unanimously perceived as an iron fist of the authoritarian state conducting repressions against citizens – was rebranded as the Police in 1990. In fact, however, this symbolic break from the past was only the beginning of transformation to democratically controlled police force. The police, particularly members of anti-riot units, were well trained in using, frequently excessive, force during anti-communist demonstrations, when they rarely met with resistance or violent response. However, in confrontation with large, violent crowds of football hooligans they not only lacked tactics and experience, but also had no proper gear that could ensure their safety. A police officer recalls putting down a stadium riot which broke out after the Legia Warsaw vs GKS Katowice game in 1995 as follows:

> Nobody could control the situation. Everyone lost their head in this hell. (...) We went on the pitch completely unprepared. (...) Our commanding officers treated us like cannon fodder. They shouted 'Attack!' even though we were outnumbered one to ten. We looked death in the face.
> (Legia Warszawa – GKS Katowice, Awantura podczas finału!, 2016)

Lack of proper training and equipment and the constant threat of injury fuelled aggression also on the part of the police, which led to a spiral of violence. It took many years for policymakers and the bodies responsible for police training to tap the experience of Western, particularly British, police forces in crowd policing and preventive actions. The measures developed by Clifford Stott and implemented under his guidance in the United Kingdom

108 *Polish political elites versus football fandom*

were finally adopted also in Poland. Stott even came over to coach Polish officers, but this happened only in course of preparations for Euro 2012 (for a thorough description of legislation and policy measures see Drzazga 2016).

Although the rise of football-related violence was frequently reported by the media, it was mostly viewed as an aspect of other social problems of the transforming state, society and economy. A general rise in violent crime was considered a side effect of the transformation and the overarching processes of deindustrialisation, pauperisation and restoration of capitalist order, which proceeded at an unprecedented pace. No major political party saw putting the issue of football-related violence on their agenda as politically promising, and thus there were no political campaigns concerning fans – they did not seem to be a convenient internal enemy. Newly emerging radical right-wing groups, usually associated with the skinhead movement, gained ground in the terraces (see the previous chapter). Although largely successful in recruiting young members, they have never been able to capitalise on this at the national level. In fact, none of the heavily conflicted far-right parties achieved any significant political success. However, as it will be shown in the next subchapter, right-wing orientation became a trademark of Polish fandom.

'Let's fight them like in the West': elite-engineered moral panics and legal attempts to control the terraces

In the second half of the 1990s, when the political and economic situation in Poland became more stable, the problem of football hooliganism was identified as one of the most significant social diseases. Numerous articles reported the violent incidents and the increasing level of aggression of fans and the inapt attempts of the police to control the phenomenon, the fans were commonly described as thugs, uncivilized threat for otherwise modernizing society (Meller, 1997). In some cases, journalists were successfully 'trolled' by members of fans' firms into reporting the fake news about the skills and techniques of their members. This was, for instance, the case of an article published in 1997 in *Polityka* [Politics], one of the largest weekly magazines. The readers were offered an example of 'modern style hooliganism' when hooligans used specially trained dogs to sneak mobile phones to the stadium's away fans' sectors so that they cannot be traced while agreements are made where and when to meet for a fight (Meller and Pytlakowski, 1998, p. 5; see also Dudała, 2004, pp. 137–138).

Reactions of the general public and the political circles to the growth of football-related violence largely followed patterns observed elsewhere. This could be described using the concept of elite-engineered moral panics (Goode and Ben-Yehuda, 2009, pp. 62–66). In this application of the famous concept proposed by Stanley Cohen, ruling political circles allied with mass-media and, quite often, business actors define a certain social phenomenon as a serious threat to social order. Moral outrage driven by liberal elites acting in defence of 'normal' citizens fuels public support for more restrictive legal

Polish political elites versus football fandom 109

solutions. In political narratives and public discourse elites can therefore be presented as responding actively and efficiently to social threats. In some cases, this can also successfully turn the attention of public opinion away from other issues (Woźniak, 2013a). Following Amanda Rohloff (2011; 2013), who combined the moral panics approach with the operationalisation of the civilising processes drawing on Elias' works, the moral panic surrounding football-related violence in the country can be seen as part of a wider discourse of civilising Poland and Poles (see Kossakowski, 2019). In the narratives of the Polish media, the need to cope with such pathological phenomena was substantiated by the necessity to catch up with Western standards. Modernisation of the economy and society after the decades of stagnation on the 'wrong side of the Iron Curtain' was widely viewed as the process of catching up with the West.

Most discussions about football-related violence in Poland typically made direct references to the British case and used the narrative of how the hooligan problem had been solved under Margaret Thatcher. Her name was associated with the unquestionable success of the tough rule of law and the zero tolerance approach to policing football fans as the best way to cope with hooliganism (Sahaj, 2007, pp. 283–288). This was no different to a self-orientalising discourse about the Western way of approaching a variety of socio-economic issues. The solutions implemented in the UK were frequently misinterpreted or distorted in Polish political and media discourse, yet they served as allegedly evidence-based proof supporting new measures. Fans and journalists with more in-depth knowledge about the UK-style struggle against hooliganism coined the ironic catchphrase 'they have managed to cope with that in the West' [*na zachodzie sobie poradzili*]. Commonly used as a tag, it also functions as the name of a Facebook fanpage commenting on the news about disorder during football games abroad (see for instance: weszlo.com, 2017a; 2017b).

How to control fans: futile legal attempts

The first attempts at introducing legal regulations in this area were undertaken in mid-1990s and reflected the growing appreciation in Poland of pan-European legal regulations. Dominik Antonowicz and Mateusz Grodecki (2018, p. 499) write:

> In 1995, Poland ratified the European Convention on Spectator Violence and Misbehaviour at Sports Events and in Particular at Football Matches (Council of Europe, No. 120). It signalled external (European) expectations to address the problem of hooliganism and modernize football fandom culture that cultivated the anarchic spirit of the 1980s.

The Law on the Safety of Mass Events, which came into force in 1997 (*Ustawa z dnia 22 sierpnia 1997 roku o bezpieczeństwie imprez masowych*), defined stadiums as a particular type of venue governed by stricter regulations; it also introduced new penal measures, including stadium bans. The implementation of the Law

110 *Polish political elites versus football fandom*

marked the beginning of a new era in football-related policy-making in Poland. In her legal analysis of this field Edyta Drzazga stresses the crucial role of the European Union in paving the way for new solutions (2016, pp. 81–86).

Even though such regulations were not part of the *acquis communautaire*, Polish lawmakers followed the general pattern of laws adopted elsewhere. One crucial consequence of the trend was that the police disappeared from the stadiums and security and safety were privatised, which comes as an example of the peculiar effects of the new solutions. The absence of the police in the stadiums was expected to ease tension, as fan groups tend to be hostile against uniformed forces. This aim, however, could have never been achieved in Poland, where the police are very much present and visible around the stadiums, often in full anti-riot gear, even when the fans of competing clubs are on friendly terms, or when away fans have been banned from attending the game. Apart from this, the police tend to confront the crowd in cases of even minor misdemeanours, at least during the games of the Polish league. The new and more effective strategies of improving security were supposed to be based on new functions: stewards, spotters and liaisons between fan groups, clubs and the football association. Physical barriers (high fences) were dismantled not so much for safety reasons (as declared), but in order to meet formal requirements for official matches. As it turned out in early 2019, the away fans stand in one of the stadiums in lower leagues had a cage where supporters were locked during the games; the situation prompted an intervention by the Polish ombudsman (Rzecznik Praw Obywatelskich, 2019).

Zealous reforms of the criminal code and criminal procedure were introduced by the PiS government during its first term in the office (2005–2007) intended to increase the efficiency of penal measures. One new solution was a fast track criminal procedure (nicknamed twenty-four-hour courts), which was supposed to enable quick sentencing of petty offenders. Apart from other explanations, the government also presented this innovation as a means of tackling hooliganism, even though PiS had never identified hooligans as a significant threat to the social order (see Sahaj, 2007, pp. 312–314). It soon turned out that most of the cases involving football-related violence were far too complex and required a standard investigation and trial (involving analysis of CCTV footage, witness statements and, quite often, cross examination of witnesses). Most fast-tracked cases concerned petty theft, vandalism and drink driving, with drunken cyclists as the category with the most offenders. The failure of the new system became apparent with a rapidly decreasing number of cases tried (from 36,000 in 2007 to under 700 in 2012) (Antonowicz and Grodecki, 2018, pp. 502–503).

As elsewhere, the new laws favoured effectiveness over various citizens' rights. Many of the new rules infringed on privacy, as they increased security surveillance and visitor tracking, and required providing an ID and personal data in order to purchase match tickets (Drzazga, 2016, pp. 170–175). The increased number of police security checks on special trains and coach or car convoys, which sometimes also involved a search, meant that fans who were stopped on

Figure 6.1 New and more restrictive rules concerning the security of the fans require all clubs to provide separate stands for away fans, regardless of the level of the competition. Consequently, at lower leagues away fans are frequently literally caged at the stands. Photo depicts away fans sector at the stadium of Garbarnia Cracow.
Source: Michał Karaś, Stadiony.net

their way to away games frequently arrived late in the stadiums. As a result, increasingly more often such trips were not registered at all and groups of fans travelled unofficially. The new Law on the Safety of Mass Events, enacted in 2009 (*Ustawa z dnia 20 Marca 2009 roku o bezpieczeństwie imprez masowych*), provided an extensive list of various types of behaviour deemed illegal, and increased the role of stadium bans as the main form of punishment imposed on troublemakers (Antonowicz and Grodecki, 2018, p. 504). It also allowed closing the doors to the stadium (or particular stands) on request of the police or as a form of collective punishment for misdemeanours during previous games. In his parliamentary speech, the Civic Platform MP (the main government party at the time) responsible for proceedings on the proposed legislation, Ireneusz Raś, stressed the need for more efficient regulations in the face of the new challenges posed by the hosting of UEFA Euro 2012. He also directly referred to the legacy of effective war on football hooliganism undertaken in Britain under Margaret Thatcher (Drzazga, 2016, p. 206). As presented above, most of the legislative changes relating to football fandom were introduced under the influence of external pressures. However, solutions developed elsewhere were adopted according to local conditions and political needs.

PZPN and the Polish government: from enemies to allies

What also needs to be noted here is the relations between the PZPN and the Polish government. These were difficult, as the national football association successfully used its status of a non-governmental and not-for-profit organisation to avoid direct political interference. Although match-fixing in Poland had been an open secret for many years, it became a criminal offence only in 2003. In 2005 the media revealed a mass-scale corruption scandal, in fact unprecedented on the global scale. As of June 2018, 525 persons were tried on corruption charges, 452 of whom were convicted; 638 games in total were presumed to have been fixed, and 68 clubs were punished (Woźniak, 2018). The unprecedented and overwhelming scale of corruption was possible due to misconduct or negligence on the part of the PZPN, which successfully used the umbrella of FIFA and UEFA to block numerous attempts of government agencies to intervene. The threat of excluding Polish clubs and national teams from competitions supervised by these two international associations was enough for the government to step back in order to avoid a conflict with fans, who would have been outraged by such a ban. However, when in 2007, contrary to all expectations, Poland was selected as a co-host of Euro 2012, PZPN – previously blamed for negligence and corruption and despised as a relic of the communist *ancien régime* – became a key partner for the government during preparations for the event supervised by the UEFA.

The political elite viewed Euro 2012 as an opportunity for showcasing Poland as a modern state capable of hosting a sport mega event, and for confirming the success of post-socialist transformation (see Włoch, 2013; Cope, 2015; Woźniak, 2015). The event provided an excuse to impose new restrictions on football fans in the name of security in the stadiums, and brought attempts to replace traditional fans with more 'civilised' consumer-oriented spectators. In the forthcoming years this was achieved to a certain extent in the case of the fan base of the national team, but completely failed when it comes to club fandom. Nevertheless, violence was gradually pushed out of the stadiums. As Kossakowski (2017a) shows, on the basis of his extensive ethnographic research, although hooliganism continued, it changed its form (at least partially) as a result of growing pressure from the police, increased CCTV surveillance and more severe legal consequences. Hooligan fights came to be arranged in remote locations, where they rarely put others at risk. Stricter rules contributed to the emergence of what Kossakowski calls the 'parliamentarisation of hooliganism' (Kossakowski, 2017a, p. 285).

Attempts to capitalise on relations with football fans

Although in the 1990s small far-right political parties attempted to infiltrate the fan community, they were not very successful. The situation has been gradually changing since the late 1990s and early 2000s.

Polish political elites versus football fandom 113

A cover story on *Polityka* from 1998 interestingly encapsulates the processes occurring within and around football fandom during this period. The article may be viewed as a clinical example of moral panic discourse, in this case – one paving the way for a more hard-line approach to handling football hooliganism. The language it uses does not refrain from the normative rhetoric, as can be seen in the descriptions of cruel tribes at war and bloody streets where the confrontations of 'young lads turning into wild beasts' take place. The cover picture for the article shows three aggressive-looking young lads wearing the colours of Widzew Łódź in the window of a train.

Although the story paints a picture of football fans as the primitive, uneducated mob, the lad on the right-hand side of the photo was a student of the Law Faculty at the University of Szczecin at the time it was published (Wiechecki and Olczyk, 2017). He came to the public spotlight a few years later, when he became the minister of marine economy in the coalition government formed by the senior partner Law and Justice, the Self-Defence party (*Samoobrona*) and the League of Polish Families [*Liga Polskich Rodzin*, LPR]. The position gained by the latter party, led by Roman Giertych, who took the post of deputy Prime Minister in the government formed by Jarosław Kaczyński, was the first successful attempt of a far-right political formation to make it into parliament and government. In 2005, the party gained 8 per cent of the votes. Giertych capitalised politically on his previous relatively successful attempts to revive the pre-Second World War proto-fascist political movement called the All-Polish Youth (*Młodzież Wszechpolska*), whose membership was composed of radicalised young people, many of them football fans.

The case of Rafał Wiechecki, a football fan pictured on a cover of the *Polityka*, is interesting, as it counters the narrative of the mainstream media. Wiechecki graduated in law *summa cum laude* in 2002, and received a degree in economics a couple of years later. A political activist in his student years, he pursued a career in politics. When the government dissolved in 2007 and the LPR failed to make it into parliament in a snap election, he worked as a solicitor in his own law firm. Interviewed in 2017, he recalled on his first days in the office, when it was revealed that he appears in the famous cover photo:

> That's true, the media had a field day then. It's always about easy associations: a fan, a hooligan, a member of the All-Polish Youth, a shady character, not fit for the office. (…) It's obvious that on a train full of fans people don't just seat and eat crisps, but react emotionally. And this picture shows that. Donald Tusk travelled to away games himself, he called himself a diehard fan and nobody made a big deal about it. But it's my picture that's still on the Internet.

> (Wiechecki and Olczyk, 2017)

The League of Polish Families failed as a party and its leader left politics. Roman Giertych is currently a solicitor and appears in the most widely reported cases in Poland; he is among the most vocal critics of Law and

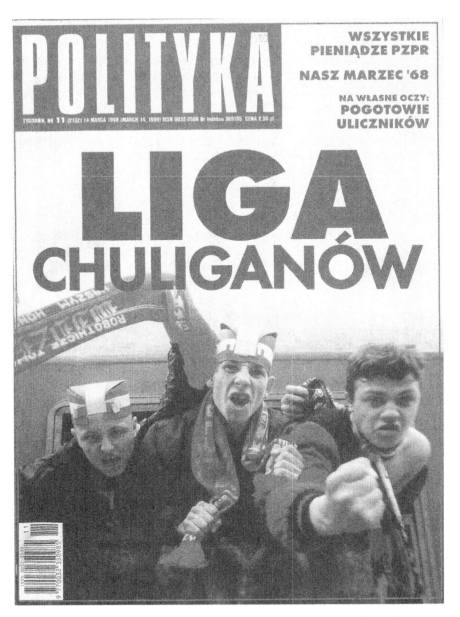

Figure 6.2 The cover of *Polityka* from 1998 with a title 'League of Hooligans' is a classic example of the narrative fuelling moral panic about football-related violence. Interestingly, the anonymous fan depicted on the photo on right ceased to be anonymous when, as a member of the radically right-wing League of Polish Families (and highly qualified lawyer), he became a Member of Parliament and subsequently a Polish Government Minister.
Source: *Polityka*, 14 March 1998.

Polish political elites versus football fandom 115

Justice. Many of the younger politicians from his party found their place in politics in new or reorganised formations, like the National Movement [*Ruch Narodowy*]. This party became part of the Kukiz'15 movement, an organisational umbrella and political platform capitalising on the popularity of Paweł Kukiz, a former rock star who won 21 per cent of votes in the presidential election in 2015. Later the same year his association of anti-establishment movements gained 8.8 percent and made it into parliament. Unlike Wiechecki, all five members of the National Movement who were elected stress their close association with radical football fan circles and present themselves as their representatives in parliamentary politics. The parliamentary election of 2015 was the first case of successful cooperation of various anti-establishment initiatives, which goes back to the first large-scale Independence March, organised in Warsaw in 2011 (see Chapter 8). The role of football fans in this event is difficult to overestimate. The massive media popularity and the increase in significance of the event was undoubtedly related to the political mobilisation of football fandom sparked by political decisions of Donald Tusk's government.

Tusk's war on hooliganism

In their article thoroughly presenting the evolution of policies towards football-related violence, Antonowicz and Grodecki (2018) argue that the Civic Platform government's hard-line approach was a conscious attempt to capitalise politically on the common despise of football fandom, which largely resulted from the public image of football fans created by the mainstream liberal media. It can thus be viewed as a policy stemming from an elite-engineered moral panic, which exaggerated threat to the general public in order to channel public fears and make people accept stricter policing.

It is quite paradoxical that the political campaign against hooligans was most intense in the 2010s, when football-related violence was in decline, a trend observed from 2000. The data from the National Police Headquarters presented by Antonowicz and Grodecki (2018, p. 498) indicate that the number of hooligan incidents at mass sporting events decreased from 1,075 in 1997 to 520 in 2000, and remained stable throughout the 2000s at a level of around 210; the figure for 2009 was 188. As shown in other chapters, violent behaviour of fans changed its forms. Spontaneous large-scale riots in the streets and stadiums gave way to *ustawki*, pre-arranged fights between hooligans trained in martial arts, usually held in remote locations. While obviously illegal, this form of violence does not pose a significant threat to bystanders and regular supporters visiting the stadiums, contrary to what was common in the 1990s. It seems that the politically motivated campaign against football fans was based on a reasonable assumption that they are not numerous enough to constitute a significant electorate. Grodecki (2016) shows that the number of supporters regularly attending games and sharing the identity of avid football fans supporting Polish clubs is not very large. Although 37 per

116 *Polish political elites versus football fandom*

cent of respondents in nationwide surveys declare they are sport fans, only about 15 per cent view themselves as fans of Polish clubs who have been affected by the new legislation. It seemed at the time that they would not find influential allies or advocates. Importantly, they were not considered a pool of voters that the liberal Civic Platform could attract and therefore they made a perfect internal enemy.

Even though, at the rhetorical level, the narratives and measures adopted by the government were aimed only against those fans who were causing trouble, many other football supporters had mixed feelings about them. No one has ever assessed the scale of the hooligan phenomenon in Poland (see Rookwood and Pearson, 2010), but there was nevertheless a sense of common fate and solidarity among different segments of fans within the fandom of particular clubs. This perception strengthened when governors of the various regions (who represent the central government in the Polish political system) began to close stadiums. This was a form of punishment of fans for any misdemeanours, including anti-government choreographies and songs during the games. A description of these politically motivated activities can be found in Chapter 8.

This kind of collective responsibility was resented also by those who were not the target of the measures undertaken by the government. Fans were yet another social category which came to be instrumentally treated in the ongoing and escalating political war between two major Polish political formations. Antonowicz and Grodecki (2018, pp. 503–504) write:

> There is no doubt that these decisions were politically motivated and such attitudes gave rise to a conflict not only with the fans, but also with the clubs, match organizers, and the Polish Football Association (PZPN). Closing stadiums became a political instrument that the state authorities used against football fans who mocked the government for taking a tough course against them and being comically submissive to UEFA.

They substantiate this observation as follows:

> To illustrate such strong claims, we quote two official reasons for closing football stadiums in Olsztyn (September 2012) and Bydgoszcz (October 2012). The first one refers to feelings that spectators might have caused during a previous football game: 'fans of both teams caused alarm and disquiet among the spectators, caused their anger, overexcitement and disgust, which, according to the Supreme Court (II K 478/33), amounts to a breach of the public order'. The governor of Kujawsko-Pomorskie region went even further in her decision to close the stadium in Bydgoszcz, foreseeing that fans 'might want to show their disapproval of government policy that aims to tackle football hooliganism (…) which might undermine a good image of Poland as a country that has successfully organized Euro 2012'.

Polish political elites versus football fandom   117

Many actions aimed against fans who allegedly posed a threat to social order were not particularly effective. This was also the case of the most spectacular of those, which earned the moniker 'the fork action'. On 2 September 2008 Warsaw police stopped 753 Legia Warsaw fans walking to Polonia stadium to attend a derby game. Six hundred of them were briefly held in custody; many of them complained about police brutality. The police reported finding several dangerous objects in their possession, including brass knuckles, mouthguards and one plastic fork which became a legend. Out of 547 people who were charged, most of them with participating in an illegal gathering, 510 were acquitted. A decade later, judgments in their cases still are not final and binding. The Polish state has already paid an equivalent of 70 thousand euros in compensation for unlawful arrest or prolonged trial. The European Court of Human Rights is currently proceeding 86 cases against Poland, which could result in more judgments finding the authorities in breach of the law (Telewizja Republika, 2018).

Who is against Tusk, he is one of ours

The early successes of the Law and Justice party on the Polish political scene came as a result of its hard-line approach to crime. The party originated from Solidarity Electoral Action [*Akcja Wyborcza Solidarność*, AWS], a multi-party platform which won the elections in 1997 and split towards the end of the term. Law and Justice, which emerged as the largest right-wing party, capitalised on the popularity of Lech Kaczyński, who served in the AWS government as the minister of justice and attorney general. Kaczyński, an activist of the anti-communist opposition before 1989 and professor of law, gained recognition owing to his strong stance against crime and corruption and his attempts to follow zero tolerance policy on petty crime. This became the trademark of the new political party and their main pledge. Kaczyński himself was elected president in 2005, and Law and Justice led by his twin brother Jarosław won the parliamentary elections the same year. As mentioned in Chapter 3, the elections of 2005 marked the end of the post-communist cleavage, which had been the underlying pattern of the Polish political scene for a decade and a half, since the beginning of post-socialist transformation.

The zero tolerance approach to crime was an important part of the PiS agenda and football hooliganism was identified in party manifesto as a threat to public safety which was to be solved by (including the fast track criminal procedure mentioned above in official party documents. (PiS, 2005, p. 144), before the crucial elections of 2005 (won by PiS), football fans were also addressed as follows: 'We will strengthen control over the funds spent on sport. It is necessary to allow Polish fans to co-decide who and how will manage Polish clubs and run Polish sports associations, such as the Polish Football Association' (PiS, 2005, p. 140). This was the first time when the issue of empowerment of Polish supporters, and their agency, was addressed, though only declaratively, at this political level. This was also the first

118 *Polish political elites versus football fandom*

political manifesto (out of 70 such documents from the period 2001–2015 examined for the purpose of this chapter) which directly referred to the topic of football fans in context other than the threat of football hooliganism.

The situation before the following general election was substantially different. Football-related topics were addressed by all major political parties, but only with reference to the UEFA Euro 2012 finals and the government policy towards fandom which was applied at the time. In its 2011 election manifesto, PiS also referred to the topic of Euro 2012, and, again, directly addressed Polish football supporters. Interestingly for a party with the words 'law' and 'justice' in the very name, and one declaring a crackdown on crime, the hard-line approach to hooliganism adopted by the ruling Civic Platform was assessed very critically:

> One cannot imagine sport without fans – they are an integral part of sport. (…) Waging a war against fans is just yet another propaganda tool of Prime Minister Tusk's and does not ensure peace in the stands. We will effectively enforce the law in order to ensure full safety of fans, including whole families willing to take part in sports events. At the same time we will enhance the status of fans' associations, which should become real partners of managing authorities in football clubs, jointly acting against stadium hooliganism.
>
> (PiS, 2011, p. 160)

In this way, the most important political document of the PiS party presented fans as an important social category which deserved protection from the oppressive state. It also clearly targeted the main political opponents: Prime Minister Donald Tusk and his party, Civic Platform. The same narrative was followed in the next manifesto, issued before the general election of 2015, which brought victory to Law and Justice. The party criticised Civic Platform for unfair and severe treatment of fans and for infringing their right to political expression; it also firmly declared: 'We will not wage war on fans for political or propaganda purposes' (2014, p. 125).

Law and Justice politicians intervened in individual cases of prominent football fans on numerous occasions. For instance, they vouched for two Legia Warsaw fans arrested in widely publicised criminal cases. One of them, Piotr Staruchowicz, was arrested on the charges of drug trafficking and spent eight months in custody. One of the most notorious faces of Polish radical fandom, he was a 'conductor', the person in charge of cheering, at the *Żyleta* [Razor] stand in Legia Warsaw stadium. In 2011 the footage showing him slap the face of Legia defender and captain Jakub Rzeźniczak appeared in the media. Because he was very active in anti-government protests against tightening the law, his arrest was widely perceived among fans as an act of vengeance of the ruling political class on one of their critics. Staruchowicz was vouched for by a number of right-wing politicians, including Zbigniew Romaszewski, a PiS senator and one of the

Polish political elites versus football fandom 119

legendary anti-communist activists from the 1960s, 1970s and 1980s, and Beata Kempa, former deputy minister of justice (Plaskota, 2016; Pasztelański, 2017).

The case of another Legia fan, Maciej Dobrowolski, became even more famous. Charged as an accessory to drug trafficking, he spent 40 months in custody without conviction. He was not released pending trial, even though charges against him were based on the statement of a single witness and never confirmed in court. The court turned down the appeals for release of the defendant thirteen times, which sparked nationwide protests among members of most Polish fan groups. The tag *#uwolnicMacka* [#freeMaciek] was trending on social media well beyond the bubbles of football fandom. Many prominent figures, not necessarily sympathising with the right of the political spectrum, including the Polish ombudsman, voiced their support for the release of Dobrowolski.

Both were finally released. Staruchowicz has already been fully acquitted by the court, and Dobrowolski received an offer of compensation for his prolonged detention. Dobrowolski's case was used by the PiS government in political campaigns: it served as proof of negligence and wrongdoings of the judicial system in Poland, which allegedly justified non-constitutional reforms launched after their victory in the 2015 general election.

Although this line of action did not necessarily increase the popularity of Law and Justice among football fans, it undoubtedly created the image of this party as the main opponent of the unlawful and politically motivated campaign against them. Since the beginning of PiS' term in the office (2015), the mainstream media have presented it as a party which instrumentally uses the penal system and legal instruments at the government's disposal for its own political goals. However, significant echelons of Polish society, particularly the youth, are fully aware that the previous government did not refrain from using the same tools to achieve its political objectives: it turned them against the groups and individuals labelled as a threat or selected as a useful internal enemy of their rule. Therefore, the large-scale protests against the abuse of power by the Law and Justice government were largely contested or ignored by younger generations.

The neoliberal belief in the free market and the reality of public expenditures on football

New regulations, which allowed for the full privatisation of football clubs in Poland, were introduced by the Ministry of Sport and Tourism in 1996. Previously, most clubs had been public or semi-public entities owned or co-owned by various public stakeholders. Every year since, more and more clubs were bought by private investors and transformed into Sport Companies Ltd. This period was characterised by the widespread belief that private ownership is a panacea to improve the quality of governance and management in any institution. The vision of Premier League-style expansion and high return on

120 *Polish political elites versus football fandom*

investments in football clubs was shared by many, including some of the richest Polish businessmen. It often happened that fans enthusiastically received the news about such takeovers: they viewed them as an unprecedented opportunity for expansion and sporting triumphs. Indeed, many of those clubs achieved significant successes, but very few turned out to be a long-term investment. Legia Warsaw, Wisła Cracow, Korona Kielce, Śląsk Wrocław, Pogoń Szczecin, Lechia Gdańsk, Widzew Łódź, ŁKS Łódź and Polonia Warsaw were all once owned by entrepreneurs who appeared on the list of 100 wealthiest Poles, an equivalent of *Forbes*' list published by the popular weekly magazine *Wprost*. The last three clubs mentioned here won the Polish League championships in the 1990s, only to go bankrupt in the following decade without bringing any harm to the owners' personal wealth. Relegated to the fifth or lower divisions of the Polish league system for financial reasons, those three clubs and many others were rebuilt from scratch by grass-roots movements of their local fans (see Kossakowski, 2017c; Grodecki and Kossakowski 2019).

As of the 2018/2019 season, only two clubs (Lech Poznań and Cracovia Cracow) in the Polish Ekstraklasa (top division) are owned by entrepreneurs listed among 100 wealthiest Poles. Many of the most prominent former owners gave up sport-related business; they sold their clubs or liquidated them when they went bankrupt. Sometimes clubs were closed down (Igloopol Dębica, Start Łódź, Odra Wodzisław), relocated (Piotrcovia Piotrków Trybunalski, Sokół Pniewy) or merged (Piotrcovia and Pogoń Szczecin; Sokół Pniewy and GKS Tychy; Lech Poznań and Amica Wronki; Olimpia Poznań, Polonia Warsaw and Lechia Gdańsk). In most of these cases fans had no say about the fate of the clubs they supported.

Corporate changes in club ownership structure sometimes led to conflicts between the owners or management and organised fandom of the club. The most spectacular case was that of Legia Warsaw, which occurred when the club was acquired by the media conglomerate ITI. The new chairman declared that a football club is a business like any other, just part of show business, and that a football game is media content, just like 'Dancing with the Stars'. It was also explicitly suggested that the new owners intended to replace the traditional fan base – which they viewed as potential troublemakers who could affect the image of the company – with new middle-class fans (Kossakowski, Antonowicz and Szlendak, 2011, p. 113). An immediate attempt to price out traditional fans (the price of match tickets went up by half) ignited a feud between them and the corporate owner, including a prolonged boycott of home games. In the long run, fans emerged victorious and the ITI corporation sold the club. The next chairman closely cooperated with fans, also with representatives of the most radical groups (Kossakowski and Bieszke, 2017, pp. 23–24; see also Chwedoruk, 2015, pp. 90–91).

In some cases (such as Śląsk Wrocław and Korona Kielce) football clubs avoided bankruptcy and relegation only thanks to local authorities, which took over full financial responsibility for their survival. Although the narrative

Polish political elites versus football fandom 121

about advantages of private ownership was widely popular, in fact all most costly investments in sport infrastructure, namely construction or renovation of stadiums, were funded either exclusively with public resources (state or municipal) or using various forms of public-private partnership, which meant that public resources were channelled into privately owned entities. This context seems important for studying relations between the world of politics and football. On the one hand, the official discourse was highly critical about how football was managed on the local level and how it was governed by the PZPN. On the other hand, local or regional authorities frequently carried the burden of financial responsibility for the existence of clubs officially owned and governed by private entities (see Woźniak, 2015; 2013b).

In some cases, this happened under coordinated political pressure from fans. In the city of Łódź, for instance, candidates representing fans of two local clubs, ŁKS and Widzew, were elected councillors from the lists of three different parties: Law and Justice, Civic Platform (otherwise widely despised by fans) and the post-communist Democratic Left Alliance. The candidates made their decision to align with particular parties on the basis of tactical assessment of their chances of making it into the city council. The councillors who officially declared themselves as spokespersons and representatives of fans used their position mainly to monitor how football-related investments, particularly the construction of two new stadiums, fully funded from the local budget, were organised and carried out (Sikora and Woźniak, 2018). Elsewhere, sport-related expenditures were usually made on the initiative of local authorities. They saw the construction of modern stadiums and sports halls as a symbol and yet another confirmation of modernisation of their towns and cities, and a proper way of investing public money, largely using also European Union resources allocated through structural funds.

Conclusion

Football fans have become an important political issue mostly from the turn of century. Along with the modernisation of Poland, accession to the European Union and ambition to be a 'civilised' member of the Western world, some liberal politicians viewed (particularly 'die-hard') fans as a 'social problem' to be resolved. The cases discussed above may be interpreted as a utilitarian approach by the political elite towards Polish football fandom. The liberal side of the political spectrum followed the British example and used the leverage of the war on football hooliganism to muster support of some segments of their electorate. The right-wing parties responded by aligning with fans against their liberal arch-enemy. Political involvement was therefore very direct. Although it did not translate into the unquestioning support of Polish fandom for any particular political party or movement, it helped in consolidating fans against the liberal establishment. Like a considerable proportion of the younger generation of Poles, they largely identified with Civic Platform, the party ruling for two terms between 2007 and 2015. As long as Polish fans take political stances,

122 Polish political elites versus football fandom

they can be perceived both as potential allies or enemies. However, any attempt to impose formal regulations on the fan world, or to capitalise politically on their sentiments or resentments, needs to take into account that football fans are unpredictable, spontaneous and unwilling to be subordinate. These features substantially hamper the potential impact of politics on fandom.

References

Antonowicz, D. and Grodecki, M. (2018). Missing the goal: Policy evolution towards football-related violence in Poland (1989–2012). *International Review for the Sociology of Sport*, 53(4), pp. 490–511. doi:10.1177/1012690216662011

Antonowicz, D., Szlendak, T. and Kossakowski, R. (2016). Flaming flares, football fanatics and political rebellion. Resistant youth cultures in late capitalism. In: M. Schwartz and H. Winkel (eds) *Eastern European Youth Cultures in a Global Context*. London: Palgrave Macmillan, pp. 131–144.

CBOS (2017). *Czy młodzi Polacy są prawicowi? Komunikat z badań nr 102* [Is Polish youth rightist? The opinion poll report no. 102]'. Warszawa: Centrum Badania Opinii Społecznej. Available at: www.cbos.pl/SPISKOM.POL/2017/K_102_17.PDF [accessed 20 October 2018].

Chwedoruk, R. (2015). Protesty kibiców piłkarskich w Polsce w XXI wieku. Analiza ruchu społecznego [Football fans protests in Poland in XXI century. Social movement analysis], *Przegląd Socjologii Jakościowej*, 11(2), pp. 84–114.

Cope, B. (2015). Euro 2012 in Poland: Recalibrations of statehood in Eastern Europe. *European Urban and Regional Studies*, 22(2), pp. 161–175.

Drzazga, E. (2016). *Chuligaństwo Futbolowe w Polsce* [Football Hooliganism in Poland]. Warszawa: Wydawnictwo Naukowe Scholar.

Dudała, J. (2004). *Fani-Chuligani. Rzecz o Polskich Kibolach. Studium Socjologiczne.* Warszawa: Żak.

Goode, E. and Ben Yehuda, N. (2009). *Moral Panics. The Social Construction of Deviance*, 2nd edn. Chichester and Malden: Wiley-Blackwell.

Grodecki, M. (2016). Liczni i fanatyczni. Skala kibicowania piłkarskiego w Polsce [Numerous and fanatical. Scale of football fandom in Poland]. In: A. Ostrowski (ed.) *Modern Futbol a Świat Kibiców 2. Interdyscyplinarne Studia nad Kulturą Futbolu* [Modern Football and World of Fans 2: Interdisciplinary Studies on Football Culture]. Wrocław: Wydawnictwo Naukowe Dolnośląskiej Szkoły Wyższej, pp. 130–143.

Grodecki, M. and Kossakowski, R. (2019). Trzy drogi odbudowy klubów piłkarskich przez kibiców [Three ways of rebuilding football clubs by fans]. In: A. Ostrowski (ed.) *Modern Football a Świat Kibiców 4: Interdyscyplinarne Studia nad Kulturą Futbolu* [Modern Football and World of Fans 4: Interdisciplinary Studies on Football Culture]. Wrocław: ATUT, pp. 165–179.

Kossakowski, R. (2017a). From communist fan clubs to professional hooligans: A history of Polish fandom as a social process. *Sociology of Sport Journal*, 34(3), pp. 281–292. doi:10.1123/ssj.2017-0019

Kossakowski, R. (2017b). Where are the hooligans? Dimensions of football fandom in Poland. *International Review for the Sociology of Sport*, 52(6), pp. 693–711. doi:10.1177/1012690215612458

Kossakowski, R. (2017c). From the bottom to the Premiership: The significance of supporters' movement in the governance of football clubs in Poland. In: B. García

Polish political elites versus football fandom 123

and J. Zheng (eds) *Football and Supporter Activism in Europe. Whose Game Is It?* Basingstoke: Palgrave Macmillan, pp. 233–255.

Kossakowski, R. (2019). Euro 2012, the 'civilizational leap' and the 'supporters United' programme: A football mega-event and the evolution of fan culture in Poland. *Soccer and Society.* doi:10.1080/14660970.2019.1616266

Kossakowski, R., Antonowicz, D. and Szlendak T. (2011). Ostatni bastion anty-konsumeryzmu? Kibice industrialni w dobie komercjalizacji sportu [The last bastion of anti-consumerism? Industrial die-hard-fans and the commercialization of sport]. *Studia Socjologiczne*, 202(3), pp. 113–139.

Kossakowski, R., Szlendak, T. and Antonowicz, D. (2018). Polish ultras in the post-socialist transformation. *Sport in Society*, 21(6), pp. 854–869. doi:10.1080/17430437.2017.1300387

Kossakowski, R. and Bieszke Ł. (2017). The pacts, the death of the Pope and boycotts. The modes of cooperation in Polish football fandom. In: C. Brandt, F. Hertel and S. Huddleston (eds) *Football Fans, Rivalry and Cooperation.* Abingdon: Routledge, pp. 17–31.

Legia Warszawa – GKS Katowice, Awantura podczas finału! [Legia Warsaw – GKS Katowice, The riot during the final!] (2016). Available at: www.nastadionie.pl/legia -warszawa-gks-katowice-awantura-finalu/ [accessed 19 June 2019].

Meller, M. (1997). Legion Łobuzów [Legion of Thugs]. *Polityka*, 17(2086), p. 18.

Meller, M. and Pytlakowski, P. (1998). Liga Chuliganów [League of Hooligans]. *Polityka*, 11(2132), pp. 3–8.

Messyasz, K. (2015). Postawy polityczne młodzieży polskiej w świetle badań empir-ycznych. [The political preferences of Polish youth in the light of empirical studies]. *Władza Sądzenia*, 7, pp. 57–79.

Pasztelański, R. (2017). Po trzech latach ławniczka nie chce już sądzić gangu „Szka-tuły". Proces od nowa [After three years the juror has not wanted to judge the gang of 'Szkatuła'. The trial from beginning]. *TVP Info.* Available at: www.tvp.info/ 30104664/po-trzech-latach-lawniczka-nie-chce-juz-sadzic-gangu-szkatuly-proce s-od-nowa [accessed 30 May 2019].

PiS (2005). *IV Rzeczpospolita. Sprawiedliwość dla wszystkich. Program Prawa i Spra-wiedliwości* [IV Republic. Justice for All. Law and Justice Manifesto]. Warszawa: Prawo i Sprawiedliwość.

PiS (2011). *Nowoczesna, solidarna, bezpieczna Polska. Program Prawa i Sprawiedli-wości* [Modern, solidarity and safe Poland. Law and Justice Manifesto]. Warszawa: Prawo i Sprawiedliwość.

PiS (2015). *Zdrowie, praca, rodzina. Program Prawa i Sprawiedliwości* [Health, work and family. Law and Justice Manifesto]. Warszawa: Prawo i Sprawiedliwość.

Plaskota, T. (2016). 'Staruch' uniewinniony od zarzutu handlu amfetaminą. 'Ten dzień przywrócił mi wiarę w praworządność' ['Staruch' justified from charges of amphe-tamine trafficking. 'This sentence has restored my faith in justice']. *Polska Times.* Available at: www.polskatimes.pl/artykul/9351466,staruch-uniewinniony-od-zarzu tu-handlu-amfetamina-ten-dzien-przywrocil-mi-wiare-w-praworzadnosc,id,t.html [accessed 30 May 2019].

Polsatnews.pl (2018). 7,5 tys. zł za ponad trzy lata niesłusznie spędzone w areszcie [7,5 thousands złotych for three years wrongly spent in a jail]. *Polsat News.* Available at: www.polsatnews.pl/wiadomosc/2018-11-07/75-tys-zl-za-ponad-3-lata-nieslusznie-sp edzone-w-areszcie-to-naplucie-mi-w-twarz/ [accessed 30 May 2019].

Rohloff, A. (2011). Extending the concept of moral panic: Elias, climate change and civilization. *Sociology*, 45(4), pp. 634–649doi:10.1177/0038038511406597

124 Polish political elites versus football fandom

Rohloff, A. (2013). Moral panics as civilising and decivilising processes? A comparative discussion. *Política y Sociedad*, 50(2), pp. 483–500. doi:10.5209/rev_POSO.2013.v50.n2.40022

Rookwood, J. and Pearson, G. (2010). The hoolifan: Positive fan attitudes to football 'hooliganism'. *International Review for the Sociology of Sport*, 47(2), pp. 149–164. doi:10.1177/1012690210388455

Rzecznik Praw Obywatelskich (2019). Po interwencji RPO klatka dla kibiców na stadionie w Daleszycach będzie zdemontowana [After the intervention of the ombudsman, the cage at the stadium in Daleszyce will be dismantled]. Available at: www.rpo.gov.pl/pl/content/klatka-dla-kibicow-na-terenie-stadionu-w-daleszycach-bedzie-zdemontowana [accessed 30 May 2019].

Sahaj, T. (2007). *Fani futbolowi. Historyczno-społeczne Studium Zjawiska Kibicowania* [Football Fans. Socio-Historical Study of the Phenomenon of the Fandom]. Poznań: Akademia Wychowania Fizycznego w Poznaniu.

Schwertner, J. (2018). Kto okradł z życia złych chłopców z Legii? [Who robbed from life bad boys of Legia?] *Onet.pl*. Available at: https://wiadomosci.onet.pl/tylko-w-onecie/kto-okradl-z-zycia-zlych-chlopcow-z-legii/7sye5fd [accessed 30 May 2019].

Sikora K. and Woźniak W. (2018). Kibice piłkarscy jako grupa interesu politycznego. Przypadek łódzkich inwestycji stadionowych [Football fans as a political interest group]. In: A. Ostrowski (ed.) *Modern Football a Świat Kibiców 3. Interdyscyplinarne Studia nad Kulturą Futbolu* [Modern Football and World of Fans 3: Interdisciplinary Studies on Football Culture]. Wrocław: Wydawnictwo Naukowe Dolnośląskiej Szkoły Wyższej, pp. 193–209.

Telewizja Republika (2018). Prawie 300 tys. złotych odszkodowań dla kibiców Legii za „Akcję Widelec" kierowaną przez resort Schetyny! [Almost 300 thousand PLN of compensations for Legia fans for 'the Fork Action']. Available at: http://telewizjarepublika.pl/prawie-300-tys-zlotych-odszkodowan-dla-kibicow-legii-za-akcje-widelec-kierowana-przez-resort-schetyny,59103.html [accessed 30 May 2019].

weszlo.com (2017a). „Na Zachodzie sobie poradzili" – odcinek kolejny. Miejsce akcji: Portugalia [They managed in the West – next episode. Stop: Portugal]. Available at: http://weszlo.com/2017/01/30/zachodzie-poradzili-odcinek-kolejny-miejsce-akcji-portugalia/ [accessed 30 May 2019].

weszlo.com (2017b). Z cyklu: „Na Zachodzie sobie poradzili" – martwe szczury na derbach Kopenhagi [From the series: 'They managed in the West' – dead rats at the Kopenhagen derby]. Available at: http://weszlo.com/2017/04/19/cyklu-zachodzie-poradzili-martwe-szczury-derbach-kopenhagi/ [accessed 30 May 2019].

Wiechecki, R. and Olczyk E. (2017). Byłem ministrem i wyszedłem z tego bez szwanku [I was a minister and I survived]. *Rzeczpospolita*, 9 July. Available at: www.rp.pl/Plus-Minus/307069928-Wiechecki-Bylem-ministrem-i-wyszedlem-z-tego-bez-szwanku.html [accessed 30 May 2019].

Włoch, R. (2013). UEFA as a new agent of global governance: A case study of relations between UEFA and the Polish Government against the background of the UEFA EURO 2012. *Journal of Sport and Social Issues*, 37(3), pp. 297–311.

Woźniak, W. (2013a). O użyteczności koncepcji paniki moralnej jako ramy analitycznej dla badań nad zjawiskiem przemocy około futbolowej. [On the usefulness of the moral panics' concept as an analytical framework for researching football-related violence]. In: R. Kossakowski et al. (eds) *Futbol i Cała Reszta. Sport w Perspektywie nauk Społecznych*. Pszczółki: Wydawnictwo Orbis Exterior, pp. 248–267.

Woźniak, W. (2013b). Polish football under transition: Catch-up modernisation gone wrong. In: D. Hynes and A. Kiernan (eds) *Football and its Communities 2012*. Oxford: Inter-Disciplinary Press, pp. 117–128.

Woźniak, W. (2015). Euro 2012 i Kraków 2022. Polskie elity polityczne wobec wielkich imprez sportowych [Euro 2012 and Cracow 2022. Polish political elites towards sport mega events]. *Przegląd Socjologii Jakościowej*, 9(2), pp. 60–83. Available at: http://przegladsocjologiijakosciowej.org/Volume30/PSJ_11_2_Wozniak.pdf [accessed 30 May 2019].

Woźniak, W. (2018). Match fixing in Polish Football (2018). Historical perspectives and sociological interpretations. *The International Journal of the History of Sport*, 35(2–3), pp. 247–263. doi:10.1080/09523367.2018.1516640

7 Contemporary Polish fandom and its civic, social and political engagement

Introduction

Previous chapters have presented various aspects of the world of Polish football fans. It can be clearly seen that over its history the structure of this fandom has undergone a significant evolution: from the culture of unorganized, spontaneous groups of – usually very aggressive – supporters, to the functional differentiation and strategic division of tasks and responsibilities observed today. In the twenty-first century, many fan groups have developed into entities with a formal status, such as officially registered supporters' associations. Apart from this, many sub-groups have started engaging in a range of activities which are not directly related to sport, like charity, social activism or political engagement. This relatively recent phenomenon should be regarded as parallel to broader changes in Polish society in general, and the emergence of civic tendencies, movements and consciousness in particular.

This chapter is devoted to a more detailed presentation of this mode of activism of Polish football fans. Opening with some general information on fan activism, it moves on to discuss the processes of the professionalisation of fandom and the development of attendant forms of activism, and presents positive and negative examples. The chapter concludes with an analysis of various consequences of fan activism.

Fan activism: a broader agenda

The issue of football fan activism is one of the most current topics in international sociology of sport (see Cleland, et al., 2018). The emergence of this phenomenon is related, as Jamie Cleland notes, to wider social changes: the transition from industrial to post-industrial society (Cleland, 2010). Transformation of football, which goes hand in hand with the commercialisation of the social world, has induced fans' reaction; in some cases, their dissatisfaction and anger stimulated protest actions. Undoubtedly, widely understood changes in football – commercialisation, mediatisation, legal restrictions – have stimulated fans' collective energy. As a

Contemporary Polish fandom   127

consequence, 'collective action' has become one of the key terms in the analysis of fan activity (Cleland et al., 2018).

However, researchers involved in this topic need to be aware that the reasons behind fans' engagement are different in particular regions. For example, the impact of commercialisation has never been important enough to trigger fan protests or an organised movement in Poland. Regardless of the country, fans most frequently engage in community-based activity. In this case, 'collective action' is multidimensional and includes protests against legal restrictions, boycotts of new club owners (e.g. when they decide to rename the club or 'sell' its soul and fan base), activity for the local community, etc. In most cases, 'collective action' is based on the human resources and social capital of groups of fans (Grodecki, 2018).

In the case of Poland, the social capital of the fan community can be understood broadly, as it is

> transferred outside the stadiums. It is used by hooligans to organize illegal fights outside the stadiums and avoid police attention or by supporters' associations for organizing certain initiatives: lobbying club authorities to make decisions; organising legal aid for fans, if needed; or generating support for local community problems.
>
> (Grodecki, 2019, p. 467)

Social connections and resources which have emerged in the structure of fandom allow supporters to undertake a wide variety of activities, both legal and illegal.

This chapter is devoted to examples of supporters' activity which go beyond the 'natural' context of supporting the local team (cheering, preparing choreographies, etc.). In order to provide a more comprehensive picture of their social activism, it is worth making an assessment of the process of institutionalisation of supporters' activity in the form of associations.

The professionalisation of fandom and supporters' associations

The process of the professionalisation of fandom, understood as the emergence of more stable and institutionally structured forms of activity, can be traced back to the turn of the century. At that time, the structure of fandom began to differentiate as some fans devoted their skills to the hooligan domain and others focused on ultras involvement. The difference in scope between their respective activity can be regarded as the most important manifestation of the process which could be called 'division of functions' (Kossakowski, 2017a). The advent of supporters' associations (the first one was established by Wisła Cracow fans in 2001) was a natural result of two major factors: the inner development of fandom culture on the one hand, and certain external pressures on the other.

The first factor – the development of resources of fan movements – was related to the tradition of fans' collective identity. Over the decades, supporters of many

128 *Contemporary Polish fandom*

clubs had developed a strong, cohesive, reliable sense of belonging and identification, first with the club (as a primary source of passion and devotion), and second with other fans of their beloved club. Naturally, the communities of fans of different clubs developed similar structures of hierarchy, merit and responsibilities. The individuals who were the strongest (in terms of physical force: strength and stamina proven in fights) and the most charismatic became natural leaders who did not have to legitimate their power in any formal or legal way. However, in the course of time the spontaneous *levy-en-masse* mode of operation of such groups turned out to be insufficient, especially in relations with external actors. This coincided with a broader transformation of the social and political environment. For example, while as recently as in the 1990s trips to away matches did not require any formalities, in the new century it eventually became impossible to manage some organisational issues involved without formal representatives. On the other hand, clubs were organisations operating in a modern, civilised way and thus could not afford to cooperate with amorphous actors. As legal entities, they demanded that fans should have some proper representation in order to avoid any problems with, or accusations from, legal authorities or the media. Without any doubt, the origins of supporters' associations in Poland are connected with the democratisation of the public sphere in the country and the normalisation of operation of institutions in the legal sense. All the factors mentioned above created a space in which the fan movement had to face the challenge of 'normalisation':

> Everything began to get normal; such things like tickets; it got impossible to get tickets in any other way than through the club administration or fan association. And that's why associations had been established: to normalise everything.
>
> (Górnik Zabrze supporter)

This statement not only indicates fans' assessment of the outside world and their awareness of their own situation, but also shows the evolution of fandom. A few decades ago, the fan movement did not care about the opinion of external others: aggression and violence were the only type of relationship here.

As listed by Jacek Burski, the reasons why fans establish their organisations are multidimensional:

> First of all, it is easier to make decisions and achieve short-term (e.g. organisation of an away trip) or long-term goals (e.g. mobilisation of supporters as part of a social campaign). Secondly, more and more fans (sometimes under pressure) take up dialogue with other actors in public debate (local authorities, clubs, players, etc.), both at the local and national level. Thirdly, fan associations take over responsibility for communication on behalf of all club supporters (…). Furthermore, formalisation means that it is possible to exert more pressure on club management.
>
> (Burski, 2013, p. 276)

As a result, the fan movement went on to discover different areas of activity outside stadiums and became part of organised civil society (Grodecki, 2015).

The second factor – external pressure – is related to changes in Polish society in the new century. In the 2000s the country experienced two remarkable events in its history: accession to the European Union (2004) and the selection of Poland as a co-host of Euro 2012 (2007). Modernising stadiums and highways, the Polish government also decided to 'modernise' football supporters, mainly by ousting hooligans from the game (see Kossakowski, 2019). It was the era of Donald Tusk, the prime minister who declared 'war' against the most ardent fans (see Chapter 6 for more details). Tusk was supported by the liberal media and pressed for a more restrictive amendment to the Law on the Safety of Mass Events. This mobilised fans, who engaged in a number of protests (Antonowicz et al., 2016). In 2007, supporters of several clubs decided to establish the National Union of Supporters' Associations [*Ogólnopolski Związek Stowarzyszeń Kibicowskich*, OZSK], aiming to integrate fans in their struggle for their interests. This reaction initially resembled some characteristics of social movements understood as 'a distinct social process, consisting of the mechanisms through which actors involved in conflictual relations with clearly identified opponents … are linked by dense informal networks [and] share a distinct collective identity' (De la Porta and Diani, 2006, p. 20). In this case, Donald Tusk and his government were a symbolic opponent (although they represented a broader mindset of the 'civilised' part the Polish establishment), and supporters consolidated their informal networks and identified themselves as a discriminated part of society. This situation seemed to be a perfect, fertile ground for a strong social movement to be born. In the course of time, however, it turned out that despite enormous human capital and resources, as well as ability for mobilisation, Polish fans were not prepared to develop a strong social movement which could use some peaceful means to change their situation. Even the National Union, an institutional umbrella, was a powerless body unable to change relations with the authorities.

However, the experience of the conflict with the government led to expanding the activity of fans. The energy of their collective identity has been used in the sphere of social, educational, political and charitable activity. Many fans have come to realise the power of fandom in terms of mobilisation and potential it can develop. In some cases, engagement in social and charity actions was part of the process of 'whitewashing' – fans tried to improve their image by presenting a better side of their 'fanaticism': 'It probably started from clearing our image, really, and showing that a fan is not just a thug or hooligan from the stadiums' (Arka Gdynia supporter). More often than not, however, their motivation was less cynical, as the broadening of the field of fandom beyond typical 'supporting' actions in fact stemmed from several motivations – the respondents indicated such factors as: the intention to demonstrate the positive side of fan activity, to use the energy and potential of the group, to work for the sake of the club, to raise the new generations of

130   *Contemporary Polish fandom*

fans, to strengthen ties in local communities, to create attitudes and values and, in a broader sense – to serve others (as one respondent mentioned: 'We just want to help'). Owing to some particular features of fan circles (hermetic structure, reluctant attitude toward others, etc.), such engagement tends to be 'quiet'; even very active supporters do not boast about their actions in the media. As a result, the image of fans which dominates in the media is associated with vandalism, hooliganism or crime.

With institutional means in the form of supporters' associations, fan circles have undoubtedly become a more reliable partner for city councils, non-governmental organisations and so on. This is apparent in the 'Supporters United' programme, a multi-actor initiative operating in seventeen cities and towns, involving fans (who provide human resources), city councils (providing facilities in local areas), the Polish Football Association (responsible for managerial support) and the Ministry of Sport and Tourism (financing the scheme). An evaluation of the programme (see Kossakowski, 2017a; 2019) indicates that when the level of trust between external actors and supporters becomes sufficient, both sides can benefit: fans build their positive image in society, and other actors can take advantage of their network, which is highly effective in terms of mobilisation and resources. As a consequence, many supporters' associations are actively involved in cooperation with different actors at the local level.

Positive impact: examples of charity and social actions

Over the course of time, supporters' associations as well as informal fan initiatives have started developing a significant range of activities going beyond fan issues. Some examples of social activity of the fan movement are presented below.

One type of involvement pursued by most groups are charity actions, including initiatives aiming to help children in need. Many supporters' associations organise them around Children's Day (celebrated in Poland on 1 June) and Christmas. In a typical scenario, their members visit orphanages, public schools or children's wards in hospitals. Some groups hold a Christmas dinner for children from poor families and for elderly and homeless people. Fans of Legia Warsaw formed a special group called 'Good People: Legia fans for children', who specialised in painting the walls of children's wards in hospitals and decorating them with cartoon characters; they have also held a public collection and bought an ambulance for the Children's Health Centre in Warsaw. Fans of other clubs organise summer camps for children from foster care institutions and from the Polish minority in the countries of the former Soviet Union. One of the most popular initiatives are Children's Day fairs, typically including a football tournament and such attractions as bouncy castles and a meeting with football players.

Contemporary Polish fandom   131

Actions held with children in mind are also related to the process of socialisation: bringing them to the stadiums and familiarising them with club colours and history is a way to raise a new generation of fans. For example, fans of Cracovia Cracow organised an event during which kids from the family stand (most modern stadiums in Poland have such terraces) prepared a dance featuring a boy and a girl in club t-shirts and a slogan saying 'The youngest in the stadium, fans at heart already'.

Most charity and social actions are possible owing to social mobilisation: their power and positive outcome rely on the mass scale of activism and not on individual skills of particular individuals. Indeed, social capital is the most decisive aspect here (Grodecki, 2018). A mass call is very effective in the case of donating blood, a very common type of action organised by fans (the most notable examples include fans of the biggest clubs, whose mobilisation brings impressive results, e.g. fans of Pogoń Szczecin donated 190 litres of blood in 2015, see Wirwicka, 2016). Social network is the most important environmental asset also in the case of initiatives which go beyond particular clubs. One such example is the action called 'Colouring': fans of different clubs renovate orphanages and day rooms for children; fans with particular skills (painters, builders, etc.) are engaged in particular tasks.

Even a brief overview of actions undertaken within one year by fans of Polish clubs, in this case Widzew Łódź, shows how diverse they are. Some are not at all connected with the club and football, others are important for fans' local communities. Last year they organised fundraisers: for the treatment of a member of the local fan club in Bełchatów who got paralysed after a serious accident; for a specialised wheelchair for a handicapped fan; for the fiancée and toddler of a fan who passed away; for a Polish children's hospice in Lithuania and for some other people in need. Sometimes these were sick children of Widzew supporters, sometimes people who have no connections with the club at all. The club and its fans also engaged in a protest demanding that traffic lights should be installed at the pedestrian crossing not far from the stadium where a young Widzew player's sister was killed in an accident. While those actions were one-off, others are continuous or held annually: fans look after the graves of the players and coaches of the club and visit them on All Saints Day (1 November); they raise funds and visit orphanages before Christmas and on Children's Day; they support the Great Orchestra of Christmas Charity, the biggest charity fundraiser in Poland; although it is run by an organisation which the Polish right considers its enemy, this does not prevent the club and its fans from supporting it (widzew. com, 2018a; 2018b; 2019a; 2019b; widzewtomy.net, 2018a; 2018b; 2019a; 2019b; widzewiak.com, 2018).

It needs to be stressed, however, that fan activism based on social capital is also an important factor when it comes to fan lifestyle. Many associations organise football tournaments to which they invite other supporters, mostly fans of 'allied' clubs and members of local fan clubs. For example, in 2018 supporters of ŁKS Łódź hosted a big tournament with 34 teams representing

Figure 7.1 Local patriotism is frequently manifested in fans' choreographies. Łódź Fabryczna (Industrial Łódź) is the celebration of the industrial heritage of the city by fans of Widzew, the club deeply rooted in the tradition of local working class.
Source: Maciej Cholewiński

ŁKS fans from Łódź, ŁKS fan clubs in other cities and supporters of 'allied' clubs (Lech Poznań, Zawisza Bydgoszcz and GKS Tychy). Such tournaments are mostly an opportunity for entertainment and socialisation: apart from playing matches, fans strengthen their bonds enjoying beer and having a good time. Since most of these events are held using public sports facilities (pitches or sports halls), they need to be organised through official channels and thus require a supporters' association for the formalities involved. Associations are also more reliable partners for occasional commemorative actions: crowdfunding for memorials to club heroes or for officially approved graffiti featuring local football legends. Their graffiti is sometimes approved by local authorities and painted on buildings which they choose. The 'division of functions' (whether formal or informal) results not only in the fact that fans with different potential are engaged in different activities. It seems that the development of the surrounding world has made fans realise – to a greater or lesser extent – the importance of new fields of activity. This also means that new media forms – fan pages, websites, forums – are gradually replacing fan magazines published in print since the 1990s.

Founding supporters' associations also opens up business opportunities, such as fan shops. For example, the Lechia Gdańsk supporters' association (called Lions of the North) is the owner of a small shop in the centre of Gdańsk, where fans can buy 'Lions' brand clothes and paraphernalia. Many associations are quite successful in the free market environment, even if capitalism 'consumes' their 'beautiful game' and transforms it into 'modern football'. It should be noted that in many cases their own products are sold along official club merchandise (e.g. official match jerseys). In general, this is allowed, subject to arrangements between clubs and associations, as long as such products do not resemble ones offered by clubs. There are no particular restrictions on the content of products designed by fans, which means that it is sometimes controversial (e.g. it refers to rival fans or politics).

Fan activism for the sake of their clubs

It is important to note that what makes the social activism of fans possible is their perception of the club as something extraordinary or even 'sacred': a symbolic universe (see Antonowicz and Wrzesiński, 2009). As the history of Polish football shows, in some cases fans have been 'pushed' into action when their beloved clubs experienced organisational and financial collapse (this phenomenon has been observed not only in Poland, see Keoghan, 2014; Cleland et al., 2018). According to some studies (see Grodecki and Kossakowski, 2019a), there have been 18 cases in Poland in which fans rescued football clubs and/or rebuilt them from scratch and later played a significant role in their running. This particular form of fan activism is referred to as 'pro-club activism' (Grodecki and Kossakowski, 2019a), in order to differentiate actions undertaken for the sake of the club from other forms of activism mentioned in previous sections.

The cases of clubs being rescued by their supporters demonstrate the resources of social capital in the fan community and the attendant 'emergency self-organisation' (Nosal and Kossakowski, 2017). They enable fans to take on their shoulders the burden of rescuing their club by taking over full or partial control of the management. One consequence of such rescue actions is the exchange of 'symbolic elites' (see Czyżewski, Kowalski and Piotrowski, 1997, p. 17), involving the replacement of business people by members of the fan community. For fans, the club is a symbol that legitimizes the existence of their community, but also individual identities. This is why they are ready to make infinite sacrifices for the 'holy symbol', unlike people who treat engagement in the club only as a job or entertainment.

The dark side of fan activism

Apart from activity incorporating football supporters in a broader, civic context, what cannot remain unnoticed is a controversial, often 'uncivilised' and illegal dimension of fan life in Poland. As mentioned above, some pro-social actions can build a positive image of fans in a broader social environment. It should be stressed that although most fans have never been involved in violence or criminal activity, some media coverage presents a negative image of fandom as such (thus reinforcing moral panic around football in general, see Woźniak, 2013). The focus on 'bad news' stems not only from tendencies in contemporary media but also from some biased attitudes of journalists (see Garz, 2014). This makes it difficult for fans to achieve a positive image in the local community (as one journalist states: 'you can perform dozens of good actions and then there is a riot, and the media write about it, and all the work gets ruined. It's like getting up over and over again' [personal interview]). Since some critical media voices put more emphasis on pathologies in the fan world, many external observers (even potentially interested in football) can view fandom as a criminal environment. This does not mean that all cases

134 *Contemporary Polish fandom*

described in the media are fake news, but their coverage certainly presents only a part of the story.

First of all, the 'division of functions' mentioned above does not change the fact that hooligan activity is still very important in the structure of fandom. What is more, although the number of hooligans is significantly smaller in comparison to all other categories of supporters, they have a decisive voice in most aspects of fan life. According to a Legia Warsaw fan, 'Hooligans are in charge in every club, every single one. If they say to ultras: 'don't prepare this choreography', the ultras will not go ahead with it, no way. It's the same everywhere and it's not a secret that hooligan groups have power'. Hooligans decide about alliances with fans of other clubs. They can break long-standing informal agreements if they find better 'friends'. In most cases, such 'friends' are better partners in criminal activities but official statements always stress that changing alliances stems from the 'objective' circumstances of the hooligan world. (In fan jargon, 'alliance' [*zgoda*] means friendly relations between fans of different clubs. Historically, 'alliances' came as a result of socialising, mainly parties heavily laced with alcohol, or personal contacts between the most charismatic fans from both sides. In recent years, however, 'alliances' between fans are increasingly 'business-related'.)

One such case was the break of a long-standing alliance between Wisła Cracow, Lechia Gdańsk and Śląsk Wrocław fans (called the Triad of the Great Cities). In 2016, the leaders of Wisła hooligans decided to form a coalition with the Ruch Chorzów hooligan crew, which was unacceptable for the other two members of the Triad. Officially, Wisła hooligans declared that the move was motivated only by hooligan considerations and involved a tactical alliance strengthening the power of hooligan crews from the region (Gdańsk and Wrocław are far away from Cracow, Chorzów is much closer). However, many of our respondents did not believe the 'official' version and claimed that the real reason behind the new 'friendship' had been related to new business opportunities, such as drug trafficking. The truth came out in 2018, when the police arrested Ruch and Wisła hooligans who had been jointly involved in organised crime (Banasik, 2018).

The domination of hooligans in the fan world is enabled by their physical strength and the fact that their culture has traditionally been at the core of fan identity. The hooligan subculture has evolved over a long period of time. As we present in Chapter 5, the violent culture of aggressive groups goes back to the 1990s. From the turn of the new century, hooligan crews underwent the process of 'professionalisation': increasingly more often only well-trained individuals (doing boxing, MMA, kickboxing, etc.) were able to meet the requirements to join. As a result, hooligans became a 'class in itself', a 'bourgeois class' which firmly dominates over the rest of fans in the stands. In recent years, some hooligan groups have started to take advantage of their dominant position and gather the resources of their entire fan communities to get rich; they feed on the ideology of solidarity of fans of the same club (see Grodecki and Kossakowski, 2019b).

The case of Ruch Chorzów fans illustrates how pathological and self-serving this kind of activity can be. Recently the hooligan crew from Chorzów exploited other fans, for example when collecting money for away trips. Regular fans paid about ten or twenty złotys (between about two and four pounds) more as the costs of transport were inflated. The surplus went to the group of hooligans, who used the money to buy weapons for their fights or to support their arrested or imprisoned mates (Pietraszewski, 2019). In case of disagreements between hooligans and regular supporters, disputes are often settled using violence. It needs to be remembered that football fan culture is not democratic: it is based on punitive imperatives, strong cohesion and absolute obedience. The Chorzów case has been widely publicised following a criminal investigation in which 52 members of the Ruch hooligan crew (known as Psycho Fans) were charged with serious criminal offences, such as drug trafficking, racketeering and extortion. While the number of those charged is rather considerable, what is important is the phenomenon itself. It appears that in many hooligan groups criminal activity is not something unusual. However, owing to their hermetic nature, it is difficult to objectively estimate its actual scale in terms of numbers; there are no statistics of hooligans involved in crime. Some media reports on police actions, arrests and publicly disclosed facts indicate that illegal practices are the case among hooligan supporters of many Polish clubs, both small and the biggest (e.g. Legia Warsaw, Lech Poznań, Lechia Gdańsk, Widzew Łódź).

The influence, impact and significance of hooligan groups have to be approached multidimensionally. They have an inclination to criminal activities because their structure and mode of operation closely resemble those of mafia culture. All of them are composed of young, strong, well-trained, extremely dedicated men (there are no hooligan groups in Poland with female members) who are 'socialised' to 'the law of the fist', hierarchical order and unconditional loyalty from the very beginning of their 'career'. Additionally, young males can perceive such groups as an attractive environment: they gain respect, they have a sense of belonging and they experience the strength of group solidarity. Some aspects are important especially for people from the underclass:

> There is this guy who in fact – that's a different side of the whole thing, another twist – in fact this hooligan group really saved his life. He lived like a bum, he had nothing to eat. And now thanks to those hooligans this guy drives a normal car, he does some business, you know what I mean. He doesn't work like other people but he does something, he gets money from somewhere; I don't ask him where this money comes from, he wouldn't tell me anyway. If he hadn't got help from hooligans he wouldn't have a job at all; he didn't learn much. Those hooligans spotted him somehow, they paid for his training to prepare him for fights. And then there was some money.
>
> (ŁKS Łódź supporter)

136   *Contemporary Polish fandom*

People socialised in hooligan groups operate on the edge of the law, which is easier thanks to a cardinal rule of the world of supporters: a total ban on cooperation with the police. Along with the threat of physical punishment, it results in a silent acceptance of the dark side of fan activism. Even if other supporters know that the leaders of the fan community are involved in criminal dealings, they prefer to stand aside and do not ask for details.

Political activism

In Chapter 6 we provide a detailed description of the relations between fans and the world of politics over the last years. We show, among other things, that in the second half of the 2000s the Civic Platform government came into sharp conflict with football supporters, which coincided with Poland's preparations for the organisation of Euro 2012. Below are examples of various forms of fan activism that refer to the world of politics, in the sense of organising own protests and autonomous initiatives or participating in political events organised by others, as well as taking the role of (local) politicians by supporters.

The 'war' against fans, initiated by Donald Tusk's government, triggered an appropriate response from fan circles. It seems that this conflict strongly influenced the consolidation of the social identity of fans and the ideological character of their community. The process of consolidation of the fan community was also reinforced by the general atmosphere of public debate on football supporters. They could get an impression that they were under attack from all sides, as the government, along with the media and public opinion, labelled them as 'deviants' 'barbarians' and so on (Kossakowski, 2015, 2017a). Paradoxically, this stimulated the uniformity of their approach and improved coordination even between fans of hostile clubs. Regardless of their animosities, fans from all over Poland were united around their slogans. The most famous one presented in match choreographies at several stadiums was 'Donald, you moron, hooligans will bring your government down' [*Donald, matole, twój rząd obalą kibole*]; another one was: 'Project Euro 2012 – stadiums: overpaid; highways: won't be there; railway stations: a splash of paint; airports: provincial; players: weak; red herring: football fans; the government: satisfied' (Antonowicz et al., 2016).

The activities which fans introduced to their repertoire at the time (fan actions reached their peak in 2011) manifested an unprecedented scale of their potential in terms of mobilisation, resources as well as intelligent, ironic content. In 2011, when Donald Tusk toured Poland during the parliamentary election campaign, fans followed him in their own coach and displayed banners saying, for example, 'And now you will only hear lies' (*Teraz Usłyszycie Same Kłamstwa*; the first letters of the words form the name Tusk). In terms of activism, all initiatives pursued by fans displayed their enormous potential, which, however, was lost. Gradually, it turned out that they did not manage to create a strong civil or social movement. Apart from street protests and match choreographies in the stadiums, they did not reach for more advanced

Contemporary Polish fandom 137

means of civil disobedience. They have never decided, for example, to hold a nationwide boycott of matches, which could have been a breakthrough. Probably, some local circumstances and 'business' relations (between fans and their clubs) were more important than the interests of the fan movement as such.

The experience of public exclusion and condemnation (fans as savagery, an ulcer on the healthy fabric of a modern and civilised society) has been one reason why the identity of fans is largely based on opposition and hostility, and why Polish fans searching for symbolic expression of such identity have turned to right-wing patterns. As we argue throughout this book, it is practically impossible to imagine that Polish football fans could use left-wing symbols (e.g. Che Guevara) as an expression of their attitudes. This is a result of the rule of real socialism in the country before 1989: many fans see being 'leftist' as being 'communist' and thus do not have means of expressing social discontent and a sense of community other than a set of conservative/patriotic symbols (more details are provided in the next chapter). Most importantly, this view is supported by leaders of this community, which means that – owing to its hierarchical order – new, young fans become familiar only with a 'ready-to-absorb' system of values. An additional explanation for such an identity configuration is also associated with the distinctive structure of the fan movement: 'militant' nature of fandom tends to promote identification with symbols referring to national and conservative ideas rather than with other sets.

This 'turn to the right' has resulted in an increasingly greater engagement in events celebrating national holidays, with their focus on history, politics and memory. Fans of many clubs are very active in the annual Independence March held on 11 November in Warsaw. They march both as a patriots (or nationalists) and football supporters – symbols of Poland (national flags, coat of arms, etc.) are displayed along club colours and crests. Mostly, such celebrations mean that fans suspend their animosities and focus on expressing both national and anti-system values. The latter mainly comes down to riots with the police, shouting slogans and firing pyrotechnics. However, despite their long engagement in the Independence March, fan circles have not transformed into a political movement (more or less extreme). As we show in the next chapter, most fans are not interested in political life in terms of institutionalised structures and party sympathies, as they prefer approaching politically sensitive topics and other actors from an anti-establishment' position. Generally, fans avoid involvement in official politics.

The engagement of fans in such celebrations is also visible at the local level. Fans play an important role in shaping local patriotism, in supporting local communities and local identity, and in commemorating important events from the history of the region. For example, Lech Poznań supporters organise a collection for the renovation of graves of the Wielkopolska insurgents (people of the Poznań region who rose up in arms against German Reich in December 1918). As one journalist states: 'Fans can express local pride. (...) Poznań citizens are not only attached to the city, they just love it. Fans not only think the same, but they are also able to articulate it publicly'.

138 Contemporary Polish fandom

Figure 7.2 Fans of Lech Poznań celebrate their regional heritage (Wielkopolska) referring also to their distinction over the fans of other teams through reference to Magnateria, the highest estate of Polish nobility in the old days.
Source: Przemysław Nosal

Fans are more willing to support and commemorate events and people related to nationhood and struggle for independence and freedom. Their glorification of brave soldiers and war heroes is certainly related to their search for role models and symbols of pride. This kind of activism is also the case among Legia Warsaw fans, who preserve and cherish the memory of the Warsaw Uprising and honour the surviving insurgents. Around every 1 August (the day the uprising broke out in 1944), Legia ultras prepare a commemorative choreography, which they present to the sound of the sirens in the stands before kick-off; some heroes of the uprising are hosted in the VIP section of the stadium on the occasion. In 2017, the UEFA fined Legia for such a performance (it included a caption in English saying 'During the Warsaw Uprising German killed 160,000 thousand people. Thousands of them were children', and received wide coverage in the international media). When fans immediately collected the money to pay the fine (35,000 euros), the club authorities donated the entire amount to organisations which support surviving insurgents.

It seems that it is easier for fans to become involved in such actions than to establish political organisations and participate in current politics. However, there are some cases when they decided to engage in political life in a formal way. Most cases concern local politics; one of them – from the city of Łódź – was presented in Chapter 6. Another notable example is that of Lechia Gdańsk fans. In 2001, when the club experienced financial and organisational collapse, they decided to draw the interest of the public and local authorities to its disastrous situation. They stood up for the 2002 local elections as

'Come on Lechia' (*Naprzód Lechio!*) grass-roots movement, which received 3.14 per cent of votes and did not go over the threshold of 5 per cent, but came to the attention of Gdańsk authorities (Kossakowski, 2017b). Lechia fans desperately looked for support for their club and their entry into politics (even if only local) was connected with football issues. This is a typical pattern, as fans view local city councils as a tool for resolving the most urgent needs of their clubs. Such was also the case of Chrobry Głogów, a club from the second level of league competition. Three Chrobry supporters stood in the local elections in November 2006. They became members of the town council, mostly owing to a considerable number of fan votes. This move did not stem from desire for power. Chrobry fans fought for their club (which was in financial and organisational difficulties at the time) and they knew that as councillors they would have a say in decisions of the town hall which concerned its survival (Kossakowski, 2017b).

Conclusion

Bob Edwards and John D. McCarthy mention the meaning of resources in successful collective action:

> The assumption that resource availability enhances the likelihood of collective action is generally taken for granted by contemporary analysts of social movements. (...) But the simple availability of resources is not sufficient; coordination and strategic effort is typically required in order to convert available pools of individually held resources into collective resources and to utilize those resources in collective action. When movement activists do attempt to create collective action ... through historical time and across geographical locations their successes are consistently related to the greater presence of available resources in their broader environments.
>
> (2004, p. 116)

As described in this chapter, the activism of Polish football fans is an excellent example of collective action that relies on various resources. Time, money and human capital – these are all easy to mobilise and use in their case. There is a multitude of examples showing that fans are able to deal with things quickly: helping people in need, raising funds or just removing snow from the pitch (which happened when their club was in financial trouble and could not afford to pay for it). But there is also a dark side of the use of fan resources: sometimes they are used for hooligan or even criminal activity. This is one of the most important constraints preventing the development of the potential of the fan movement.

Another constraint is of a more fundamental nature: it is a lack of ideas directed towards any form of social change. Polish fans differ in this respect from, for example, German fans of St Pauli, whose engagement in numerous social campaigns stems from their ideological foundation (Totten, 2015). The

140 *Contemporary Polish fandom*

political activism of Polish football supporters is usually limited to the symbolic space: they can refer to history and politics using performative means of expression like probably no one else. They undertake many small initiatives on a local scale but it is difficult to talk about Polish fan circles as a social movement in terms of sociological understanding as it is today.

References

Antonowicz, D. and Wrzesiński, Ł. (2009). Kibice jako wspólnota niewidzialnej religii [Fans as a community of invisible religion]. *Studia Socjologiczne*, 192(1), pp. 115–150.

Antonowicz, D., Kossakowski, R. and Szlendak, T. (2016). Flaming flares, football fanatics and political rebellion. Resistant youth cultures in late capitalism. In: M. Schwartz and H. Winkel (eds) *Eastern European Youth Cultures in a Global Context*. London: Palgrave Macmillan, pp. 131–144.

Banasik, M. (2018). Skruszeni pseudokibice pogrążyli „Miśka" – lidera wiślackich bojówek? [Apologetic hooligans incriminated 'Misiek' – the leader of the Wisła Kraków hooligans?] Available at: https://dziennikpolski24.pl/skruszeni-pseudokibice-pograzyli-miska-lidera-wislackich-bojowek/ar/13542155 [accessed 27 June 2019].

Burski, J. (2013). Od chuligana do prezesa – analiza przemian zachodzących w społecznym świecie polskich kibiców [From hooligan to chairman – the analysis of transformation in social world of Polish fans]. In: R. Kossakowski et al. (eds) *Futbol i Cała Reszta. Sport w Perspektywie nauk Społecznych*. Pszczółki: Wydawnictwo Orbis Exterior, pp. 269–286.

Cleland, J. (2010). From passive to active: The changing relationship between supporters and football clubs. *Soccer & Society*, 11(5), pp. 537–552.

Cleland, J., Doidge, M., Millward, P. and Widdop, P. (2018). *Collective Action and Football Fandom: A Relational Sociological Approach*. London: Palgrave Macmillan.

Czyżewski, M., Kowalski, S. and Piotrowski, A. (1997). Wprowadzenie [Introduction]. In: M. Czyżewski, S. Kowalski and A. Piotrowski (eds) *Rytualny Chaos. Analiza Dyskursu Publicznego w Polsce* [Ritual Chaos. Analysis of Public Discourse in Poland]. Kraków: Aureus, pp. 7–41

De la Porta, D. and Diani, M. (2006). *Social Movements: An Introduction*, 2nd edn. Malden MA: Blackwell Publishing.

Doidge, M. (2015). *Football Italia: Italian Football in an Age of Globalization*. London and New York: Bloomsbury Academic.

Edwards, B. and McCarthy, J. (2004). Resources and social movement mobilization. In: D. A. Snow, S. A. Soule and H. Kriesi (eds) *The Blackwell Companion to Social Movements*. Malden: Blackwell, pp. 116–152.

Garz, M. (2014). Good news and bad news: Evidence of media bias in unemployment reports. *Public Choice*, 161(3–4), pp. 499–515.

Giulianotti, R. (2002). Supporters, followers, fans and flaneurs: A taxonomy of spectator identities in football. *Journal of Sport and Social Issues*, 26(1), pp. 25–46.

Grodecki, M. (2015). Trzecia strona trybun. Działalność stowarzyszeń kibiców piłkarskich w Polsce [The third side of terraces. Activity of supporters' associations in Poland]. *Miscellanea Anthropologica et Sociologica*, 16(4), pp. 100–115.

Grodecki, M. (2018). *Życie po Meczu. Formy Wykorzystania Kapitału Społecznego Kibiców Piłkarskich w Polsce* [Life after Match. Forms of Using Social Capital by Football Fans in Poland]. Warszawa: WUW.

Contemporary Polish fandom   141

Grodecki, M. (2019). Building social capital: Polish football supporters through the lens of James Coleman's conception. *International Review for the Sociology of Sport*, 54(4), pp. 459–478.

Grodecki, M. and Kossakowski, R. (2019a). Trzy drogi odbudowy klubów piłkarskich przez kibiców [Three ways of rebuilding football clubs by fans]. In: A. Ostrowski (ed.) *Modern Football a Świat Kibiców 4: Interdyscyplinarne Studia nad Kulturą Futbolu* [Modern Football and World of Fans 4: Interdisciplinary Studies on Football Culture]. Wrocław: ATUT, pp. 165–179.

Grodecki, M. and Kossakowski, R. (2019b). *Class Wars among Football Supporters. Hooligan Bourgeoisie and Non-Hooligan Proletariat.* Unpublished manuscript.

Keoghan, J. (2014). *Punk Football: The Rise of Fan Ownership in English Football.* Worthing: Pitch Publishing.

Kossakowski, R. (2015). 'Kibole' wyklęci w poszukiwaniu autentyczności: próba rekonstrukcji polityki tożsamości polskich kibiców [Cursed 'hooligans' in search of authenticity: The reconstruction of Polish fans' identity politics]. *Kultura Współczesna*, 1, pp. 30–45.

Kossakowski, R. (2017a). *Od Chuliganów do Aktywistów. Polscy Kibice i Zmiana Społeczna* [From Hooligans to Activists. Polish Fans and the Social Change]. Kraków: Universitas.

Kossakowski, R. (2017b). From the bottom to the Premiership: The significance of supporters' movement in the governance of football clubs in Poland. In: B. Garcia and J. Zheng (eds) *Football and Supporter Activism in Europe. Whose Game Is It?* Basingstoke: Palgrave Macmillan, pp. 233–255.

Kossakowski, R. (2019). Euro 2012, the 'civilizational leap' and the 'supporters United' programme: A football mega-event and the evolution of fan culture in Poland. *Soccer & Society*, 20(5), pp. 729–743.

Millward, P. (2011). *The Global League: Transnational Networks, Social Movements and Sport in the New Media Age.* Basingstoke: Palgrave Macmillan.

Nosal P. and Kossakowski, R. (2017). Doświadczenie czarnego łabędzia, mity logistyczne i okręt Tezeusza: trzy mechanizmy wytwarzania i wzmacniania zbiorowej tożsamości kibiców [The experience of black swan, logistic myths and the Ship of Theseus: three mechanisms of creation and reinforcement collective identity of fans]. *Kultura i Społeczeństwo*, 61(2), pp. 3–28.

Numerato, D. (2015). Who says 'no' to modern football? Italian supporters, reflexivity, and neo-liberalism. *Journal of Sport & Social Issues*, 39(2), pp. 120–138.

Numerato, D. (2018). *Football Fans, Activism and Social Change.* Abingdon: Routledge.

Pietraszewski, M. (2019). Kibole z Psycho Fans oskarżeni. 'Mają na koncie zabójstwo' [Hooligans from Psycho Fans group accused of murder]. Available at: http://ka towice.wyborcza.pl/katowice/7,35063,24756300,kibole-z-psycho-fans-oskarzeni-ma ja-na-koncie-zabojstwo.html [accessed 22 September 2019].

Totten, M. (2015). Sport activism and political praxis within the FC Sankt Pauli fan subculture. *Soccer & Society*, 16(4): 453–468. doi:10.1080/14660970.2014.882828

widzewtomy.net (2018a). Zbiórka dla Romka przed meczem z Olimpią [Fundraiser for Romek before Olimpia's game]. Available at: www.widzewtomy.net/zbiorka-dla-rom ka-przed-meczem-z-olimpia/ [accessed 30 May 2019].

widzewtomy.net (2018b). Zbiórka na wózek dla Artura [Fundraiser for Arthur's wheelchair]. Available at: www.widzewtomy.net/zbiorka-na-wozek-dla-artura-wcia z-trwa/ [accessed 30 May 2019].

142 *Contemporary Polish fandom*

widzewtomy.net (2019a). Pomóżmy rodzinie Sebastiana [Let's help Sebastian's family]. Available at: www.widzewtomy.net/pomozmy-rodzinie-sebastiana/ [accessed 30 May 2019].

widzewtomy.net (2019b). Pomagamy Kasi [We're helping Kasia]. Available at: www.widzewtomy.net/pomagamy-kasi-zbiorka-funduszy-na-meczu-z-row-em/ [accessed 30 May 2019].

widzew.com (2018a). Widzew znów gra z WOŚP [Widzew joins WOŚP fundraiser again]. Available at: www.widzewtomy.net/widzew-znow-gra-z-wosp-co-przekaza l-na-licytacje/ [accessed 30 May 2019].

widzew.com (2018b). Maciek walczy w guzem mózgu [Maciek fights a brain tumour]. Available at: https://widzew.com/-/maciek-walczy-z-guzem-mozgu-widzewiacy-poma gamy- [accessed 30 May 2019].

widzew.com (2019a). Zbiórka dla polskiego hospicjum na Litwie [Fundraiser for Polish hospice in Lithuania]. Available at: https://widzew.com/-/zbiorka-dla-polskiego-hosp icjum-na-litwie [accessed 30 May 2019].

widzew.com (2019b). Widzew włącza się do walki o bezpieczne przejście [Widzew joins the fight for a safe crossing]. Available at: https://widzew.com/-/widzew-wlacza -sie-w-akcje-walki-o-bezpieczneprzejscie [accessed 30 May 2019].

widzewiak.com (2018). Trwa zbiórka dla chorego Antosia [The fundraiser for sick Antoś]. Available at: www.widzewiak.pl/newsroom/35363,Trwa-zbiorka-pieniedzy-dla-chorego-Antosia [accessed 30 May 2019].

Wirwicka, A. (2016). Kibice oddają krew. Ostatnio zebrali ponad 180 litrów [Fans donate the blood. Recently they donate more than 180 litres]. Available at: https:// szczecin.onet.pl/kibice-oddaja-krew-ostatnio-zebrali-ponad-180-litrow/7xzwepg [accessed 24 June 2019].

Wouters, C. (1986). Formalization and informalization: Changing tension balances in civilizing processes. *Theory Culture and Society* 3(2), pp. 1–18.

Woźniak, W. (2013). O użyteczności koncepcji paniki moralnej jako ramy analitycznej dla badań nad zjawiskiem przemocy około futbolowej. [On the usefulness of the moral panics' concept as an analytical framework for researching football-related violence]. In: R. Kossakowski et al. (eds) *Futbol i cała reszta. Sport w perspektywie nauk społecznych* [Football and the Rest. Sport in the Perspective of Social Sciences]. Pszczółki: Wydawnictwo Orbis Exterior, 248–267.

Z historii Lechii Gdańsk [From the history of Lechia Gdańsk] (n.d.). Available at: www.lechia-gdansk.pl/page/show/historia [accessed 27 September 2019].

8 Ideology on Polish terraces

Introduction

In previous chapters we have outlined a broad context of Polish football fandom, which was necessary as no social group functions in a vacuum. Writing about Polish fans, it was therefore important to present a historical overview concerning the country and its football, and the development of the phenomenon of fandom itself. We have also presented how the relationships between the worlds of politics, football and fans have been evolving in contemporary Poland since the post-1989 systemic transformation. This outline of the context and issues concerning Polish history helps us to understand the ideological profile of Polish fans, which has been shaped by a number of cultural and historical factors. This chapter presents a more detailed picture of their ideological involvement, including examples of ideas, values, behaviours and attitudes that they currently promote.

We begin here with an analysis of quantitative data from independent studies on the political sympathies of Polish fans (e.g. in terms of political party preferences). Then we move on to investigate fans' narratives about their political worldview – on the basis of qualitative interviews we demonstrate how they justify their loyalty to particular ideas. The third part of this chapter concerns examples of match choreographies, slogans and banners that express the ideological foundation of Polish fandom in a symbolic and performative way.

Quantitative data on the political preferences of fans

The inspiration for this section came from the empirical research which allowed for the first quantitative generalisations concerning the patterns of political attitudes of Polish fans. The data collected by Radosław Kossakowski in 2017 (see also the Methodology section in the Introduction) confirm that they are oriented towards the right (for more details, see Kossakowski and Besta, 2018). When it comes to political parties, survey participants generally favoured right-wing and nationalist formations. The National Movement commanded the strongest support (27 per cent) and was followed by the Kukiz'15 Movement (19.7 per cent), 'KORWiN' (the political

144 *Ideology on Polish terraces*

movement led by Janusz Korwin-Mikke, a vehement opponent of the European Union, 18.1 per cent). The leading parties in the Polish parliament – Law and Justice [*Prawo i Sprawidliwość*, PiS], the winner of the parliamentary election in 2015 and the election to the European Parliament in 2019, gained only 4.5 per cent, and the Civic Platform [*Platforma Obywatelska*, PO], a centre-liberal party which was the senior coalition partner in the 2007–2015 government, even less – 4.2 per cent. Other political parties (including left-wing ones) gained below 2 per cent (19.7 per cent of respondents did not identify with any party).

Similarly, the survey conducted in February 2017 by the polling company Sport Analytics confirms the assumptions about a well-defined and clear political identification of fans. The sample of 1,508 questionnaires was selected using stratified sampling from the database of 8,090 questionnaires. Here, the Kukiz'15 Movement received the biggest support (24 per cent), ahead of 'KORWiN' (19 per cent) and the National Movement (16.5 per cent). The ruling Law and Justice party was supported by 13.3 percent of the respondents, while two liberal parties: Civic Platform and Modern [*Nowoczesna*] received 4.9 and 4.2 per cent respectively (Chmielowski, 2017).

The movement called Kukiz'15 was founded after Paweł Kukiz, a rock musician and a celebrity, came third in the presidential election of 2015, winning 21 percent of the votes (42 per cent in the 18 to 29 age group). His organisation (never officially registered as a political party) is an association of various anti-establishment movements, from right-wing nationalists to activists demanding legalisation of soft drugs, with the introduction of single member constituencies as the major demand. The National Movement is one of the far-right parties which cooperated with the Kukiz'15 organisation before the elections. Five members of the National Movement made it to the parliament as representatives of Kukiz'15. They are closely associated with radical football fan circles and should probably be perceived as the very first institutional representation of football fandom in Polish parliamentary politics. They co-organise the annual Independence March, which gathers fans from all over Poland (see Chapter 7). The third choice is KORWIN (since renamed as the Liberty Party [*Wolność*]), a radical right-libertarian and Eurosceptic party. Its former name was an acronym identical to the surname of its leader, Janusz Korwin-Mikke, ex-member of the European Parliament (he resigned his seat in January 2018), notorious for his misogynist, homophobic, racist or anti-Semitic remarks (see for example Day, 2014; Szczerbiak, 2014). These parties and movements, organised and supported mainly by younger people, mostly males, proved very effective in mobilising the electorate using social media and web-based communication tools (Lipiński and Stępińska, 2019).

Political sympathies in terms of party preferences could be one variable of ideological engagement. However, not less important seems to be self-perception in terms of values. In their study, Radosław Kossakowski and Tomasz Besta (2018) included measures of cultural and economic conservatism. The

Ideology on Polish terraces 145

latter highlights the 'free market' ideology, with no limits to private initiative, and opposes progressive taxation, welfare state, etc. In the domain of culture and values, right-wing ideology favours tradition and well-established social roles in the context of marriage, gender roles, or same-sex relationships. In the case of economic right-wing beliefs, one item was used with a scale anchored at 1 ('I support progressive taxation, welfare-state, the state has a role in economy') and 10 ('I support totally free market economy, the state has no role in regulating markets'); and one item for the cultural dimension, on a scale from 1 to 10 ('When it comes to cultural issues, my opinions on religion, gender roles, same-sex marriages or abortion, are': 1 = left-wing/liberal/progressive to 10 = right-wing/conservative/ traditional). In both cases, the average index confirms right-wing preferences. In the case of economic dimensions, it was 6.88, and in case of moral/cultural values the index was even higher at 8.28

The above findings are evidence of a strong ideological attitude. From one point of view, it could be stated that fans are not a representative group – the majority of Polish society has different political preferences. In the sample from Kossakowski and Besta's study, most of the respondents were men (87.4 per cent) and the average age was 26 years. Interestingly, however, there is an important 'turn right' in the case of young males in the Polish population as such (see Pacewicz, 2019). Men aged 18–30 express their preference of right-wing parties far more often (62 per cent) than left-wing and centre ones (only 33 per cent). This is significantly different than in the case of women of the same age, 55 per cent of whom favour left and centre parties, and 43 per cent – right-wing ones. (Generally speaking, young people were more inclined to support conservative parties in the parliamentary election of 2015 than that of 2011, see Szafraniec and Grygieńć, 2019). And it is hardly surprising that right-wing tendencies dominate at Polish stadiums. Some studies devoted to gender issues show that Polish fandom culture is ruled by male fans – both in terms of discourse and practice (Antonowicz et al., 2018; Jakubowska et al., 2019). When it comes to gender-related content presented in ultras choreographies, Polish examples are related to hegemonic masculinity and stress the significance of physical and mental strength (see Kossakowski et al., 2020).

Quantitative data provide a general picture and give some insight into political preferences. They indicate what kind of values and parties fans tend to prefer. However, numbers are not enough to answer the questions: 'What are the roots of fans' political preferences?' and 'What is their perception of particular topics?'

The next part of this chapter is organised as follows. One subchapter is devoted to three issues (presented in three headed sections): fans' narratives on their right-wing ideology, fans' reluctance to leftist ideas, and their views on engagement in institutional politics. The following subchapter includes a number of headed sections concerning fans' opinions on particular issues (gender, refugees, etc.).

146 *Ideology on Polish terraces*

Political statements in fans' narratives

This subchapter reviews the attitudes of fans and their axiological stance towards particular issues. It is based on extensive qualitative studies encompassing a broad spectrum of themes and approaching the multidimensional experience of being a member of football fandom.

Why we are right-wing?

The Polish fan scene is peculiar and uniform in terms of political orientation, as it is dominated by groups and people holding strong right-wing views. The quantitative data presented above show a clear dominance of such convictions. Qualitative studies, in turn – mainly in-depth interviews, but also participatory observations – make it possible to investigate this phenomenon in a more nuanced manner: they can provide an answer to the question where this ideological dominance comes from. Analysis of fans' narratives allows to identify several factors at play here.

One topic that often appears in their narratives is references to history – to the communist heritage, which they unequivocally assess negatively, and which, according to some informants, still has an impact on the Polish present.

> The consequences of transformation, well.... Transformation didn't go exactly the way we would have wanted. You see, the more time passes from the symbolic fall of communism (*komuna*), and the more anniversaries of freedom we celebrate, the more it turns out that it wasn't exactly what underground activists had imagined in 1980.
>
> (ŁKS Łódź supporter)

> Perhaps it's connected with this anti-communist tradition. Well, I mean, Polish fans are mostly nationalist; you can easily see that even when just you look at their flags. And that's probably where it comes from, I mean this sort of general aversion to the communist system (*komuna*), aversion to the left; it's historically conditioned. And that's where this general clear-cut split in current politics comes from: either you support PiS [Law and Justice], which means that you're a patriot, or you support the Civic Platform or the SLD – which are pretty much one and the same thing when it comes to what fans think about them – and that means that you are for the erosion of values, you support gender [issues], you're for all the evil you can see in the world today. And so that's probably where all of that comes from – it's this anti-communist tradition of the fan movement in Poland.
>
> (Arka Gdynia supporter)

> It probably comes from history (…). There was a communist system (*komuna*) here for forty odd years, and so it's kind of natural that there is this thing about resistance of sorts that's really strong. And people

Ideology on Polish terraces 147

probably had this association of the communist system with the police. And another thing is that patriotism is something that sort of keeps us together; but being a patriot and being a leftist – it just doesn't go together a bit.

(Legia Warsaw supporter)

The historical explanation is sometimes related to the history of the club, especially such as Polonia Warsaw, which cultivated national values and symbols in the final phase of the period of Poland's partitions ('Polonia' means Poland in Latin; the club was founded in 1911):

It seems to me that we are right-wing. The history of the club is very strongly connected with the history of Poland and we are even obliged to be more right-wing. I mean, right-wing.... it's such a marked word. It's more a matter of being patriots of flesh and blood; we will always participate in patriotic initiatives.

(Polonia Warsaw supporter)

What could be viewed as paradoxical – in recent years there was a left-wing group operating in the structure of Polonia fandom (more details in the following section).

Many respondents referring to the historical context also mentioned the influence of the skinhead subculture in the 1990s. As we showed in Chapter 5, that decade was a period of anomie and instability.

There's no denying that the skinhead movement used to be strongly connected with fandom, and I think this patriotism is, in a way, a light version of that movement.

(Arka Gdynia supporter)

Many old-school fans go back to the skinhead movement. There are a lot of guys in Legia stadium I remember from the old days when we used to run around in flyer jackets and we had bald heads.

(Legia Warsaw supporter)

Another respondent mentioned the influence of skinhead culture on the development of right-wing and patriotic tendencies among fans:

Back in the 1990s there was the skinhead subculture and the punk subculture; there were *Sieg Heil* shouts, there was national socialism, there was more of that than of patriotism. Don't let's cheat ourselves, that's what it was like. Perhaps except some people who were a bit more interested in history – they were students or just were into it and had a real interest – all others didn't really care much about it. I think that later on many of those people who grew up in the 1990s began to mature and

148 *Ideology on Polish terraces*

look for something like their own national identity; that's why it became more visible. People began to feel that, in a way, it's them who make this country, and that how they shape the awareness of young people, young fans, may bring about in several years' time, in a decade or so, what in fact we have here today. I think that it's the activity of those people in the mid-1990s, the late 1990s, the early 2000s: [such topics as] Lwów [Lviv], the Cursed Soldiers – all that slowly began to emerge then and it fell on fertile ground. You see, apart from some strictly fan things, fan culture didn't really have any great models to follow.

(Motor Lublin supporter)

Interestingly, some informants stated that being a patriot and a person with right-wing sympathies is obvious and natural, and that being a supporter and follower of a local club contributes to being a supporter and follower of the state and nation:

In fact, I've always considered myself a patriot. And being a patriot is kind of obvious when you become a fan. I mean, when you're a fan, the way you treat the club – that the club is the most important for us, that we are with the club, that it's Arka [club] above all – well, it's something like, I mean, we are Poles at the same time, and so I think that just like we support our club so strongly, we pretty much the same way so strongly support our state.

(Arka Gdynia female supporter)

It's hard to say why, but fans are patriots and that's it. I was raised as a patriot; I'm a patriot and so is my friend here. And this patriotism (…) is some kind of a value. Even fans of clubs which hate each other have been able to stand shoulder to shoulder and celebrate an important holiday [together]. And this also proves that fans are people who have their values and are faithful to them.

(Lechia Gdańsk supporter)

Perhaps it's about attachment to traditional values as something stable; like faith, tradition, for example; well, they are kind of typical right-wing values. So perhaps it's simply some kind of a social, psychological type of person that is conditioned in this way.

(Wisła Płock supporter)

As we describe in other chapters, another factor that encouraged the emergence of more politically oriented tendencies was the political situation in Poland. A very important breakthrough, which drove the ideological involvement of supporters, was the 'war' with Donald Tusk's government before and after the Euro 2012 tournament:

The political situation in the country was conducive to that. When Donald Tusk started the war against fans it was obviously something that consolidated people somehow, something that stirred their resistance. It's always like that: when there is a problem – you take a side and you have someone to fight against, you have an enemy that you can identify. And in this case the enemy marginalised the Cursed Soldiers. The whole thing was kind of obvious. But there was also this kind of spirit of the old Solidarity movement – manifestations are banned, so let's organise manifestations; free press is banned, so let's print our own newsletters illegally; that sort of thing.

(Motor Lublin supporter)

The history of the country and football clubs on the one hand, and stories of people's own beliefs on the other, seem to be the most important threads in explaining the right-wing views of Polish fans. The mono-ideological landscape of Polish fandom also draws the focus to those fan narratives that explain the lack of leftist ideas and the absence of left-wing groups.

The absence of the left wing

As mentioned above, the world of Polish football supporters is uniform in terms of ideology. This does not mean, however, that there have never been any left-wing groups in its history. The last organised left-wing fan group operated on the terraces of Polonia Warsaw. This club emerged at the beginning of the twentieth century in the circles of local *intelligentsia* (a specifically Eastern European status class, see Pikora, 2013). This tradition remained an important point of reference for the fans. Throughout the entire post-war era Polonia remained in the shadow of Legia Warsaw, the central military club, which was privileged in a number of ways. Polonia was victimised for alleged resistance to the regime and spent 41 years of this period in the lower echelons of Polish football competition (the last season Polonia played in a higher division was 2012/2013; today, the club competes in the fourth level of the league system). It was perceived as a non-mainstream club with very diverse fandom. Nevertheless, the group of fans associated with anti-fascist and anarchist group called the Black Rebels (black is the traditional colour of the club) was effectively silenced and pushed out of the stands by their radical right-wing adversaries from the same club. A violent clash between the two groups during a Polonia home game in 2013 was the only example of ideological tension of this kind within Polish fandom. The incident erased the last instance of political pluralism in the stands. A Polonia fan comments on the developments at the time as follows:

There were no hostilities between those groups for some time; they had a kind of rough respect to each other. And then, well… there was generational change, the Smolensk totemism [a peculiar 'cult' of the victims of

150 *Ideology on Polish terraces*

> the Smolensk plane crash, including President Lech Kaczyński, ed. auth.], radicalisation caused by I don't know what... And among our guys there was also generational change, there were patriotic sentiments, and apart from that there was also classic struggle for influence in the stadium. And on top of that, the old generation [of Polonia fans] stepped back for a while, and the thing is that they had protected this truce between the two groups.
>
> (Polonia Warsaw supporter)

As it is today, Polonia supporters with left-wing sympathies continue to operate under the name Black Rebels and support various anti-discrimination campaigns. Although the group is very active in social media, it does not appear as an organised formation in the stands.

In the opinion of most supporters, the absence of leftist groups, and, above all, the inability to form them today, results primarily from the historical context. As viewed in the fan world, leftism has too many associations with communism, which is clearly apparent in such firm statements as the following:

> people in other countries don't really know what communism was; they have a wrong idea of what it was. Our parents and us – we know what evil it was and that's why there is no room for the left in the stands. I tell you, I see a guy wearing a Che Guevara T-shirt; I ask him if he knows who he was; he doesn't. 'So why are you wearing it then?', I say. That

Figure 8.1 Lech 100% Anti-Antifa. The banner on Lech Poznań stands exemplifies refusal and condemnation of any groups which may be associated with left wing values.
Source: Przemysław Nosal.

Ideology on Polish terraces 151

whole thing is going to fall through sooner or later. In Italy, they have Livorno; but something like that just can't happen here.

(Lechia Gdańsk supporter)

I think it results from history a bit. (...) In the stadiums you generally met with anti-communist attitudes. (...) So, that anti-communism was also linked with the way people were brought up in their families. I mean, it was obvious that parents who accepted or taught those attitudes to their kids – I mean those anti-communist, anti-system attitudes – taught them about the Katyń Massacre, taught them about all that; and that's where all this comes from. That's what I think.

(Lech Poznań supporter)

Well, I think that it's a historical thing most of all. I mean, it's like, fans kind of draw on the tradition of those earlier periods, when the left as such was clearly connected with communism and, on the other hand, also with the state apparatus. And, as I see it, that's something that very strongly defines all this, and something that can be clearly seen in most Polish clubs; and it's also a sort of continuation of anti-communist tradition.

(Legia Warsaw supporter)

Another supporter mentioned how the experience of life under communism influenced the socialisation of fans in their families, and, more importantly, how it shaped their worldview. In his view, this experience is something that French or Italian apologists for communism are not able to understand:

We live in a peculiar country: France or Italy have never had such experience of communism as we have. We remember what it was like when the communist system [*komuna*] in Poland was over and the transformation began. And I think that in the families of 80 or 90 per cent of fans in Gdańsk, the cradle of the Solidarity movement, there are people who challenged the communists, which means that about 80 or 90 per cent of fans here have this hatred of the communist party, of the communist system, from their families. And that means that they have this right-wing attitude; it may not be very precisely defined or very conscious; it's more like 'get a commie' sort of thing, or this anti-communism thing as such. It's a Polish thing in general, and especially here, in Gdańsk. Italians don't understand that, they are very happy about their Che Guevara banners; the communist party used to get 10 per cent of votes there.

(Lechia Gdańsk supporter)

One more element which explains why referring to contemporary leftist values seems unacceptable in the fan circles was mentioned by a Legia Warsaw fan:

152 *Ideology on Polish terraces*

And another thing is that, as I see it, the opinion about the left tends to be very clear; it's viewed as progressive, blindly progressive, really. And fans are strongly for the traditionalist approach. Of course, there are also extremist groups, but a general understanding is, I mean, it's something that I'd call a more historical approach, in a way. It's about the tradition of the state, about memory of our identity, about being proud of this country. And the left is associated with all those things that are opposite, sort of. I don't know, things like no limits, understood as no limits to identity, a complete mix of cultures, forgetting where you are from, where your roots are; all those things mean completely forgetting about the past.

(Legia Warsaw supporter)

On the other hand, one Widzew Łódź supporter points out a narrative – which is present not only in the liberal media – that associates national symbols with extreme political views. In his opinion, this approach is counterproductive: the rejection of liberal, progressive values may be associated with being 'anti' and lead to embracing right-wing and conservative values. It is worth remembering, however, that, as it is today – also thanks to the narratives promoted by the camp of the ruling Law and Justice party – pro-national attitudes are treated more favourably:

When I put up the national flag on 11 November [Independence Day] or 3 May [Constitution Day, commemorating the Polish Constitution of 1791], I just know that some of my neighbours look at me, well.... And sometimes I'm off to a match wearing a fan scarf, and on top of that I have a doggy that happens to be a bullterrier. (...) It's a sort of a pack: a bald head, a bullterrier and the national flag. (...) But I think it's something that comes from this media terror, that if you say you're a Pole it immediately means you're some sort of a Nazi, right? That you're just... And the more people keep telling you you're evil, just evil and evil all the time, there is this moment when you finally tell them 'just leave me alone for fuck's sake'.

(Widzew Łódź supporter)

According to other studies in this field (Kossakowski et al., 2018), fans in Poland reached for right-wing, conservative symbols – especially in ultras choreographies – in the absence of other symbols of rebellion and resistance. For historical reasons, leftist symbols were hardly possible to implement here, even if their use is quite natural for many groups in Western Europe. As the respondents mention, the left 'has bad connotations'. It is striking that thirty years after the fall of communism as a socio-economic system the memory of it still determines attitudes towards the values that are promoted by contemporary left-wing movements. As the following sections of this chapter show, even the issues that practically did not exist as socio-cultural phenomena in public awareness before 1989 (e.g. refugees from the Middle East, LGBT rights) are subject to resistance and rejection by football supporters owing to what they call anti-communism.

Ideology on Polish terraces 153

Being political outside the party system

Polish fans are primarily characterised by a culture of rebellion and resistance, which is apparent in their opposition against any attempts to control them from outside (see Kossakowski, 2015). There are many reasons for this attitude. First of all, it is a consequence of years of functioning on the edge of the law (which requires 'hiding', strategies to mask one's identity, etc.) and the attendant need to keep 'strangers' as far as possible from the details of the life of the group. There is also the desire to establish own rules and modes of action, and to protect the unlimited freedom of expressing emotions and ideological attitudes. The 'anti' attitude (anti-establishment, anti-mainstream, anti-media, etc.) gained importance in the period of conflict with Donald Tusk's government (see Chapter 6), and it was then that the aversion to institutional politics clearly intensified. Most informants strongly rejected the idea of engaging fandom in official support for political formations:

> We don't get involved in political affairs. Who will be up there ... we don't care. If they don't interfere with us, we don't.... There's surely no way that we do some sort of action and this minister comes over to take pictures to use them in his political campaign.
>
> (GKS Tychy supporter)

> We have different political views, we try to put politics aside in such places as fan projects. Let it be recorded as my personal opinion – this place is completely apolitical, neutral.
>
> (Polonia Warsaw supporter)

> No, I think that the fan environment should be apolitical; in my opinion it must not be mixed up in politics.
>
> (Kielce City Council)

> We should be apolitical. We are citizens, we have the right to vote and to express that voice in the elections but we should stay away from politics because people can use it in an offensive way. It's easy to get pigeonholed, and to lose a lot.
>
> (Miedź Legnica supporter)

One of the respondents, a Legia Warsaw fan, referred to a specific slogan displayed by Legia ultras, which he interpreted as a manifestation of an extreme and uncompromising approach to all 'external factors' that might possibly interfere with the structure of the fan culture:

> Any time there's been some kind of involvement – for example in the case of Legia – in some sort of a political issue, even if it was something that fans supported, at some stage all those politicians, let me put it

154 *Ideology on Polish terraces*

straight, have always been told to go to hell. On all such occasions fans always think that there is something in this slogan that was once displayed in a Legia choreo: 'Ultras – we hate everyone'. Personally, I think that it's quite apt, although perhaps it kind of goes a bit too far, it's negative. But on the other hand, it shows this identity, this idea of, kind of, being a bit of a lone wolf, someone who will always follow their ideals, which of course can be different sometimes. But there is this thing that someone like that will not join anyone, will not be part of a bigger puzzle. We are completely independent. I think that fans in Poland take great care not to get pigeonholed and not to let others take advantage of them. Although I'm pretty sure they sometimes can be taken advantage of without realising it.

(Legia Warsaw supporter)

Keeping distance from institutional politics is a kind of protection against the danger of loss of certain values that fans associate with their own environment:

Researcher: Can this ideological involvement of fans, which is so visible these days, lead to some kind of a political movement?
Respondent: No, it can't.
Researcher: And why not?
Respondent: Because it would be the greatest mistake. I always keep saying in all kinds of meetings that the fan movement must keep its identity. All that we did here in Gdańsk back in the 1980s – I was involved in the fan movement in the period, I was also a member of the Federation of Fighting Youth – we did out of patriotic motivations; it wasn't about politics.

(Lechia Gdańsk supporter)

If freedom, understood very broadly, has been our ideal since the 1970s – sometimes it's been anarchy, but let's call it freedom and … absence of any control whatsoever – it's kind of obvious that we won't constrain ourselves by turning into some sort of a political formation.

(ŁKS Łódź supporter)

Interestingly, some fans admit that although the stadiums are dominated by people with right-wing sympathies, at the same time there is a general agreement that views on political issues should not be the subject of dispute in the stands:

There is this unwritten rule that there are no arguments about political issues in the stands. Although most people have patriotic or right-wing views, we don't argue about such topics.

(Legia Warsaw supporter)

When analysing the fan environment, it should be borne in mind that despite their common political views, for many supporters it is not politics that is the most important thing in the context of sport and football at all. One of them sums this up as follows:

> This environment is mostly right-wing, but it's difficult to say that we all have the same political views. Anyway, a friend of mine nicely captured this by saying that we are divided by everything, but we are united by only one thing – Lech [Poznań].
>
> (Lech Poznań supporter)

The club is the foundation on which fan communities and identities are born. They acquire a political character over time, even if only in a discursive and narrative layer. A lack of involvement in institutionalised politics and reluctance to political parties do not prevent Polish fans from expressing views on moral, historical, social and political issues, which are not only of interest to political parties and the media, but also concern society in general. Consequently, they should be considered a group that, although defending the borders of their environment, nevertheless takes part in the public discussion on such topics. Their ideological positions and the ways in which they express them are described in the following sections.

Dimensions of ideological involvement of Polish fans

Commercialisation of football is a particular process which transforms the domain of sport into a space of entertainment, business and media spectacle (Dixon, 2013). One of the dimensions of this process is the transformation of fans' habits and culture – mostly – from the cultural practice of the traditional working class to more family- and middle-class oriented product. To enable this change, some new legal regulations introduced in many countries address such burning and politically important issues as aggression, physical violence or vandalism (Tsoukala, 2009). But apart from reducing violence, the expected outcome also includes more 'civilised' patterns of behaviour, for example when it comes to stadium language (Flint and Powell, 2014). A commercialised football arena should free from violence, but also free from divisive political commentary. Modern football is supposed to be a sport without any ideas which are not related to the game. For example, in official competitions organised by FIFA or UEFA any content associated with politics is forbidden. Many clubs have been fined for their own fans' political choreographies and slogans. However, probably the most infamous case were the fines imposed on England, Northern Ireland, Scotland and Wales national teams for wearing poppies to commemorate Armistice Day during their World Cup qualifiers in 2016 (Slater, 2017).

As we show throughout this book – political ideas are in fact very common in choreographies and celebrations not only in Poland but across Europe.

156   *Ideology on Polish terraces*

Polish football fans, then, are not unique in terms of political engagement but they seem to be unparalleled when it comes to its content. In the sections above we have provided some explanations concerning the absence of leftist groups and ideas on Polish terraces. In the following parts we would like to focus on core ideas that fans support: they cultivate a traditional, conservative way of thinking and they are faithful to right-wing politics. These aspects can be investigated at many different levels.

Fans and Catholicism: intertwined identities

As we mention in the chapter devoted to fan activism, the club is sometimes regarded as a 'sacred' entity, at least by some fans. Religious metaphors describing relations between the club, the team, the stadium and the fans have been investigated in the context of fans' engagement and identity (see Antonowicz and Wrzesiński, 2009). A 'fervent faith' in the club sometimes leads to 'irrational' behaviours, when fans treat the stadium as a 'cathedral' or when they set a special place at their homes which they decorate in club colours and use it to keep their memorabilia (a 'temple'). Some legendary players (like Maradona), in turn, are elevated to 'divine' status (Kossakowski, 2017a). In Poland, many 'hardcore' fans regard flags and scarves in club colours as 'sacred' symbols. Sometimes this leads to 'holy wars', when fans of rival teams hunt for flags of their opponents. Once seized, those symbols are defiled, most often in front of the humiliated rivals.

In Poland, fans regard club symbols as sacred not only in the context of matches. As most of them cultivate a conservative, traditional set of values, they seriously consider their relations with the Roman Catholic Church and Catholic teaching. This relationship has two different dimensions: one is a private world of faith which is unrelated to the fan world, and the other involves the introduction of religious aspects into the sphere of fandom. The latter is apparent in two major phenomena. First, references to religious values and symbols in fan activity during matches. Second, collective participation in religious practices – devoted football supporters attend an annual Fans' Pilgrimage to the Jasna Góra Monastery in Częstochowa (the most important Roman Catholic sanctuary in Poland), an event which seems unique on the European scale.

References to religious values and symbols are an important element of the performative dimension of fandom in general, and ultras' activity in particular. In search of components of group identity, fans create a common iconography strengthening and popularising the unifying symbols and narratives. The sacralisation of history and religious tropes are clearly visible in most ultras' choreographies (Wasilewski, 2016), which often include overt references to religious elements. For example, a Legia choreography featured the face of Christ accompanied by the inscription 'God save the fanatics'. Wisła Cracow fans, in turn, displayed a choreography with the sentence reading 'God, have mercy on our enemies because we don't have it', placed over the drawing of a

Figure 8.2 Religious motifs are recurring tropes in ultras' choreographies. One of the most famous one claimed: 'God Save the Fanatics' and was displayed by Legia Warsaw fans during the friendly charity game with ADO Den Haag in 2010.
Source: Albert Jankowski, available at Wikimedia Commons (Public Domain)

machete-wielding Wisła hooligan standing among the graves decorated with the scarves of the local rival club. This syncretic and eclectic symbolic sphere combines a variety of tropes, mixing the sacred with the profane. Holy pictures and religious references mix with vulgar and aggressive statements against the enemies, creating a seemingly chaotic and paradoxical bricolage of symbols and meanings, easily recognised and adopted within the fandom. All these aspects can be viewed in terms of 'boundary-setting rituals' (Polletta and Jasper, 2001), which separate potential challengers and strengthen the internal solidarity of fans. As most of their ideas are demonstrated to a broader audience in a performative way, they establish 'symbolic boundaries' (Lamont et al., 2015). Such a ritual 'energizes the participants and attaches them to each other' (Alexander, 2006, p. 29), thus strengthening their collective identity.

One outstanding example of the performative creation of 'symbolic boundaries' is a choreography presented by Legia Warsaw fans in Glasgow during a Europa League qualifier against Rangers at Ibrox Park (August 2019). They unfurled a gigantic banner of Pope John Paul II with the motto 'Be not afraid' (his words referring to welcoming Christ in the life of every believer). One of the leading figures among Legia ultras in the away stand was Artur Boruc, a renowned goalkeeper who had played for Celtic Glasgow

158 *Ideology on Polish terraces*

(Rangers' fierce enemy) in 2005–2010. He is a recognisable figure owing to his provocative behaviour on the pitch: he earned the nickname the Holy Goalie for making a sign of the cross in front of Rangers fans. The attitude and behaviour of Legia fans was certainly provocative, as Rangers supporters are widely known for their Protestant sympathies (Kelly, 2011).

The religiosity of fans is also demonstrated during their annual pilgrimage to the most important Polish sanctuary – Jasna Góra in the city of Częstochowa. At the time of the pilgrimage, hundreds of fans participate in the Holy Mass during which the priests bless their club scarves and flags. Religious faith is intertwined with the 'faith' of fandom, and the supporters of hostile clubs suspend all animosities at this time. The pilgrimage includes various elements. First of all, Holy Mass serves to unite all the fans and other participants. The significance they attach to club symbols can be felt during the service. It would be an overstatement to say that they are perceived as more important than symbols of Catholic faith (the Holy Cross, images of Christ and Our Lady, etc.) but there is a common agreement – among fans, monks and priests alike – that blessing club symbols is something normal and acceptable. No one views it as a kind of blasphemy or profanation of a sacred place and holy rituals. What is more, many members of the local monastic community participating in fans' pilgrimage (Jasna Góra is a monastery of the Order of Saint Paul with a community of monks living there on a permanent basis) seem to support the idea of the event, and many of them stress a 'good spirit' in fan circles. It probably stems from the fact that the pilgrimage is mostly focused on topics that are not related to football as such – there are talks (mostly concerning historical topics), concerts (singers and bands with a patriotic repertoire) and films (religious and historical documentaries, etc.). On the other hand, a very important moment of the pilgrimage is a firework show in the evening. The sight of hundreds of fans firing flares on the ramparts that surround the monastery (which once was also a fortress) could come as a shock for ordinary believers unrelated to the fan world. The light of the flares (the show is always presented after dark) illuminates dozens of club flags and patriotic banners displayed by the assembled fans.

Talking about the pilgrimage, one of the priests summed up its significance as follows:

> This pilgrimage is an ideal, authentic opportunity for religious work in the fan circles, which are not always perfectly what we would like them to be. Those young people can get to know more about Christian values here. For some of them, it's a rare opportunity to visit such an extraordinary sanctuary. Apart from this, they also receive a very good explanation of patriotism. (…) The participants invoke the motto 'God, Honour and Motherland' (*Bóg, Honor, Ojczyzna*), like the generations of our parents and grandparents. And that's the foundation on which we need to build a community, especially on the centenary of Poland's independence, and especially among the young people who aren't particularly involved in the

Ideology on Polish terraces 159

Church and stand by. On this pilgrimage they get a clear message that they need to engage in the social life of the country and the Church. And this does not mean engaging in struggle in the literal sense of the word, but cherishing patriotic and religious traditions from generation to generation.

(Rajfur, 2018)

It seems the pilgrimage is consistent with a broader relationship between faith, nationhood and Polish history. It would be quite difficult to imagine such an event if fans were attached to leftist ideas, for example. Their 'faith' in their clubs goes hand in hand with religious faith and political statements and attitudes of fandom. In this case, it is reasonable to interpret the ideological attitude of fans in the light of the concept of the 'ideological thickening of populism' (Kotwas and Kubik, 2019). This means that populism – understood as an idea dividing social world into 'good people' (right-wing fans, real Poles, etc.) and 'bad elites' (or broadly perceived 'others') – is reinforced with additional ideological aspects, for example religious ideas, nationalism, etc. As we try to demonstrate throughout this book, the world of fans is founded on many antagonisms (they can be regarded multidimensionally – as football-related ones and ones based on political differences). The political antagonism corresponds to populism understood as a vision of a black-and-white social order: there are 'us', fans and 'them', the bad media, the government, mostly viewed as the post-communist elites. This dichotomy is thickened by additional layers of nationalism, patriotism, anti-communism and Christian background.

Anti-establishment and belated anti-communism

Using the metaphor from the paper by William McDougall (2013), a claim can be made that Polish football supporters are exclusively 'right-footed'. This certainly refers to those who are actively engaged in fandom at the level of Polish league competitions. The long-lasting and overwhelming dominance of right-wing ideology in the stands stems from particular historical conditions. As discussed above, to a considerable extent this actually mirrors the situation on the Polish political scene and the attitudes of the younger generation. Harsh conflicts between the supporters of various teams are not in any way connected to political divisions, but the political context may be a reason for malicious reactions from the rival fans. For instance, the radical right-wing fans of Śląsk Wrocław were met with jeers on the terraces nationwide after they lost their colours (flags and scarves) to Sevilla FC fans during the away game in 2013. The main reason was that Sevilla fans strongly associate themselves with left-wing ideology. On the other hand, Polish anti-fascist or anarchist groups which may engage in violent confrontations with ultra-right groups, including those composed of football fans, are generally weak and operate outside of the fandom and terraces. As a consequence of a number of factors described above, it was not possible for Polish fans to adopt leftist symbols as their group symbols of resistance. Patriotic and nationalist symbols

160 *Ideology on Polish terraces*

better conformed to their values and thus came to be used as a means of presentation of their anti-system and anti-communist attitudes.

Anticommunism is an idea that connects fans across Poland. This clearly stems from the history of the country. Although surveillance of Polish football fans and repressions against them were limited in comparison with, for instance, East Germany (Grix, 2012; Wojtaszyn, 2012), expression of political views in the stands was rare during the socialist period (1945–1989), with the notable exception of the terraces of Lechia Gdańsk fans (the name of the club derives from a traditional Polish male name Lech, the mythical founder of the Polanians, the most prominent of the West Slav tribes settled between the Odra and the Vistula, the central and western part of Poland as it is today, see Davies, 2005, p. 52). Gdańsk was the cradle of the Solidarity movement (the first trade union independent from communist authorities, established in 1980) and many of the local anti-communist activists were regulars at Lechia games (Wąsowicz, 2012). As one Lechia fan claims: 'People remember that stadiums were a stronghold of freedom; stadiums and churches'.

The most memorable example of political involvement occurred during the match between Lechia Gdańsk and Juventus Turin in the Cup Winners' Cup, held on 28 September 1983, just weeks after the official suspension of martial law introduced in Poland on 13 December 1981. The match became an anti-communist manifestation. In spite of the efforts of the security police, Lech Wałęsa, the leader of Solidarity and Nobel Peace Prize winner (the decision was announced just a week later), sneaked into the stadium (Nawrocki, 2012). Although the significance of Lechia for the anti-communist movement before 1989 should not be downplayed, this kind of involvement was not a frequent phenomenon among fans in the period. In most of the cities it was rather hooligan subculture formed by young members of pauperised working class that dominated the terraces in the late 1980s and in the 1990s. Anti-leftist and anti-communist sentiments (which in the case of Poland seem fully intertwined) emerged in parallel. This could be explained by the ideological influences of the older generation of fans who really (like in Gdańsk) or allegedly, were involved in anti-communist opposition.

It should be mentioned that today most ultras groups in Poland are actively involved in performing anti-communist content, and anti-communist slogans are common in Polish stadiums. One of the most popular are 'Red is Bad' and 'Good Night Left Side', accompanied by the crossed-out hammer and sickle. Such performances tend to the most frequent around 13 December, the anniversary of the introduction of martial law in Poland in 1981. For example, in December 2012, Lechia ultras presented a giant crowd flag with the image of General Wojciech Jaruzelski (who was responsible for the decision taken in 1981) burning in the fires of hell (with the devil pointing a trident at him) and an inscription reading: 'You sold the nation and hell will take you' [*Za naród sprzedany, piekło cię pochłonie*].

Even though the promotion of communist ideology is formally banned and there is no single political party referring to communism in Poland, it still remains an umbrella term present in stadium choreographies. Former members of the communist party are frequently mentioned on the banners, as are journalists working for the media that are critical towards right-wing ideology. In one of the choreographies displayed by Lechia Gdańsk fans, former prominent communist officials were shown as effigies hanged on the trees. One of the figures portrayed Adam Michnik, one of the leaders of anti-communist opposition, who had spent a few years in communist prisons and was under surveillance of the communist secret police from 1965 until the collapse of the system. Michnik currently is the editor-in-chief of the *Gazeta Wyborcza* [The Electoral Newspaper], the leading Polish broadsheet daily, which is a proverbial enemy for right-wing fans as it represents the liberal-leftist establishment (Sandecki, 2013). The Lechia ultras' performance was highly criticised in the media for using means of expression utterly unacceptable in democratic discourse and for inciting to violence. But in the eyes of fans, any values associated with the left are criticised and ridiculed by making references to the tyranny of political correctness.

Anti-communist slogans and banners can be regarded as a manifestation of being 'anti-system' or 'anti-establishment' – the 'anti' attitude seems to be one of the main features of the fan community. Their 'anti-communism' stems from historical background even if its contemporary implementation could be regarded as inadequate or old-fashioned. But it is crucial as it seems to be an important 'forerunner' of their 'anti' attitude in general. Being 'anti-system' (anti-establishment, anti-mainstream) also brought about a particular structure and a particular set of behaviours typical of fans. Ever since their early days as structured entities in the 1970s, fan circles have been marked by a violent attitude, very often on the edge of the law. This naturally stimulated their struggle against the authorities: law enforcement services, the government and so on – the 'system' in general. But this 'natural' scheme has been reinforced by some changes occurring in the new century. As we have mentioned in previous chapters (see Chapter 6, for example), the political agenda of 'war against fans' during the preparations for the Euro 2012 finals had a significant impact on 'anti-establishment' tendencies. Apart from banners featuring slogans directly targeting the government, some more general statements were presented as well.

One of them was a large-scale choreography performed by Śląsk Wrocław ultras. The giant banner featured a boxing match scene: the victorious fighter climbs the ropes raising his arms in a gesture of triumph; the tattoo on his back reads 'Great Śląsk' (*Wielki Śląsk*, the name of Śląsk Wrocław supporters' association); his knocked-out opponent wears a suit and tie. The caption below read 'Politics will not defeat a fanatic' [*Polityka nie pokona fanatyka*]. The performance was presented in 2013, at the time when the Civic Platform was in power. The same year saw the release of a documentary entitled 'The Rebellion of the Stadiums' [*Bunt stadionów*]. The film presents a broad range of actions undertaken by fans in the course of their struggle against the government.

162   *Ideology on Polish terraces*

At that time, being 'anti' also meant being against the mainstream media which supported the government and were critical about fans. The two 'greatest enemies' were the *Gazeta Wyborcza* daily and the TVN broadcasting company. Legia ultras presented a large card stunt [*kartoniada*] featuring the slogan 'Bullshit' [*Gówno prawda*], styled to resemble the *Gazeta Wyborcza* logo. In another choreography (Ruch Radzionków ultras), the crossed-out logos of the PZPN (Polish Football Associations), the police and the TVN were accompanied by the caption 'Your propaganda is as strong as it was under communism, but the truth is on the side of this stand right here' [*Wasza propaganda silna jak za komuny, ale prawda stoi po stronie tej trybuny*]. Other choreographies were radically anti-system: 'Everyone is shouting out loud here: fuck the system! No one will destroy fanaticism' [*Krzyczymy głośno tutaj wszyscy: jebać system! Fanatyzmu nikt nie zniszczy*, Polonia Bytom].

As in the case of any cultural-social dimension, fans' political sensitivity and 'anti' attitude keep changing. As it is today, fans do not present anti-government content as the Law and Justice party and its government tend to avoid a conflict with them. Additionally, in terms of moral values, both sides seem to support a similar set of principles (however, owing to their own particular style, fans present them in a more radical way). Being 'anti' has changed also due to influences not directly related to the government. Recently, fans have expressed some resistant ideas against variously defined 'Others': refugees on the one hand, and LGBT movements on the other. These examples are investigated in the following sections.

Re-emergence of nationalism and patriotism

In the early 2000s fans were already presenting ideologically or politically themed choreographies, mainly anti-communist or celebrating the anniversaries of historical events, including the theme of Polish military victories and atrocities suffered during the Second World War. Special attention has always been paid to the Warsaw Uprising of 1944, an attempt of the Polish underground Home Army to liberate the capital from the German occupation. The Uprising failed after 63 days, causing the death of at least 15,000 soldiers and between 150,000 and 170,000 civilians, who were mass murdered by the German Army (the number of victims is difficult to estimate), as well as a complete destruction of the city. The Red Army marching from the east slowed down its offensive in the summer of 1944, and the fighters received little or no support from the outside, neither from the Soviets nor from the Western allies (Davies, 2003). The event has been very frequently commemorated by Polish football fans, not only in the capital city.

The performance prepared by Legia Warsaw ultras in August 2017 stirred a considerable controversy. During a Champions League qualifier they presented the text (in English) reading '1944: During the Warsaw Uprising Germans killed 160,000 people. Thousands of them were children', accompanied by the image of a Nazi soldier holding a gun to a child's head. It came as the

Ideology on Polish terraces 163

latest episode in a long series of themed choreographies. Fans of Legia are known for their Warsaw Uprising celebrations, in which they cooperate with club management – during a game played around 1 August (the anniversary of the event), Legia hosts some surviving heroes in the VIP section and the Polish national anthem is played.

The repertoire of symbols adopted by fans was quickly commercialised. This can be evidenced by the emergence of new brands of 'patriotic' clothing and ultras gear (e.g. Red is Bad, Semper Patria, Surge Polonia). First popular among radical football fans, they became part of the mainstream and are greatly successful among non-football related audience. The Red is Bad company received huge publicity when Andrzej Duda, President of Poland, was photographed wearing clothes with its trademark during, paradoxically, an official visit to the Republic of China. As of August 2018, the products of this company are sold in official shops in Polish historical museums (Prze-ciwnicy UE współpracują, 2018). This visual manifestation of banal nation-alism, strengthened by the official memory policy of the current Polish government, is an example of the synergy between the grass-roots resurgence of pro-nationalist tendencies within the football fandom and the official poli-cies of the state.

Although aesthetically spectacular, in many respects fans' ideologies are based on banal patriotism or banal anti-communism, which manifest them-selves almost exclusively in the adoption of 'simple' symbols of difference and can be related to the phenomenon of 'shallow ideologization which in many cases goes no deeper than the display of symbols and paraphernalia' (Spaaij and Viñas, 2013, p. 105). In this case, wearing a club/patriotic T-shirt or waving a club flag does not need to be a manifestation of a profound belief system, but can refer to a sheer need for belonging and identification, particularly impor-tant for young males in the contemporary era, when many traditional points of reference and visions of identity are being contested. As we show in the next section, especially the Cursed Soldiers are regarded in terms of role models. This strengthens the sense of community and collective identity even if it is only superficial and has neo-tribal characteristics (Maffesoli, 1996).

Interestingly, one of the fans mentions what he calls 'competition about who is more patriotic' among fan groups today:

> Being a fan is a tribal thing, it has typical tribal attributes. I think that the pendulum has swung a bit too far; I mean this competition about choreographies and the same slogans. We've recently even joked that it's also competition about who is more patriotic. Luckily this patriotism isn't very confrontational – I mean those choreographies. We had a laugh with some friends about how far it's going to get – commemorating more and more of those heroic generations of Poles. We joked that someone is soon going to rediscover the Battle of Cecora [1620], that the whole thing is getting deeper and deeper into the past. First it was the Solidarity movement [1980s], then the Second World War, and at this stage – when

164 *Ideology on Polish terraces*

it comes to this historical memory – we are unfortunately getting to the November Uprising [1830].

(Polonia Warsaw supporter)

Although this 'competition' should be regarded as a metaphor, it is certain that patriotic themes flourished rapidly, especially in the first half of the 2010s. However, some political content was visible already in the 2000s, when it was mostly related to the anti-communist theme. For example, at the turn of the century some ultras groups displayed crossed-out images of Che Guevara or the hammer and sickle; the slogan 'Good night left side' has also been common ever since. It is important to note that large-size choreographies appeared in Polish stadiums together with first ultras groups and were first displayed in the early 2000s (with the exception of a Legia group called *Cyberf@ni* (Cyberf@ns), established in 1999). In the 1990s, political content was limited to small flags with the Celtic cross (as it was a period of influence of right-wing skinheads, see Chapter 5). One of the respondents confirms that the 'patriotic trend' in the fan circles gained momentum at the turn of the 2010s:

Well, around 2007 or 2008, if someone was into patriotism, into all that patriotic sort of stuff, people looked at him like an alien, like a crank, right? And then, just a year or two later, sometime around 2010, everyone was on about it, right? And so there was this boom around that time. I'd say that fans were apolitical back around 2004; really, most of them. They were into business, parties, working out, but surely not into patriotism. And today it's all about patriotism, right?

(Legia Warsaw supporter)

Many respondents stress the connection between being a fan of the local club and being a local and national patriot. The flourishing of patriotic choreographies has gone hand in hand with participation in some patriotic initiatives, such as celebrations of important national anniversaries (e.g. the annual Independence March described below). In this regard, the majority of fans are consistent – fans should take part:

We have participated and we will participate as fans in the celebration. It's also politics. When we go, we go as a group – fans.

(Lech Poznań supporter)

The majority of interlocutors noted the importance of the concept 'patriotism':

In recent years, fans have started to approach patriotic issues differently. They stress them quite a lot. (…) In Poznań, fans are focused on pro-national patriotism.

(Poznań journalist)

Ideology on Polish terraces 165

Many motifs related to patriotism are incorporated into match choreographies across Poland. Sometimes this comes in reaction to current affairs or current events, like the death of President Lech Kaczyński in a plane crash in 2010, when ultras from many clubs prepared special choreographies to commemorate the victims of the tragedy. For example, Lech Poznań fans presented a giant crowd-flag obituary: 'R.I.P Smoleńsk 10.04.2010'; there was also a large card stunt featuring the Polish national flag, and the accompanying caption (a quotation from Pope John Paul II) read: 'Let's leave aside words, let there remain just great silence' [*Oszczędźmy słów, niech pozostanie wielkie milczenie*].

The repertoire of symbols and motifs differs depending not only on the circumstances and the occasion, but also on the local context. In terms of commemorative practices (even if they are often limited to changing the graphics of Facebook profiles), it is the Warsaw Uprising that seems to be the most widely celebrated; occasional choreographies are displayed not only by Legia Warsaw ultras. In general terms, the engagement of fans certainly depends on how they perceive their role beyond their 'ordinary' duties (supporting the team, etc.), what kind of involvement they consider important and what resources they have at their disposal. In many cities they can employ the resources they typically use for their fandom activity. In some of them they also have their local centres – facilities operating thanks to participation in the programme called 'Supporters United' [*Kibice Razem*], aiming to develop cooperation between football authorities, the Ministry of Sport and Tourism, local councils and local fan circles. The inspiration for launching the programme came from the initiative of fan projects in Germany. As it is today, there are 17 local Supporters United centres in Poland. Each centre has its own premises, two employees with background in local fan circles, and financial resources from the Ministry and local councils (for more details see Kossakowski, 2017b; 2019).

The centre in Kielce, for example, puts a strong stress on historical education, e.g. organising meetings with war veterans:

> I think we should organise such actions as much as possible. (…) [Organise] talks with historians. We work with such organisations as the patriotic 'Third Way'. They want to organise history tutorials. We are open to this, of course. This can also mean watching historical films.
>
> (Korona Kielce supporter)

The Third Way (*Trzecia Droga*) is an organisation which admits to nationalist as well as anti-globalist, anti-system ideas.

In other cities the prevailing view is that the club and its fans play an important role in shaping local patriotism, supporting local communities and local identity, and commemorating important events from the history of the region. Lech Poznań supporters contribute to celebrating the anniversary of the Wielkopolska Uprising:

166 *Ideology on Polish terraces*

Fans have engaged in commemorating the Wielkopolska Uprising for years. Restoring memory and creating a bond of local patriotism is certainly a benefit for the city.

(Poznań City Council)

Fans can express local pride. (…) Poznań citizens are not only attached to the city, they just love it. Fans not only think the same, but they are also able to articulate it publicly.

(Poznań journalist)

Activities undertaken by Lech Poznań fans include not only occasional choreographies and participation in official anniversaries of the Uprising: their supporters' association organises a collection of funds for the renovation of graves of the insurgents, which started as a small initiative:

In 2009 we started an action aiming to restore the memory of the Wielkopolska insurgents. It all started from selling T-shirts and buying commemorative candles with the profits. It turned out that the action grew so much that the following year we started to collect funds for the renovation of their graves, not just for the candles. (…) We decided: alright, we'll renovate as many graves as we can.

(Lech Poznań supporter)

The first collection raised 8,000 złotys (about 2,000 euros); as more people became engaged in the following years, the amount kept growing: in 2017 they collected almost 200,000 złotys (about 50,000 euros).

For many fans, soldiers and insurgents are role models so restoring their memory (and graves, which are often neglected) seems obvious.

On 27 December each year [the anniversary of the Wielkopolska Uprising] we present a commemorative choreography using flairs. Thanks to this spectacular show, it suddenly turned out that people started talking about how important the uprising really was. We succeeded in restoring the memory of the Wielkopolska Uprising. We turned to our sponsors for funds to organise a historical re-enactment event.

(Lech Poznań supporter)

Engagement in commemorating local heroes seems to be related to being a fan of the local team. When asked about this, one respondent interpreted being a fan along with such notions as tradition, local identity and history:

I think that to be a fan means … first and foremost to be … a Poznań person, a Wielkopolska person, a person who has a stronger [local] identity that an average citizen; a person who is more devoted to tradition.…

And somewhere there on the way there is football, but it isn't the most important in all that. The most important thing is definitely to fulfil the need to belong. And probably this need underlies our historical consciousness as well. The tradition of the Wielkopolska Uprising – that's the central point, I think.

(Lech Poznań supporter)

Supporting the local team is associated with local patriotism by definition:

I think that we should be local patriots. (...) I love Zabrze and I love Silesia. (...) I can't imagine supporting my team if I'm not a local patriot. Well, you know, let's say I support Poland today, and Mexico tomorrow. It's as if I didn't care, isn't it?

(Zabrze City Council)

Local identity is part of fan identity not only in the case of Poland. Many studies (see Castillo, 2007; Kossakowski, 2013; Russell, 2016) show connections between fandom and locality in different countries and explore fans' topophilia in a broader sense (their emotional attachment to the stadium, but also to such places like local pubs, streets, districts and cities as well). Polish fans refer to their local identity in many different ways, for example by forming local district fan clubs (which display small-size flags in club colours bearing the name of the district) or painting graffiti on walls. It should be mentioned, however, that national or local identity demonstrated by Polish fans goes hand by hand with – sometimes very radical – antagonistic attitude towards national or local identity of others. On the one hand, Lech Poznań fans organise a successful collection for the renovation of graves of the Wielkopolska insurgents. On the other, following a Europa League qualifier in Vilnius (where some cars of Lech fans were vandalised by the rivals) they displayed an extremely controversial anti-Lithuanian banner during the second leg in Poznań: 'Lithuanian peasant, kneel down before your Polish master' [*Litewski chamie, klęknij przed polskim panem*]; a few members of the Lech ultras crew were charged and convicted of insulting members of another nation.

Local identity is also important when it comes to the biggest national event referring to history: the annual Independence March, celebrating Poland's independence in 1918. On 11 November thousands of Poles march on the streets of Warsaw. Football fans are also there and they make their presence very visible. Although the march is a national event, they take part as representatives of their local clubs: they display both the national symbols and club paraphernalia, as being a supporter of a local club does not interfere with the national spirit – pride in national symbols is an extension of pride in club identity. Club and national symbols overlap and make up a cohesive system of symbols, which makes it possible even for fans of hostile clubs to walk shoulder to shoulder in the march. According to an account of a Legia fan, their ordinary animosities are suspended:

168 *Ideology on Polish terraces*

> I'll never forget what it was like when we went out of the Źródełko [Legia fans' local pub]. We are marching as Legia fans. I look around and I can see Lech Poznań in balaclavas next to us. In a moment we are joined by Lechia Gdańsk and Wisła Cracow with their faces covered. (…) We were there all together marching shoulder to shoulder. There was no aggression even though those were not the most peaceful crews of the fan crowd. (…) We have to remember that for Lech we are the enemy number one. Still, they stood there in their balaclavas next to us and no one even thought of attacking the others. It was a really big thing.
>
> (Marsz Niepodległości, 2011, p. 5)

For many years of their participation in the march, suspending their animosities served two principal goals. Officially, most of them gathered to celebrate the most important national holiday. On the other hand, however, for many fans, particularly those most militant, the event was a perfect opportunity for a battle with the police. Especially under Donald Tusk's government, most marches were accompanied by street riots, which usually involved confrontations between allied hooligans of various clubs on one side, and uniformed services on the other. For some fans, participation in the march was an expression of their anti-system attitude with all violent consequences of the fact:

> We live in the times when there isn't much action in the stadiums at all. So it doesn't come as a surprise to any clever person that if there is this once in a year opportunity for fan hordes to frolic a bit like in the old times – and at the same time get their own back on the hated authorities for all the repressions, the clampdown and invigilation – then. (…) It's easy to be anonymous in a crowd of thousands of people after dark, and the will to fight is all the greater in the atmosphere of patriotic and anti-system elation.
>
> (Nadchodzi, nadchodzi, Marsz Niepodległości!, 2014, p. 6)

However, no political formation of any kind has emerged as a result of this mobilisation. This confirms our observations stressed in previous chapters, that despite unprecedented opportunities in terms of mobilisation of human resources the fan environment is not able to transform into any organised political entity. It seems that, for most rioters, clashes with the police have been – most of all – an occasion for violent and aggressive performance of force. Sometimes, there have also been confrontations with other actors, as some left-wing and anarchist groups organised counter-demonstrations.

The participation of fans in the Independence March is consistent with the performative form of their ideological engagement, which could be referred to as 'performative banal nationalism' (to develop Benedict Anderson's concept, see Anderson, 1991). It may be only 'banal' (when people put hats with national symbols on their heads or paint their faces in national colours) but in the case of more engaged fans it is often quite sophisticated in terms of aesthetic form: their choreographies are often an outstanding spectacle that ordinary 'banal nationalists' would never prepare. According to quantitative data presented above, most fans have right-wing, nationalist attitudes, which means that their performances actually stem from their principles. However, all their nationalist and patriotic shows begin and end at the performative level – they have never entailed further steps in terms of setting up a political formation (which does not mean that they will not lead in this direction in the future).

The performative nature of fans' participation in the march goes hand in hand with the growth of the symbolic meaning of the event in recent years. As Marta Kotwas and Jan Kubik observe: 'the organizers of the March have been gradually strengthening the symbolic link between a radically nationalistic vision of Polishness and a traditionalist version of Catholicism' (2019, p. 461). This perfectly exemplifies the 'ideological thickening of populism', a concept that Kotwas and Kubik introduce in their article. As we show in previous sections, this also seems to reflect a general ideological attitude of Polish fans. Football identity, nationalist ideas and Christian beliefs march together, symbolically united.

Cursed Soldiers: in search of role models

In recent years, an increasing number of historical choreographies have been devoted to restoring the memory of the so-called Cursed Soldiers (*Żołnierze Wyklęci*), members of military formations fighting against both Nazi Germany and, later, against the communist regime in Poland. The term covers guerrilla forces operating towards the end of the Second World War, some of which continued into the years of communist Poland. Their stance was characterised by radical anti-communism, and they engaged in military struggle against various formations and institutions of the communist regime. Rafał Wnuk (2016), a historian specialising in the post-war resistance movement, argues that the term was coined in the 1990s by the Polish radical right with a view to creating a new myth. The anti-communist discourse of fight against the oppressors whatever the circumstances, of bravery, honour and loyalty to brothers in arms inspired football fans – they pledged their allegiance to the Cursed Soldiers (it is worth adding, however, that fans glorify them without any doubts or reservations; they do not take into consideration that some of them admitted to anti-Ukrainian and anti-Jewish pogroms):

> My godson is with ultras and I've learned a lot from him about the 'cursed soldiers'. No one has ever taught me about it at school. And they [fans] have this positive energy, they come back home and tell you about this. (...) For fans, a hero is always someone associated with their environment, the terraces, their club, and they support them. But they also look for new heroes and find those who were never mentioned before.
>
> (Lech Poznań supporter)

170 *Ideology on Polish terraces*

Figure 8.3 Mural with the inscription: "All hail the memory of Cursed Soldiers". alongside the emblem of ŁKS Łódź football club.
Source: Wojciech Woźniak

Cursed Soldiers were excluded from official narratives and neither did they feature in fans' choreographies in the communist period (Legia Warsaw supporter: 'It seems to me that it's also a matter of fight against communism and this topic has been forgotten as no one mentioned those soldiers at all'). This is why some performances actually pointed out education as the key to restoring their memory (e.g. a banner displayed by Śląsk Wrocław fans stated: 'Listen children, are you taught who Cursed Soldiers were?'). Before the Cursed Soldiers entered the official pantheon of national heroes, they had become a theme of match choreographies (the first one was presented by Śląsk Wrocław ultras in 2011, the year of introduction of the National Day of Commemoration of Cursed Soldiers). Fans participated in commemorative ceremonies, visited cemeteries, met with the surviving members of the 'cursed' guerrilla forces and wore clothes with symbols relating to them. This coincided with the growth of banal patriotism and banal anti-communism in the stands, where every opponent was easily labelled as a successor of communism (including not only the Polish government, but also the European Union and UEFA). A member of the fan movement who documents political engagement of football fandom explains the phenomenon of reverence to the Cursed Soldiers among the fans as follows:

> [They] are perceived as ideal role models, romantic and tough-minded fighters for a lost cause who were fighting in the name of honour, principles and their oath of allegiance. In addition, they fought against communists

Ideology on Polish terraces 171

and – according to fans – Polish elites who try to destroy fandom descend from the communist circles. Therefore, fans feel they are not only successors, but also continuators of the Cursed Soldiers' struggle.

(Jantych, 2016, p. 137)

The idea of searching for role models was mentioned by our respondents. This is how one of them explained the significance of Cursed Soldiers:

> As I see it, that was a moment of a kind of ideological chaos; there was no distinct figure, I'd say, no distinct ideology that fans would find appealing. And such an ideology has to fulfil some criteria; the first thing is that it has to be distinct, it has to appeal to steadfast people, people who go against the current of the surrounding reality. And thanks to Professor Janusz Kurtyka, the head of the Institute of National Remembrance, by the way, and thanks to the engagement of President Lech Kaczyński, the National Day of Commemoration of Cursed Soldiers was introduced in 2011. And from then on fans' energy went in a positive direction, in fact. And I think that such values like steadfastness, refusal to make compromises, make it possible for fans to identify with Cursed Soldiers.
>
> (Lechia Gdańsk supporter)

A Widzew Łódź fan explained that the observed turn to Polish war heroes stems both from the need of a point of reference and from hostile discourse on fans:

> I remember one meeting with war veterans; they were two old fellas. I know the kind of stories they told from my family home. (…) My family is from Warsaw, and so it's the Home Army and all that, you know. And when they were talking I kept looking at all those young guys (…) they sat there, they looked at those soldiers … and they sat there all the time … they sat there and just kept listening; they showed them respect; they helped them to stand, they helped them with their cup of tea, that kind of thing. You know, when this guy tells you that they made him stand in cold water for the whole day and night; holy shit, man, that's something. (…) And [when he tells you] that he put up a Polish flag and the secret police got him, and they beat him, and he got sent to the mines. And those young guys sit there, they listen to all that and then they say 'Fuck, man, so what's that all about?' You see, the thing is they write in the papers that those people are Polish anti-Semites, you know, fascists, Nazis and all that … and this guy right here tells you that he knows for a fact that the officer [in charge of his case] was a Jew. Well, you know … everyone has this need, sort of, to search for some kind of a point of reference, something that, I don't know, something that would be pure, that would be good, you know. I mean, when everyone tells you that you're a fucking hooligan, that you're a thug and so on, at some point

172 *Ideology on Polish terraces*

either you tell them to piss off, or you want to find something that will make you better after all, right?

(Widzew Łódź supporter)

Such comments confirm that fans search for their role models only on the right side of the political spectrum. Glorification of war heroes, people who sacrificed their lives for their country, comes as a result at least two factors. Firstly, the structure and cultural-moral tissue of fandom culture. Most fan groups view the structure of their world in terms of guerrilla units and strongly emphasise being ready to fight and inflict violence – features saturated with masculinity based on physical stamina. This is reinforced by years of developing only rightist attitudes in the fan circles. Combined, these traits have a significant impact on the paths of inspiration. Any 'dark sides' of role models are simply ignored: they do not exist in fan performances or discourse. The second factor, in turn, is related to external imperatives: promotion and commemoration of heroes of Polish history by the Law and Justice government. The memory politics of this party is based on the principle of presentation of Polish history without any 'dark sides'.

As one means to this end, the government relies on the Institute of National Remembrance [*Instytut Pamięci Narodowej*, IPN], established in 1999 with the support of all major political parties except the post-communist SLD. IPN is one of the key institutions in Poland, responsible for the design and implementation of memory policy on both national and local level. Apart from conducting historical research, it also has public prosecution powers (in the cases of crimes against the Polish nation). The Institute is generously funded from the state budget and thus can offer good working conditions for its staff. Nevertheless, the politicisation of IPN increased in pace and intensity following the elections of 2015, when it was taken over by more ardent supporters of the victorious party. Increasing national pride among Poles and informing about Polish martyrdom are now openly declared aims of the Institute.

In the search of the Other

The fact that fans are highly focused on national, patriotic and local contexts has some consequences as regards relations with actors who do not come under categories of 'familiarity'. These consequences are even greater in view of the patterns of fan behaviours and their antagonistic orientation: 'others' are not only 'not welcome' but they are also treated with extreme language or pictured as a threat.

Contrary to other national contexts, none of the Polish fan groups opts for more openness and multiculturalism. The attempts to 'kick racism out of the stadiums' undertaken by anti-racist watchdogs along with pan-European organisations like UEFA or FARE are perceived by Polish fans (but also by some Polish Football Association officials) as part of the leftist cultural agenda and therefore neglected even by those fans who do not engage in

Ideology on Polish terraces 173

chauvinist of xenophobic behaviours (racist incidents in Polish stadiums have been reported to UEFA by a Warsaw-based organisation called Never Again, allegedly associated with leftist and anarchist movements). This does not mean that racism is an inherent element of their ideology. Partly because of the strict policies of the national football association, the instances of racist chants or choreographies are rather rare (significantly less prevalent than in the case of the Russian league, see Arnold and Veth, 2018). Serious racist incidents occurred in the 1990s and the early 2000s (throwing bananas at black players, monkey chants); following the media pressure and legal regulations, as well as the 'civilising' process of fandom, such attitudes seem to have significantly decreased.

As it is today, however, the fear of terrorism, allegedly stemming from the acceptance of refugees from the Middle East, has been successfully fuelled by right-wing parties since the election campaign of 2015. Poland's refusal to accept any refugees and the fear-mongering of the current government have led not only to serious tensions with the European Commission and other EU member states, but also to a significant change in attitudes as measured by public opinion polls, which show a general trend of growing chauvinism and fear of refugees (nearly 60 per cent of the Polish population are reluctant to accept refugees in the country, see Leszkowicz-Baczyński, 2018). In this respect, the terraces follow the social sentiments. There are no 'Refugees welcome' banners in the stands, and anti-refugee chants can be heard during some of the games. In this context, it is crucial to remind that contemporary Polish society lacks intercultural experience. For instance, the issue of migrants' children on the national team, topical in most European countries, has been absent in sports and political debates in Poland.

In our view, the anti-establishment attitude of fans to some extent stems from the widespread belief that the political and economic elites are successors of the compromised and despised circles of communist elite. A considerable number of anti-establishment actions are oriented towards identifying a well-described and conceptualised enemy which could serve as an imagined threat. Those actions are often 'against' (or 'anti') someone (a certain group), e.g. against Jews, Muslims or refugees on the one hand, and LGBT people on the other. Since the beginning of the European refugee crisis Polish political debate has been dominated by 'strong and forceful anti-immigrant rhetoric of discrimination or even outright hate toward migrants and, in particular, asylum seekers arriving in Europe' (Krzyżanowski, 2018, p. 76). This could be perceived as a political strategy undertaken by the Law and Justice party, one that helped to pave the way to its victory in 2015 elections. Although Polish fans officially declare they are anti-elitist and anti-establishment, in this respect their resentment is very much in line with the official line of the ruling political elite.

The most vivid example is the issue of refugees. As the Polish government refused to accept them during the migrant crisis, the number of refugees from Muslim countries in Poland is very low. Nevertheless, many fans at the stadiums use slogans suggesting that refugees pose an imminent threat to the Polish majority. Lech Poznań fans chanted 'All Poland, sing with us / Let's

174 *Ideology on Polish terraces*

fuck out the refugees' and displayed a banner saying: 'For us it's simple and clear / We don't want refugees here'. Fans of Lech boycotted the Europa League match against Belenenses Lisbon in protest against UEFA's decision to donate one euro from each ticket sold to the cause of refugees. Lechia Gdańsk ultras, in turn, displayed a banner reading 'Welcome to hell, stray sheep', and many fans groups presented the slogan 'Europe, Wake Up!'. Although these banners and chants are the sole 'material' sign of the refugee presence in Poland, they give people the impression that they are here and have criminal intents. Under the circumstances, the fans 'have to' react.

The issue of refugees also serves to stress the nationalist idea of exclusively Polish character of the country. For example, fans of Piast Żmigród presented a choreography featuring the motto 'Poland for Poles', accompanied by crossed-out images of a mosque, a figure of a man resembling a Muslim believer, the crescent and star (a symbol of Islam) and the abbreviation ISIS. The central part of the banner featured Poland's coat of arms, the Celtic cross and the crest of the club. The need of defence against Islam was also expressed by Śląsk Wrocław ultras, who displayed a large choreography featuring the image of a knight in armour (with the logo of Śląsk on his shield) 'defending' the European continent against the Muslim invasion from the sea. The image was accompanied by a caption reading: 'When the Islamic plague is flooding Europe, let's stand in defence of Christianity'. As mentioned above, the attitude of fans is a case of 'ideological thickening': anti-refugee and anti-Muslim expressions are based on a mix of nationalism, militant spirit, religious background, ethnocentrism and antagonism. This narrative would not be as attractive for fans if it did not directly refer to the long-established *topos* of Poland as the *antemurale christianitatis*, the bulwark of Christendom in Europe (Zubrzycki, 2011).

As mentioned above, the issue of refugees is not the only one. A similar mechanism operates in the case of anti-Jewish attitudes of the fans. The figure of a 'Jew' is used as the enemy, 'Other', particularly in the city of Łódź, where the fans of both local clubs (ŁKS and Widzew) allege that their rivals are 'Jews', while they all are labelled this way by fans from other cities. A similar strategy is implemented to insult the local rivals in Cracow (Wisła vs Cracovia). In the environment of football fans, the figure of a 'Jew' should not be interpreted as an indicator of anti-Semitism targeted against the ethnic group but as a historically developed way of expressing contempt (Burski, 2015). Polish fans have created their own 'Other' in order to construct strong boundaries of their fan communities and enhance the 'We' identity. Created by some rightist fans, their self-made enemy is the alarm which stimulates the rightist activities of the others. It facilitates gathering, ensures the ideological cohesion of the group and enhances collective reactions of its members.

Conservative attitudes to gender roles and sexual identity

The ideological dimensions of Polish fandom investigated above reveal a particular image: patriotic/nationalist attitudes are permeated with religious

Ideology on Polish terraces 175

values, reluctance to acknowledge the Other, references to militant heroes and historical events, and they are complemented by some moral values concerning gender roles and sexual identity. This conservative 'package' brings us to consider the latter issue and the issue of the status of women in fandom culture. The existing 'analyses provide evidence that female supporters are either marginalised (not being counted as regular fans), patronised or instrumentalised by their male peers. These strategies are visible both in language and in the social contexts in which women on the stands are described' (Antonowicz et al., 2018, p. 1). Women are accepted in the ultras circles as long as they follow the rules of this environment, which are set by males. In their study, Antonowicz et al. demonstrate that male ultras do not perceive female members of the fan world as 'real fans'. Even when female fans try to pursue typical traditional patterns of fan craft (e.g. violently react to rival fans), their efforts are belittled or considered ridiculous. Female fans are not allowed to take part in hooligan fights (which can be understood as today they are an exclusive domain of men training martial arts), but sometimes they are also banned from trips to away matches.

Although there are no female fans in the top echelons of the fan world (even though some of them are active both in ultras groups and supporters' associations), this does not mean that they are not respected by male fans – in fact, they are. This stems from the traditional attitude, according to which a man should respect and protect women. In this approach, women are considered naturally weaker and inclined to be engaged in a different set of actions. This is confirmed by remarks from a female fan of Arka Gdynia:

> Well, women work with kids here. For some time we've been running this place for children in the stands; we take care of kids. We also prepare school kits, Christmas gifts, we organise children's tournaments. In general, we look after kids.

Some respondents stress that a ban on women's travel to away matches with hated rivals stems from safety considerations: men do not want to put women at risk. This indicates a traditional point of view, according to which a man is responsible for women's safety and makes a decision for them. A female fan confirms that the world of the most engaged fans is a male world:

> Well, it's always been… a thing for guys, yes. Away trips are for guys. Well, it's because, I don't know, because a girl can't defend club colours, for example, right? There are away trips that are only for guys. Because… because everyone knows that there are some rules here.
>
> (Śląsk Wrocław supporter)

What is more, female fans are confronted with peculiar stadium language, which in the case of Poland is extremely vulgar and contains many homophobic references, as one of the ways of offending rivals is to attribute them

176 *Ideology on Polish terraces*

with female or homosexual features. This 'feminisation' of opponents aims to humiliate them by presenting them as 'weaker' and sexually exploited. It also confirms the view that only men can be real fans. As there is no way for fans to cross the border between them and leftist ideas, there is no way to accept 'Other' in terms of sexual orientation. Fandom culture can be described as 'homohysterical' (Anderson, 2009), one in which heterosexual hegemonic masculinity (Connell, 1987) is the pattern and homophobia is intensified. In the fan world, hegemonic masculinity stems from a strong character of bonds between men, which can be described as homosocial (bonds between people of the same gender which are not of romantic or sexual nature, see Lipman-Blumen, 1976). Homosocial bonds between fans are set and strengthened through exclusion of anything that could be considered 'unmanly'. It is important, then, to exclude and depreciate women (due to their 'weak' nature) and gay men (due to their non-heteronormative sexuality). This attitude is revealed in stadium chants: 'Zagłębie is an old slut with a dick down her throat'; 'Legia is an old slut, Legia is fucked, Legia's got to be fucked'; 'Arka Gdynia is a slut and a pig'; 'Suck on a dick, you cunts'. Importantly, in the fan world such degradation does not involve a physical act, and it is the narrative element that is used as a tool of humiliation. It reduces other fans to an object serving the purpose of satisfying sexual needs, which reduces their status to that of a 'victim'.

Traditional patriarchal masculinity manifests itself in total opposition against any attempts to recognise the rights of sexual minorities. Homophobic slurs can be heard in the chants of most Polish firms and there has never been a single action to put an end to homophobia in the stands. Such behaviours have recently intensified and gained even more prominence in reaction to a declaration of support to LGBT rights signed by the Mayor of Warsaw (who is a member of Civic Platform). Although the document does not have any legal effect in terms of regulations, it comes as a clear statement that Warsaw authorities are going to respect those rights. The declaration stirred a huge opposition in conservative circles. Some municipal councils of smaller towns (with Law and Justice majority) declared them 'LGBT-ideology free'. As such declarations are contrary to the constitution, they only come as an ideological statement.

The Warsaw declaration prompted an immediate reaction from the fan circles. Ultras from many clubs prepared and displayed banners explicitly condemning any attempts for equal rights of LGBT people. They used their typically antagonistic and uncompromising style: extremely resistant, homophobic and vulgar. Legia Warsaw fans reacted with a banner reading 'Warsaw free from faggots'. Fans from other clubs demonstrated similar discourse: 'Sodomites, deviants, faggots, paedophiles from LGBT – hands off our children!' (Lechia Gdańsk); 'The whole Poland screams: Deviant ideology will not spoil our children!' (Wisła Płock); '100% Anti-LGBT' (Jagiellonia Białystok); 'Faggots, paedophiles and deviancy will get hammered anytime and anywhere' (LGBT crossed out) (Śląsk Wrocław); 'Lubin & Gdynia against deviants' (LGBT crossed out) (Zagłębie Lubin and Arka Gdynia); 'A simple message for Poland: Let's protect our children' (LGBT crossed out) (Wigry

Suwałki); 'Stop the depravation of Polish children' (LGBT crossed out) (Raków Częstochowa); 'This is Poland, not Brussels, there is no support for deviancy here!' (Zawisza Bydgoszcz); 'Sick ideas of leftist scum – fuck off from our children!' (Ruch Chorzów); 'Stop the leftist propaganda' (Dolcan Ząbki). Many ultras also presented a simple crossed-out LGBT acronym. It was clearly visible that fans across Poland reacted in a similar way.

Most reactions of fans were limited to the performative dimension. At some point, however, this changed: during the March for Equality, organised by LGBT groups in the city of Białystok (20 July 2019), counter-demonstrators, some of them football fans, attacked the participants (see: Santora and Berendt, 2019; Tara and Darwish, 2019). They resorted not only to verbal but also physical violence – there were stones thrown at those marching. Interestingly, fans of the local team, Jagiellonia, published an appeal inviting fans of all Polish clubs to join their protest against the march. This initiative received many voices of support on fan forums, for example:

> Respect to Białystok for a decisive move. As someone has just mentioned [on this forum], so far it's been only in Lublin that people tried to oppose the rising tide of the so-called equality marches. The faggots [pedały] are very cleverly entering [the mainstream of] our society without any opposition. It's time to show our strong objection to LGBT and gender. Banners in the stadiums are not enough (...). What we need is determined action to make people AWARE of the great devastation of mentality, particularly among the young generation, caused by the anti-values presented at those parades. It's POLAND here, not Brussels, there is NO support to deviance here!
>
> (Ogólnopolski zjazd kibiców, 2019)

The most aggressive anti-march protesters were detained by the police. In reaction to the aggression demonstrated in Białystok, marches for tolerance and against homophobia were organised in a number of cities across the country. Polish football fans are not the only group which is against LGBT rights: the same attitude prevails in various right-wing circles. Although fans declare their opinions in the most uncompromising way and are thus certainly more visible, it has to be stressed that Polish society is strongly divided over the LGBT issue.

Conclusion

The collective identity of fans can be described as 'exclusionary', one that discourages a coalition with movements devoted to other values. Fans in Poland construct their collective political identity by means of particular 'frames', understood as interpretative and discursive sets developed through time and dependent on many internal and external factors; these factors come from cultural and social surroundings (see Goffman, 1974). The frames in question can be described as a mosaic of traditional, conservative, right-wing

178 *Ideology on Polish terraces*

puzzles saturated with reluctance to 'other' frames both on the ideological (e.g. liberal, progressive principles) and the practical level (practice stems from ideological assumptions; in this context, fans do not accept alternative lifestyle, same-sex marriage, etc.).

As we present throughout this book, this ideological mosaic, a frame of their ideology, stems from many aspects. It has developed as a result of some historical transformations and relations with official politics. On the other hand, this ideological frame is constructed in view of the external audience, the enemies to tackle, as well as organisational and human resources. All these factors have an impact on possible options that fans can implement on a daily basis. Since their 'frames' are highly exclusionary, the freedom of activism and cooperation is strictly limited. Along with the limitations investigated in this and the previous chapter (control by hooligans, which prevents involvement of actors supporting different ideologies, etc.), this means that the prospects for the growth of fandom into a significant political and social movement seem to be rather limited. Even the most hard-core attitude needs to be expressed in a more sophisticated way than offensive chants or repugnant slogans. So far, the Polish fan environment has not reached beyond this kind of means.

References

Alexander, J. C. (2006). Cultural pragmatics: Social performance between ritual and strategy. In J. C. Alexander, B. Giesen and J. L. Mast (eds) *Social Performance. Symbolic Action, Cultural Pragmatics, and Ritual.* Cambridge: University Press, pp. 29–90.

Anderson, B. (1991). *Imagined Communities: Reflections on the Origin and Spread of Nationalism.* London: Verso.

Anderson, E. (2009). *Inclusive Masculinity: The Changing Nature of Masculinities.* New York: Routledge.

Antonowicz, D. and Wrzesiński, Ł. (2009), Kibice jako wspólnota niewidzialnej religii [Fans as a community of invisible religion]. *Studia Socjologiczne*, 1(192), pp. 115–149.

Antonowicz, D., Jakubowska, H., and Kossakowski, R. (2018). Marginalised, patronised and instrumentalised: Polish female fans in the ultras' narratives. *International Review for the Sociology of Sport.* doi:10.1177/1012690218782828

Arnold, R. and Veth, K. M. (2018). Racism and Russian football supporters' culture. *Problems of Post-Communism*, 65(2), pp. 88–100. doi:10.1080/10758216.2017.1414613.

Burski, J. (2015). Pomiędzy realnym a skonstruowanym. Antysemityzm kibicowski [Between reality and construction. Antisemitism of football fans]. In R. Kossakowski, J. Kurowski and J. Nowakowski (eds) *Modern Futbol a Świat kibiców. Interdyscyplinarne Studia nad Kulturą Futbolu* [Modern Football and World of Fans. The Interdisciplinary Football Studies]. Pszczółki: Orbis Exterior, pp. 225–240.

Castillo, J.C. (2007). Play fresh, play local: The case of Athletic de Bilbao. *Sport in Society: Cultures, Commerce, Media, Politics*, 10(4), pp. 680–697. doi:10.1080/17430430701388822

Connell, R. (1987). *Gender and Power.* Cambridge: Polity Press.

Chmielowski, P. (2017). Sondaż wyborczy kibiców piłkarskich [Political survey of football fans]. Available at: http://sportanalytics.pl/news.php?&id_news=247 [accessed 20 October 2019].

Ideology on Polish terraces 179

Day, M. (2014). Polish MEP says 'n———' in EU parliament. *The Telegraph.* www. telegraph.co.uk/news/worldnews/europe/poland/10974032/Polish-MEP-says-n–in-EU-parliament.html [accessed 20 September 2019].

Davies, N. (2003). *Rising '44: The Battle for Warsaw.* New York: Macmillan.

Davies, N. (2005). *God's Playground. A History of Poland in Two Volumes. Volume I. The Origins to 1795.* Oxford: University Press.

Dixon, K. (2013). *Consuming Football in Late Modern Life.* Farnham: Ashgate Publishing.

Flint, J. and Powell, R. (2014). 'We've Got the Equivalent of Passchendaele': Sectarianism, Football and Urban Disorder in Scotland. In M. Hopkins and J. Treadwell (eds) *Football Hooliganism, Fan Behaviour and Crime. Contemporary Issues.* Basingstoke: Palgrave Macmillan, pp. 71–91.

Goffman, E. (1974). *Frame Analysis.* Cambridge: Harvard University Press.

Grix, J. (2012). *Sport under Communism – Behind the East German 'Miracle'.* Basingstoke: Palgrave Macmillan.

Jakubowska, H., Antonowicz, D., and Kossakowski, R. (2019). Bracia po szalu i sąsiadki zza miedzy. Narracje o męskości w środowisku kibiców piłkarskich [Brothers in scarves and female neighbours. Narrations about masculinity in football fans environment]. *Studia Socjologiczne,* 1(232): 95–115.

Jantych. (2016). *Kibice w Polityce w Latach 2004–2016* [Fans in Politics in 2004–2016]. Warsaw: PZI Softena.

Kelly, J. (2011). 'Sectarianism' and Scottish football: Critical reflections on dominant discourse and press commentary. *International Review for the Sociology of Sport,* 46 (4), pp. 418–435. doi:10.1177/1012690210383787

Kossakowski, R. (2013). Proud to be Tukker. A football club and the building of local identity: The case of FC Twente Enschede. *Przegląd Socjologiczny,* 62(3), pp. 107–117.

Kossakowski, R. (2015). 'Kibole' wyklęci w poszukiwaniu autentyczności – próba rekonstrukcji polityki tożsamości polskich kibiców [Cursed 'hooligans' in search of authenticity: the reconstruction of Polish fans' identity politics]. *Kultura Współczesna,* 1, pp. 30–45.

Kossakowski, R. (2017a). Religia [Religion]. In H. Jakubowska and P. Nosal (eds) *Socjologia Sportu* [Sociology of Sport]. Warszawa: PWN, pp. 205–217.

Kossakowski, R. (2017b). *Od Chuliganów do Aktywistów. Polscy Kibice i Zmiana Społeczna* [From Hooligans to Activists. Polish Fans and the Social Change]. Kraków: Universitas.

Kossakowski, R. (2019). Euro 2012, the 'civilizational leap' and the 'Supporters United' programme: A football mega-event and the evolution of fan culture in Poland. *Soccer & Society,* 20(5), pp. 729–743. doi:10.1080/14660970.2019.1616266

Kossakowski, R. and Besta, T. (2018). Football, conservative values, and a feeling of oneness with the group: A study of Polish football fandom. *East European Politics and Societies,* 32(4), pp. 866–891. doi:10.1177/0888325418756991

Kossakowski, R., Antonowicz, D., and Jakubowska, H. (2020). The reproduction of hegemonic masculinity in football fandom. An analysis of the performance of Polish ultras. In R. Magrath, J. Cleland and E. Anderson (eds) *The Palgrave Handbook of Masculinity and Sport.* London: Palgrave Macmillan, pp. 517–536.

Kossakowski, R., Szlendak, T. and Antonowicz, D. (2018). Polish ultras in the post-socialist transformation. *Sport in Society,* 21(6), pp. 854–869. doi:10.1080/17430437.2017.1300387

Kotwas, M. and Kubik, J. (2019). Symbolic thickening of public culture and the rise of right-wing populism in Poland. *East European Politics and Societies: and Cultures,* 33(2), pp. 435–471. doi:10.1177/0888325419826691

180 Ideology on Polish terraces

Krzyżanowski, M. (2018). Discursive shifts in ethno-nationalist politics: on politicization and mediatization of the 'refugee crisis' in Poland. *Journal of Immigrant & Refugee Studies*, 16(1–2), pp. 76–96. doi:10.1080/15562948.2017.1317897

Lamont, M., Pendergrass, S. and Pachucki, M. (2015). Symbolic boundaries. In J. Wright (ed.) *International Encyclopedia of Social and Behavioral Sciences*. Oxford: Elsevier, pp. 850–855.

Leszkowicz-Baczyński, J. (2018). Ewolucja przekonań Polaków wobec 'Obcych' jako efekt kryzysu migracyjnego w Europie [Evolution of Poles' convictions toward 'Others' as effect of migration crisis in Europe]. *Colloquium Wydzialu Nauk Humanistycznych i Spolecznych*, 2, pp. 31–48.

Lipiński, A. and Stępińska, A. (2019). Polish right-wing populism in the era of social media. *Problems of Post-Communism*, 66(1), pp. 71–82. doi:10.1080/10758216.2018.1484667

Lipman-Blumen, J. (1976). Toward a homosocial theory of sex roles: An explanation of the sex segregation of social institutions. *Signs*, 1, pp. 15–31.

Maffesoli, M. (1996). *The Time of the Tribes. The Decline of Individualism in Mass Society*. Thousand Oaks: SAGE.

Marsz Niepodległości [Independence March] (2011). *To My Kibice* 12(123), pp. 4–11.

McDougall, W. (2013). Kicking from the left: The friendship of Celtic and FC St. Pauli supporters. *Soccer and Society*, 14(2), pp. 230–245. doi:10.1080/14660970.2013.776470

Nadchodzi, nadchodzi, Marsz Niepodległości! [It is coming, it is coming, Independence March!] (2014). *To My Kibice*, 12(159), pp. 4–13.

Nawrocki, K. (2012). Więcej niż mecz. Lechia Gdańsk-Juventus Turyn [More than match. LechiaGdańsk-Juventus Turin]. In S. Ligarski and G. Majchrzak (eds) *Nieczysta Gra. Tajne Służby a Piłka Nożna* [Dirty Game. Secret Services and Football]. Chorzów: Videogaf, pp. 151– 159.

Ogólnopolski zjazd kibiców w Białymstoku [All-Poland gathering of fans in Białystok]. (2019). Available at: https://stadionowioprawcy.net/news/ogolnopolski-zjazd-ki bicow-w-bialymstoku/ [accessed 11 October 2019].

Pacewicz, K. (2019). Młodzi mężczyźni na wojnie o wartości. Dlaczego popierają Konfederację? [Young men in war for values. Why they support Confederation?]. Available at: http://wyborcza.pl/7,75398,24820306,mlodzi-mezczyzni-na-wojnie-o-wartosci-dlaczego-popieraja-konfederacje.html [accessed 1 October 2019].

Pikora, M. (2013). Kibice piłkarscy jako wspólnota ludyczna. Próba analizy socjologicznej [Football fans as a ludic community'. Sociological analysis]. In: R. Kossakowski et al. (eds) *Futbol i Cała Reszta. Sport w Perspektywie nauk Społecznych* [Football and the Rest. Sport in the Perspective of Social Sciences]. Pszczółki: Wydawnictwo Orbis Exterior, pp. 287–302.

Polletta, F. and Jasper, J. (2001). Collective identity and social movements. *Annual Review of Sociology*, 27, pp. 283–305. doi:10.1146/annurev.soc.27.1.283

Przeciwnicy UE współpracują z Muzeum II wojny światowej. Koszulki Red Is Bad obok pamiątek [Opponents of the EU cooperate with Second World War Museum. Red is bad t- shirts among the souvenirs] (2018). Available at: http://wiadomosci.ga zeta.pl/wiadomosci/7,114883,23760844,antyunijna-firma-odziezowa- sprzedaje-swo je-produkty-w-muzeum.html [accessed 11 October 2019].

Rajfur, M. (2018). Ks. Isakowicz-Zaleski: Dobrze, że paulini przyjmują kibiców na Jasnej Górze [Father Isakowicz-Zaleski: it is good that the Pauline Fathers host fans at Jasna Góra]. Available at: https://wroclaw.gosc.pl/doc/4453450.Ks-Isakowicz-Zaleski-dobrze-ze-paulini- przyjmuja-kibicow-na?fbclid=IwAR0DwqhyOQeP1g5uhEvQfRF07KXlN TxqhiwcbI-5X9mAfKVjuVWj0RQl4fU [accessed 4 October 2019].

Russell, D. (2016). The historical significance of locality and regional identity to football. In J. Hughson, K. Moore, R. Spaaij and J. Maguire. *Routledge Handbook of Football Studies*. Abingdon: Routledge, pp. 18–29.

Sandecki, M. (2013). '170 tys. zł na edukację kibiców Lechii. Czyli od Hessa do Jaruzelskiego' [170 thousand for education of Lechia fans. From Hess to Jaruzelski]. Available at: http://trojmiasto.wyborcza.pl/trojmiasto/1,35612,15127395,170_tys__zl_na_edukacje_kibicow_Lechii__Czyli_od_Hessa.html [accessed 8 October 2019].

Santora, M., and Berendt, J. (2019). Anti-Gay Brutality in a Polish Town Blamed on Poisonous Propaganda. The *New York Times*, https://www.nytimes.com/2019/07/27/world/europe/gay-pride-march-poland-violence.html [accessed 20 October 2019].

Szafraniec, K. and Grygień, J. (2019). Prawicowość młodych Polaków. Kontekst wyborów parlamentarnych z 2015 roku [The right-wing ideas between young Poles. The context of parlament election in 2015]. *Studia Socjologiczne*, 2(233), pp. 5–35.

Slater, M. (2017). FA claims victory in row over players wearing commemorative poppies as Fifa backs down on ban. Available at: www.independent.co.uk/sport/football/football- poppy-ban-fa-fifa-a7965206.html [accessed 4 October 2019].

Spaaij, R. and Viñas, C. (2013). Political ideology and activism in football fan culture in Spain: A view from the far left. *Soccer and Society*, 14(2), pp. 183–200. doi:10.1080/14660970.2013.776467

Szczerbiak A. (2014). The congress of the new right is the latest anti-establishment party to have success in Poland, but it may struggle to secure long-term support. Available at: http://blogs.lse.ac.uk/europpblog/2014/06/10/the-congress-of-the-new-right-is-the-latest-anti- establishment-party-to-have-success-in-poland-but-it-may-struggle-to-secure-long-term- support/ [accessed 8 October2019].

Tara, J., and Darwish, M. (2019) Polish city holds first LGBTQ pride parade despite far-right violence. *CNN*, https://edition.cnn.com/2019/07/21/europe/bialystok-polish-lgbtq-pride-intl/index.html [accessed 20 October 2019].

Tsoukala, A. (2009). *Football Hooliganism in Europe. Security and Civil Liberties in the Balance*. Basingstoke: Palgrave Macmillan.

Wasilewski, K. (2016). Media and the sacralization of history. *Central European Journal of Communication*, 1, pp. 114–130. doi:10.19195/1899–5101.9.1(16).8

Wąsowicz, J. (2012). Futbol i polityka. Przypadek kibiców Lechii Gdańsk [Football and politics. The case of Lechia Gdańsk fans]. In S. Ligarski and G. Majchrzak (eds) *Nieczysta Gra. Tajne Służby a Piłka Nożna* [Dirty Game. Secret Services and Football]. Chorzów: Videograf, pp. 130– 150.

Wnuk, R. (2016). Wokół mitu 'żołnierzy wyklętych' [On the myth of 'cursed soldiers']. *Przegląd Polityczny*, 136, pp. 184–187.

Wojtaszyn, D. (2012). Kibice w socjalizmie. Trybuny piłkarskie w NRD. Studium historyczno- społeczne [Fans in socialism. The football terraces in DDR. The historical-social study]. Wrocław: ATUT.

Zubrzycki, G. (2011). History and the national sensorium: Making sense of Polish mythology. *Qualitative Sociology*, 34, pp. 21–57.

9 Polish national team supporters

From the politicisation to the depoliticisation of fandom

Introduction

Studies on football fans are mostly focused on club supporters. For many reasons they provide more material to analyse in terms of stadium activity, political commitment or involvement in local issues. On the other hand, national team supporters are perceived as less multidimensional object of study, and the scope of issues raised here is rather limited. The available works contain the reflection on fandom and national identity (e.g. Foot, 2016; Giulianotti, 2005; Gibbons, 2011), the national carnival during sport mega-events (e.g. Giulianotti, 1995) or fans' attitudes to the political regime (e.g. Kassimeris, 2012). Most often the authors do not offer a more global perspective on national team fans (e.g. Molnar, 2007; Kittleson, 2014). As a result, this category of supporters is under-researched.

However, national team fandom offers a number of issues to examine, and it is worth mentioning here at least two of them. On the one hand, fans of national teams are permanently transforming: they are affected by many factors (social, economic, political) and react to them. The fandom of respectively the 1990s, 2000s or 2010s was substantially different, and its members used diverse forms of expression, cooperation or consumption. They also presented various patterns of supporting (cf. Hughson and Poulton, 2008). Consequently, the historical perspective on national team fans provides a broader understanding of wider social processes, especially when we consider such serious social changes as the fall of communism in Poland. Nevertheless, in most studies, this category of fans is perceived as a stable group which is not subject to transformations.

On the other hand, the very idea of the relation between fans, the national team and nation-state politicians is changing. National team fandom is strictly political because it legitimises the state and its authorities (e.g. Chehabi, 2002; Freeman, 2005). Fans are an important agent of this politics of symbols (Zald, 1966): they are the eye-catching vehicles for the flags, emblems, colours and anthems. This kind of pop-patriotism remains the crucial aspect of banal nationalism (Billig, 1995) and reinforces the role of nation state in everyday life (Edensor, 2002). Therefore, the relationships in the triangle 'fans – national team – politicians' are more complex. For example, fans can support or reject the national team. At the same time, they can use national team matches to reject national authorities. Politicians, in turn, can support the national team but reject the unsubordinated fans, and so on.

This chapter considers the transformation of supporters of the Polish national team. Although it mostly focuses on their political commitment, another goal of this chapter is to present the bigger picture of fans' transformation with regard to changes in sport, and to social, media and economic changes.

In order to make this reasoning clear it is necessary to make some initial remarks. National team fans are a very heterogeneous group, consisting of various communities of supporters. Nevertheless, in this chapter these fans will be described as a whole. Adopting this assumption makes it possible to focus on the global processes of transformation of fandom instead of the more common reflection on its social composition. The chronology suggested in this chapter, in turn, is intended to emphasise the most important aspects of this transformation. As a result, the periods vary in length. Finally, it is important to stress again that this chapter is not a history of Polish national team or its fandom. The topic is defined in more narrow way – it concerns the changing socio-political contexts of Polish national team supporters. The chapter consists of ten sections presenting ten periods of their political involvement.

1921–1939: state-building in the stadiums

Poland regained independence on 11 November 1918, after 123 years of partitions by Austria (later Austria-Hungary), Prussia and Russia. The Polish Football Association (PZPN) was established a year later, in 1919. The Polish national team played its first official international match on 18 December 1921 in Budapest (Poland lost 0–1). In those times the national representation was primarily a symbol of the newly born nation state. In other words, the official team became an important symbol of political sovereignty, and played the same role as other symbols of statehood – independent government, army, currency or cultural institutions. All of them meant that the Polish nation was – again – an integral part of the post-war new order.

Furthermore, international matches were also an indicator of international relations. Considering that the rivals on the pitch were recruited from among diplomatic allies, Poland frequently played with Hungary, Romania, Yugoslavia, Finland or Sweden. At the same time, it did not compete with the Soviet Union, and the German team was the rival only in the 1933–1938 period, when Germany was undergoing transformation into the Third Reich and Poland was ruled by the *Sanacja* regime (an authoritarian political movement in interwar Poland).

Polish national team matches received great attention from the very beginning. They were one of the most popular forms of mass entertainment and stirred considerable interest in the sport in the 1920s. Although the tickets were cheap, and even poor people could afford them, the social composition of the stands was differentiated: there were workers, intelligentsia, military,

184   *Polish national team supporters*

men and women, younger and older people. In the 1920s, match attendance was generally over 10,000, and in the 1930s – over 20,000. The last match before the Second World War, played with Hungary (4–2) at the stadium in Warsaw, was observed by 25,000 fans. Home games were usually hosted by the biggest Polish cities: Warsaw, Cracow, Poznań and Lviv.

Considering away matches, there is no data about the participation of Polish fans. However, they eagerly followed press reports on the team's 'big adventures': matches during the Olympic Games in Paris (1924) and Berlin (1936), or at the World Cup in Brazil (1938). The newspapers provided extensive coverage of the expeditions, including the trip, the country and its culture, organisation of the event, stories about the players, match reports and so on. The mass popularity of those reports created the emotional attachment to 'Our Boys' and thus contributed to the emergence of 'imagined fandom' – the narrative of common representation (cf. Anderson, 1991).

Moreover, the existence of the Polish team boosted the spirit of community and national identity among fans. Before and during the First World War they could support the various local football clubs but did not have any representation in terms of national team. The national squad provided the platform for sharing a sense of belonging with others. It gave fans the sense of 'reification' or 'objectification' of the nation-state. In this way, the official national football team embodied an abstract construct of the nation.

Another reason for the significance of the national team was that it gave ethnic minorities a sense of belonging to the Polish nation. In the 1920s and 1930s the football squad of Poland was composed of Poles, Jews (e.g. Jozef Klotz, the scorer of the first goal ever for Poland, in the match with Sweden in 1922, Leon Sperling or Ludwik Gintel), Germans (e.g. Fryderyk Scherfke, the scorer of the first goal ever for Poland at the World Cup, in the match with Brasil in 1938, Emil Goerlitz) and Silesians (e.g. Ernest Wilimowski, the first player to score four goals in a single World Cup game, Jerzy Wostal). The pre-Second-World-War team had been the most multicultural sport assemblage until the 2010s squad (more details below in this chapter). The making of one common sports team, then, was a way of creating a sense of one nation.

1947–1969: (official) pro-socialism of the national team

After the Second World War Poland became a country under Soviet domination. The new regime imposed communist rules: state socialism, dependence on the Soviet Union, the leading role of the Polish United Workers' Party (PZPR), centralisation, nationalisation, etc. (Kenney, 1997; Kersten, 1991; cf. Radziwiłł and Roszkowski, 1995). Moreover, following the destruction of the Polish Jewish population in the Holocaust and changes to the national borders during the Potsdam Conference, for the first time in its history Poland became an ethnically homogeneous nation state without prominent minorities (Fleming, 2010).

Polish national team supporters 185

The new conditions also affected the national team. The period between 1947 and 1969 was marked by its very strong politicisation and the absence of any serious acts of resistance on the part of fans. The team was fully controlled by authorities and used for socialist propaganda as a symbol of the 'Polish working class'. The impact of communist politicians was apparent even at the organisational level. The national team was managed by a board rather than one head coach. Composed of the coach and politicians, who were direct nominees of the ruling communist party, the board was politically dependent. In the 1947–1960 period the composition of this body changed twenty times. In this way, politicians, together with the training crew, decided about the selection of players and match tactics. The choice of rivals was also political. Apart from the World Cups and EURO qualification matches, the opponents were teams from fellow communist countries: Bulgaria, Romania, Czechoslovakia, Yugoslavia, Albania and East Germany.

This political interference could have been the reason behind the team's poor performance. The squad did not qualify to seven consecutive international tournaments: World Cups (1958, 1962, 1966, 1970) and European Championships (1960, 1964, 1968), and suffered many spectacular defeats (e.g. the highest defeat ever: 0–8 against Denmark in 1948). Nevertheless, the authorities styled the footballers as socialist heroes, the so-called 'udarniks' (shock workers). Such players as Gerard Cieślik, Ernest Pohl, Stanisław Oślizło or Lucjan Brychczy were communist celebrities – they visited schools and factories, appeared on television, gave interviews and met members of the communist party.

In spite of this combination of political interference, poor results and the 'socialist football celebrity culture', the team attracted great interest of the audience. The matches had the highest attendance in history: in 1957–1961 it was often over 100,000, for example: Poland vs Soviet Union (2–1) in 1957, Poland vs Spain (2–4) in 1959, Poland vs Yugoslavia (1–1) in 1961. National team matches were widely available (cheap and heavily promoted by the state propaganda), as they were politically accepted entertainment during the Stalinist and early-post-Stalinist period.

The first mentioned match, Poland vs Soviet Union in 1957, was probably the most political Polish match in history. It also comes as a rare example of political resistance of football fandom in those times. The game was held on 20 October 1957 as part of the World Cup 1958 qualifications. It was the first competition between Poland and the Soviet Union hosted by Poland after the Second World War, that is, from the beginning of Soviet domination. In addition, relations between the two countries were strained following the 1956 crisis (see Kramer, 1998). Poland had lost the away game in Moscow (0–3) in June 1957, and the rematch was to be played four months later in Chorzów, one of the biggest Silesian cities.

On the day of the match fans were gathering at the stadium from the early morning. A few hours before the first whistle there were over 100,000 of them in the stands. There were hostile whistles directed against the Soviet team and loud anti-communist slogans. The frightened Soviets decided to warm up on

186 *Polish national team supporters*

the side pitch rather than the main one to avoid the insults. During the match most of the Polish spectators booed and screamed at the guest team. The emotional game was won by Poland (2–1) as Polish striker Gerard Cieślik scored twice. Polish fans celebrated the score as a victory over the occupying power. And it did not matter that the win was not decisive – Poland ultimately did not qualify for the 1958 World Cup finals, having lost the play-off game at a neutral ground in Leipzig (0–2) (cf. Dmowski, 2015, pp. 179–180).

This match, however, was one of the few moments when fans openly expressed their anti-Soviet – and not just anti-establishment – attitude. The reason why they were so rare was probably the oppressive security apparatus, which blocked any internal criticism, even during football matches. To sum up, this period was characterised by high politicisation of the national team and minor acts of resistance.

1970–1989: the golden age of Polish football … and political propaganda

The period 1970–1989 is considered the golden age of Polish football. During those two decades, apart from the successes of Polish clubs in European competitions, Poland won the gold medal at the Olympic Games in 1972 and silver in 1976, and came third at two World Cups, in 1974 and 1982. James Montague writes about this period as a time 'when Poland (almost) ruled the soccer world' (Montague, 2012).

These achievements were obviously exploited by the socialist propaganda machine, as political authorities were the effective 'owners' of the national team at the time. They took care of the players – they were 'professional amateurs', officially employed in the military, factories, mines or railway companies on fake contracts, and received salaries for their sporting duties. Apart from better salaries than blue- or white-collar workers, they also had privileged access to limited resources, such as flats, cars, telephone lines or furniture.

In return, they played a significant role in the propaganda machine. Such footballers as Kazimierz Deyna, Grzegorz Lato or Jan Tomaszewski became role models of communist success. Even the legendary head coach Kazimierz Górski was 'a real socialist man', an icon of modesty and hard work. They appeared in the media and visited schools and workplaces as 'socialist celebrities'.

Members of the national team were also frequent guests at the meetings with politicians (especially good-bye and welcome parties before and after football events). Their achievements were viewed as achievements of the socialist system and communist authorities. In the era of PZPR First Secretary Edward Gierek (1970–1980) football victories were an element of the country's leap forward (see Lepak, 1988; Jung, 2017). Under the rule of Stanisław Kania (1980–1981) and General Wojciech Jaruzelski (1981–1989), in turn, national football was part of 'normalisation' in the time of crisis. The political discourse used the success of the national team as proof of efficiency of the socialist system.

The successful team became a vehicle for the 'traveling propaganda'. Its matches were hosted in various cities across the country – Chorzów (the main football arena in the 1970s), Warsaw, Cracow, Łódź, Poznań or Bydgoszcz. The games attracted great interest. In the 1970s stadium attendance often exceeded 90,000, and in the 1980s it was between 70,000 and 80,000. Television broadcasts and radio transmissions of all the matches were extremely popular. In these terms, the fans legitimised the system.

The national team was also a tool for external propaganda. The 1970 and 1980s were the period of many foreign tours lasting several weeks each (e.g. the United States, Canada and Mexico, South America, North Africa, Japan and India). These expeditions consisted of football staff (players, coaches), representatives of the authorities (sometimes there were more politicians than footballers) and members of secret services. The aim of those tours was primarily to create a positive international image of the communist regime: the team played a number of – mostly unimportant – friendly matches, which provided the opportunity to show up to the Polish diaspora at the stadiums and to meet local politicians. The trips also offered opportunities to do some smuggling and unofficial private trade, both for footballers and accompanying officials.

Considering heavy restrictions on foreign travel, those international tours, and foreign matches in general, were a window on the world. Communist authorities limited access to passports, and citizens had to apply for approval before each journey abroad. In effect, all the footballers played in the Polish league (they were only allowed to sign for foreign clubs over the age of thirty). National team matches, then, were a rare opportunity to visit other countries.

It seems that national team fandom was exclusively focused on the sporting aspect of the game. Especially the 1970s were characterised by the total absence of political manifestations in the terraces. Victories of the national team redirected attention from social issues to the issues of sport. They were 'opium for the masses', a distraction from the difficulties of daily existence and a confirmation of the right choices undertaken at the top level of policy-making. They perfectly fitted in with the 'success propaganda' [*propaganda sukcesu*] of the Gierek era, an illusion of prosperity achieved thanks to large foreign loans taken out by the communist government. Besides, at home matches fans were supervised by the security service and sometimes even the army. At the same time, they could not participate in away games. There was not much chance for any acts of political resistance at the stadiums. That is probably the reason why such events as workers' strikes in 1970 and 1976, the formation of Solidarity in 1980 or the proclamation of martial law in 1981 were not echoed in the stands.

It is important to note that at the same time, though infrequently, some acts of resistance occurred during club matches (mainly in Gdańsk). Still, some signs of political awakening were also apparent among fans of the national team. The most spectacular was an anti-communist manifestation that took place during the Poland vs USSR match (0–0) on 4 July 1982 at the World Cup in Spain, when martial law had already been in force for more

188 *Polish national team supporters*

than half a year (read more in Chapters 3 and 4). The moment when Polish fans unfurled a big white and red Solidarity banner was broadcast live all over the world. However, in Poland the game was broadcast with a couple of minutes' delay, which allowed state-controlled Polish television to remove the shots with Solidarity banners and substitute them with previously recorded images of football stands from a completely different game. Following pressure from the Soviet television, the Spanish police intervened and removed the banners in the second half of the match. Nevertheless, other fans at the stadium supported the Polish fans and chanted: 'Solidaridat! Polonia!'. This incident became an important moment for the Solidarity movement.

In contrast to the 1947–1969 period, the 1970s and 1980s brought success of the national team and slow political awakening among its fans. The golden age came to an end after 1986: the team failed to qualify for the 1988 European Championships and the 1990 World Cup. In 1989 the communist regime collapsed, and the ensuing transformation changed Polish football and its fandom.

1990–1996: a nation in transformation, a team in transformation, fandom in transformation

The triumph of Solidarity in partially free elections in June 1989 led to the fall of communism in Poland (all seats in the newly formed Senate, the upper chamber, and 35 per cent of seats in the Sejm, the lower chamber, were democratically elected; the remaining 65 per cent of Sejm seats and the post of president of the country were reserved for the PZPR). The state was transforming: from communism to democracy, from socialism to capitalism, and from welfare state to free market. Those systemic shifts affected all spheres of public life, including football.

Although the changes concerned the most important areas of football, some of them were rather peculiar. The evolution of the Polish Football Association (PZPN) and Polish sports authorities can be described as 'skipped transformation'. The domestic league suffered from a number of very serious problems: corruption, match fixing, bankruptcy of many clubs, the exodus of top players, decrepit stadiums, hooligan riots and so on (read more in Chapter 5).

The national team was also 'lost in transition'. Its practical conditions – in terms of financing, equipment, infrastructure – were very poor. In addition, they were coupled with a great organisational disorder. Since former communist activists were unable to deal with the new, democratic and free-market reality, the key arrangements were makeshift and inadequate. The team did not have a proper national stadium ('homeless national team'), it was affected by marketing turmoil and problems with equipment (e.g. a number of broken sponsorship deals, rotation of suppliers), and suffered from a constant rotation of coaches and internal conflicts.

Sports performance was also below expectations. The golden generation of the 1970 and 1980s had finished their careers, and the new players did not guarantee the same level. The Polish national team was viewed as 'a bad team

Polish national team supporters 189

with good players', who focused on their club careers because they earned much more money there. Indeed, the national team offered relatively poor conditions (in terms of remuneration, bonuses, accommodation, etc.) for footballers, especially those playing in foreign clubs. The result involved a number of embarrassing defeats, some 'shameful wins' (e.g. 1–0 against San Marino after Jan Furtok's hand goal in 1993), a streak of 13 matches without a win (1995–1996) and failure to qualify for any international tournaments between 1986 and 2002.

Another considerable problem was the rising hooligan violence. Hooligans took over control of the terraces both at club and national team matches, which was particularly evident in the domestic league (read more in Chapter 5). Organised hooligan groups caused many riots: fights between fans of different Polish clubs (e.g. Poland vs England in Chorzów in 1993, the biggest stadium riots in the national team's history, a Pogoń Szczecin fan was killed by Cracovia hooligans before the game); fights with foreign fans (e.g. Poland vs England in Poznań in 1991; Slovakia vs Poland in Bratislava in 1995, the most serious hooligan violence abroad in the 1990s), and fights with the police. The Poland team matches were mainly the opportunity for violent clashes between hooligans from all over the country motivated by hatred between 'crews' from various clubs. As a result, many supporters who did not accept violence avoided these games. The level of attendance dropped to about 7,000–8,000, and the PZPN tried to manage the situation by hosting them in smaller cities and towns (e.g. Mielec, Brzeszcze, Radom, Gdynia, Iława, Jastrzębie, Ostrowiec Świętokrzyski).

Fans of the national team became a 'political problem'. Since most of them were perceived as a threat to public order and safety, politicians declared 'a war against hooligans'. It was the first time when legal regulations were aimed specifically against football-related violence: 1997 saw the introduction of the Law on the Safety of Mass Events, which gave the police more powers in this respect. Although violent football supporters became public enemies, those politically motivated regulations affected them only to some extent. The 1990s, then, seem to be the golden era of football hooliganism also in the context of national team games.

1997–1999: the advent of marketing

The situation changed in the late 1990s. After the defeats of 1990–1997, the PZPN nominated Janusz Wójcik as the new head coach; the decision was made under an enormous pressure from fans. He was a former coach of the Polish Olympic football team which won silver in Barcelona (1992). Besides, as a former member of the communist party (PZPR), he was friends with many influential politicians. This was one of the reasons why they started to appear at national team matches (e.g. President Aleksander Kwaśniewski and many government ministers); it is worth noting that they had avoided the stadiums in the early 1990s.

190 *Polish national team supporters*

In addition, Wójcik had an exceptional instinct when it came to public relations. He gave many TV interviews, had good relations with the press and attended a lot of meetings with fans. Apart from his communication skills, his expensive suits and gold jewellery also went down very well in that era. He sounded like a strong figure in relations with the fossilised PZPN. In his public appearances he stressed that the national team needs proper funding. He famously demanded of the PZPN president: 'Cash, my honey bear, give me the cash!' [*Kasa, misiu, kasa*]. All this made his period a symbol of consumerisation and commodification of the national team.

The impression that 'something new is coming' was strengthened by the new media reality. The broadcasting rights to Poland team matches in the EURO 2000 qualifications were sold to a paid channel (*Wizja Sport*). It was the first time ever when Polish public television had no rights to live broadcasts of national team games – they were available on a public channel (free of charge) with a three-hour delay. The revolution also included other areas. The late 1990s was when national team fan merchandise became widely available. Fans could buy not only magazines, posters, cards, stickers and so on, but also official (and unofficial) jerseys and scarves. They began to be perceived as the target of marketing.

The climate around the national football team significantly improved. There was a positive atmosphere, political attention, professional training conditions and friendly media coverage. It is hardly surprising, then, that fans expected achievement on the pitch. That wind-of-change feeling was strengthened by good results in 1998 and by wins in the first two matches of the EURO 2000 qualifications. However, Poland lost the crucial games and did not make it to the finals. Janusz Wójcik was fired towards the end of 1999.

Although it initially looked different, the Wójcik period finished like many other before. Still, this short period is important for two reasons. Firstly, democratically elected politicians began to appear in the stadiums and the national team became politically trendy. Secondly, fans were offered 'national team goods' – gadgets, media, matches – and became (early) consumers.

2000–2002: the new age of commodification of the national team

After 16 years of absence from major international tournaments, Poland qualified for the 2002 World Cup finals in Korea and Japan. The victorious coach Jerzy Engel and his players became media stars, and each successful match consolidated fans around the national team.

The fans gave unprecedented support to the team: the stadiums were full regardless of the profile of the game. At the same time, hooligans were less active and focused on club rivalry. That situation made room for new match consumers – families with children, women, groups of friends and business-related people. Another new development was official sponsorship deals, which meant that supporters were offered a wide range of national team paraphernalia. All those 'normalisation' processes contributed to the

Polish national team supporters 191

transition from fans to fandom: the fans started to share not only the common idea of one Polish team but also the cultural meaning of the matches. Without hooligans, they became a group with a common goal – to support the national team and consume the event. The fandom was consolidated despite internal diversity. Consumer goods (fan paraphernalia) strengthened a sense of community and led to the development of the 'banal' side of patriotism.

The early 2000s was when fans, to some extent, became exposed to globalisation processes in football. The 2002 World Cup qualification round was the first time when they were so strongly represented at away matches abroad (e.g. a few thousand fans travelled to Norway and Wales). Another manifestation of the global nature of football was the naturalisation of foreign players. The best-known example is the case of Emmanuel Olisadebe, a Nigerian-born player who was granted Polish citizenship after three years spent in the country. That situation provoked a debate on Polish racism (acts of racism against Olisadebe appeared at league matches). The process of accepting Olisadebe as a member of the national team was highly connected with his goals that were crucial for qualifying for the finals. Many fans came to call him 'our Oli' and acknowledged his Polish identity (see Nosal, 2009; Longman, 2002).

The 2002 World Cup tournament was the symbolic opening of the new millennium, marking the end of the era of Polish football at the periphery of the game. For the first time since the democratic transformation it was again at the core of international competition, and became part of the global football industry, with sponsors, advertising, media interest, celebrities, etc. (Jawłowski, 2007). Polish players played in the best leagues, in Germany, England, Italy, France or Holland. The question before the 2002 World Cup finals was not: 'Is Poland a member of the football world' but rather: 'Is Polish football ready to reach the top of world's football?', or, more generally: 'Is Poland ready to be part of the modern world?'

However, the expedition to South Korea showed the old social inequalities. The match tickets and the trip were so expensive that only a very small group of fans could afford them – typical fans-consumers did not seem to be wealthy enough. In effect, the World Cup trip was a celebrity affair. The representation of Polish fans consisted of politicians (for example, President Aleksander Kwaśniewski), actors and singers (for example, the Polish national anthem before the match South Korea vs Poland was sang by the popular singer Edyta Górniak). Apart from that, the trip was a real experience of 'Otherness' both for fans and the players. It was somewhat of an anthropological meeting with a different culture (habits, hospitality, language, patterns of support) and its infrastructure (new technologies, new roads, new stadiums).

The 2002 World Cup became a lost opportunity. Having suffered two defeats (against South Korea and Portugal) and won only the last match (against the United States), which was worthless in terms of promotion, the Polish team failed to make it beyond the group phase.

192 *Polish national team supporters*

2003–2009: transformation is over: 'small stabilisation' and the post-transformation crisis

Although Poland suffered a defeat at the 2002 World Cup, it confirmed its status as a mid-range European team in terms of football performance. The team had its ups and downs – it failed to qualify for EURO 2004, made it to the World Cup in 2006 and EURO in 2008, and was not good enough to play at the 2010 World Cup finals – but in general it kept up the level. That period, however, also brought tension within fandom.

After a long break, fights among different hooligan groups broke out during national team matches. The fan community reacted with the so-called Poznań Pact, an informal agreement between the most influential fan groups supporting different clubs, concluded in December 2004 in the city of Poznań. One of the key principles was the suspension of all animosities during national team matches. Step by step, most groups of hardcore supporters abandoned the national team and focused only on their clubs. The Poland matches were thus attended mostly by fans-consumers, the so-called 'picnic fans'. That shift led to high stadium attendance during the following tournaments. Qualification matches were played in Warsaw or Chorzów, and friendly ones in smaller cities and towns (Szczecin, Płock, Bydgoszcz, Bełchatów, Ostrowiec Świętokrzyski, Grodzisk Wielkopolski or Wronki).

Good results of the national team made its matches a significant issue on the domestic political agenda. Prime Minister Kazimierz Marcinkiewicz (2005–2006) visited the players in their dressing room before the first game at the 2006 World Cup finals, against Ecuador. The next prime minister, Donald Tusk (2007–2014), attended almost every home match and the most important away matches. After the Austria vs Poland game (1–1) he even wanted to 'kill the referee' Howard Webb (see: Kill the referee, 2009). President Lech Kaczyński (2005–2010) attended Poland matches at the 2006 World Cup and EURO 2008. He even commented on the controversial penalty in the game against Austria (1–1) during the EURO 2008: 'I don't believe in a penalty in the last minute when the host is losing'. Besides, he famously mispronounced the names of two Polish players (Roger Guerreiro: 'Roker Pereiro', Artur Boruc: 'Artur Borubar'). Moreover, the Austria vs Poland (1–1) game at EURO 2008 was the first time ever when two presidents – a former one, Lech Wałęsa, and the one in the office, Lech Kaczyński – met at a national team match. The period 2003–2009 was the moment of intensive politicisation of the Polish national team. The games were the scene of a political spectacle and the fans were the audience.

The fans were also to face the next steps of globalisation processes in football. After the World Cup in 2006, Leo Beenhakker, a well-recognised Dutch coach, became the first foreign head coach of Poland national team in the post-war era. The world-famous former Real Madrid and Dutch national team coach introduced himself as 'the man of the world' who would be responsible for the transfer of knowledge to Poland (not only to Polish football). The best illustration of his involvement are the quotes: 'You should leave your wooden cabins!' (to Polish football authorities); 'Everyone has a talent! Believe in yourselves!' (to Polish footballers). Another issue was 'foreigners' in the Polish squad: the naturalisation of Brasilian player Roger Guerreiro and French-born Ludovic Obraniak (who did not speak Polish but had a Polish grandfather). All those steps taken by Beenhakker challenged the Polish mentality. Although his way of thinking was different to what fans were used to, he got great results and qualified to EURO 2008, which earned him great praise.

This peaceful period was over with the great crisis of 2009. Triggered by poor results of the team, it can be attributed to various reasons. The Polish squad suffered a number of shameful defeats in 2009. Not only did it fail to qualify for the 2010 World Cup finals, but also came the lowest in the FIFA ranking since 1998 (56th). The head coach Leo Beenhakker was dismissed by Grzegorz Lato, the head of PZPN, during a live TV interview (September 2009). Nominated as the new coach, Stefan Majewski had no record of coaching successes in football and was very unpopular (the fans nicknamed him 'Talib' on account of his allegedly unforgiving attitude to footballers). Moreover, hooligan riots during national team matches were back (the most spectacular example is the Slovakia vs Poland game (2–1) in Bratislava in October 2008). The atmosphere around the team was dense.

A wider problem was the relations between fans and the PZPN. In October 2008 Grzegorz Lato – a former world-famous player, top scorer of the 1974 World Cup – won the election and became the chairman. However, he represented 'the old' in Polish football. He was supported by older members of PZPN and was strongly associated with the post-communist political camp. From 2001 to 2005 he was a member of the Senate (the upper chamber of Polish parliament) representing the SLD, a post-communist party. His election met with dissatisfaction among fans. In the background there was a great corruption scandal in Polish football, which was associated with a group of older football activists (cf. Woźniak, 2019, pp. 252–256).

All those developments led to the greatest protest of Poland national team fans, a multi-dimensional action directed against football authorities under the slogan 'The end of PZPN' [*Koniec PZPN*], which started in late September 2009, after the lost qualifications to the 2010 World Cup and hiring Stefan Majewski. There were a number of demonstrations in front of the PZPN building. Most of the fans boycotted the qualification match Poland vs Slovakia (0–1) in Chorzów in October 2009 – there were only 5,000 spectators in the stadium with the capacity of 50,000. During league matches fans sang the most popular stadium chant in those times – 'Fuck the PZPN'. There were also protest letters signed by 100,000 fans and sent to the FIFA and UEFA, and a website reporting all protest activities (koniecpzpn.pl).

The protest of 2009 was the first out-of-stadium collective action of Polish national team supporters. It involved a range of coordinated activities, which showed their commitment and their causative potential. The protest made

194　*Polish national team supporters*

them a subject rather than an object of national football, even though the results of 'The end of PZPN' boycott were rather limited.

2010–2012: preparing for EURO 2012

On 18 April 2007, Poland and Ukraine were announced the co-hosts of the EURO 2012 finals. In the initial period of preparations, the discussion about the event mostly focused on organisational issues. Since the tournament was perceived as a modernisation project, the key topics in public discourse were airports, railways, stadiums, hotels, security and so on (see: Woźniak, 2013; Kowalska, 2017). However, national team fans also had undergone the process of politicisation.

At the basic level, fans became the audience of a political campaign in the stadiums. Top politicians travelled around Poland opening new stadiums, and fans were supposed to admire the organisational efficiency of the authorities. Politicians thus gained a great opportunity to appear at mass events. For example, President Bronisław Komorowski officially 'opened' the National Stadium in Warsaw during the Poland vs Portugal match in February 2012 with more than 53,000 spectators present (cf. Woźniak, 2015).

Owing to EURO 2012, fans became the target of intense marketing effort. It was a time of special offers on official paraphernalia or media coverage. However, the parallel goal of this commodification process was the progressive pricing-out (see Saner, 2011; Warwick, 2014). The tournament provided an opportunity to change the social composition of the national team audience – to push lower-class fans out of the stadium and to attract higher classes. Football authorities and football market used the opportunity of mega-event to make fans consumers rather than supporters.

The key mechanism was the price of a ticket. Tickets to Poland friendly matches before EURO 2012 and during the finals themselves were perceived as very expensive (see Williams, 2012). Another tool of the pricing-out policy was the Official Polish Team Fan Club (2011–2012), whose membership gave priority access to EURO 2012 tickets.

As a result, the audience in the stadiums came to be composed of members of, at least, the middle class. The main role assigned to a fan was that of a consumer, and national team matches became 'pure entertainment' or 'just fun'. The proverbial figure of a fan was the so-called 'picnic fan' (*piknik*, a fan who eats and drinks, blows a vuvuzela and does not support the team) or 'Johnny' (*Janusz*, a stereotypical moustached male fan, heavily equipped with free gadgets). Hardcore fans boycotted Poland's friendly matches and the entire EURO 2012 finals. Moreover, there were a number of banners against 'dyed foxes' (second- or third-generation Poles with very weak ties to Poland: French-born Damien Perquis and Ludovic Obraniak, German-bred Sebastian Boenisch, Eugen Polanski and Adam Matuszczyk; see Castels, 2012), mega-event politics (see Studenna-Skukwa, 2012), the commercialisation of football (see Gońda, 2013), as well as some street demonstrations against holding

Polish national team supporters 195

EURO 2012 in Poland (the main slogans: 'Bread, not circuses' and 'Nobody asked us if we want EURO 2012!').

Another issue related to fans was the perceived threat of violence: both Polish and foreign media were dominated by the moral panic discourse (Wawrzyczek, 2017). The deliberations at home were focused on hooligan riots during several Polish league matches (e.g. Ruch Chorzów vs Górnik Zabrze in 2009), the Polish Cup Final in 2011 in Bydgoszcz (fights between Legia Warsaw and Lech Poznań fans) and even Polish national team games (e.g. Polish hooligan riots during Lithuania vs Poland friendly match (2–0) in Kaunas in March 2011). Prime Minister Donald Tusk declared the policy of 'zero tolerance' against hooligans (read more in Chapter 6), including police checks and surveillance. In response, hardcore fans protested against the government; their main slogan was: 'Donald, you moron, hooligans will bring your government down!' (see Kossakowski, Szlendak and Antonowicz, 2018, pp. 856–857). It was a period of serious friction between political authorities and football fans in Poland, probably the highest in the twenty-first century.

Reports of those events in foreign media gave the impression that Polish fans are violent, and that the terraces in Warsaw, Gdańsk, Poznań or Wrocław are unsafe and unfriendly. The moral panic was stirred by such programmes as BBC One Panorama, Euro 2012: 'Stadiums of hate' episode on Poland. Football celebrities also warned of Polish fans. For example, Sol Campbell dissuaded the England fans from attending Euro 2012 in Poland 'because you could end up coming back in a coffin' (Stadiums of hate, 2012).

In conclusion, it needs to be stressed that the pre-EURO 2012 period was the time when supporters of the Polish national team received political attention. On the one hand, the event was regarded as an opportunity to change the composition of fandom and build a new class of fans. On the other hand, the rejected old-school fans were still perceived as a serious threat to the tournament.

2012: celebrating EURO 2012

Apart from the sports context, EURO 2012 was also a political event which attracted top home and foreign politicians to the stadiums. The opening match, Poland vs Greece, was an opportunity for an extraordinary political meeting: the game was attended by the current President of Poland Bronisław Komorowski (2010–2015) and his two predecessors – Lech Wałęsa (1990–1995) and Aleksander Kwaśniewski (1995–2005). There were also government officials – Prime Minister Donald Tusk and many members of his cabinet. All of them participated in all the matches played by Poland at EURO 2012 and some knockout phase games.

The most important foreign guests at the opening match were President of Ukraine Wiktor Ianukovych and President of Hungary Viktor Orban. The list of top foreign politicians in Polish stands during other EURO 2012 matches was longer: German Chancellor Angela Merkel, Italian President Giorgio

Napolitano, Felipe VI of Spain, Albert II Prince of Monaco, Czech President Vaclav Klaus, Russian Foreign Minister Sergey Lavrov, Irish President Michael Daniel Higgins, Croatian President Ivo Josipović. EURO 2012 brought together key European politicians, which made the tournament not only sport but also political mega-event. However, it did not have any particular international consequences.

The most important political legacy of EURO 2012 was image enhancement: Poland presented itself as a modern, well-organised, open society and country (see Kossakowski, 2017). The fans had a significant role in this public relations effect. Poles enthusiastically engaged in the event: the stadiums were full and TV broadcasts of matches were immensely popular (e.g. the Poland vs Russia match had 14.7 million viewers and 16.23 million in the peak). Polish fans turned out to be friendly hosts to foreign supporters. The matches were an opportunity to have fun, and the atmosphere was described as a 'carnival' or 'football feast'. The carnival went on not only in the stadiums but also in the streets and in fan zones (cf. Lauss and Szigetvari, 2010). Fans were focused strictly on entertainment and did not engage in politics (there were no political slogans, chants or banners).

The media vision of fan violence did not materialise apart from one significant incident in Warsaw, where Polish and Russian hooligans fought their battle before the game between the two teams (see Riach, 2012; Press Association, 2012a; 2012b). A high number of arrests among Russian fans led to a minor diplomatic crisis in Polish-Russian relations (see Press Association, 2012c). Nevertheless, the situation calmed down and was not politically exploited.

EURO 2012 consolidated the new model of Polish national team fandom: mainly middle-class, not involved in political issues, perceiving the match as an opportunity for entertainment. Focused on consumption and pop-patriotism, such fandom can be described as 'picnic' or 'carnival'. The shift from hardcore fans to cheerful consumers became a fact.

Figure 9.1 Crucial legacy of Euro 2012 was the new and very modern sport infrastructure including the National Stadium in Warsaw, pictured here. At least in case of the fandom of Polish national team, modernization of infrastructure attracted new, consumer-oriented spectators.
Source: Grzegorz Kaliciak, Stadiony.net

2013–2019: the time of advancing professionalisation

The post-EURO 2012 time brought a new sporting crisis. Under the new head coach, Waldemar Fornalik, the team did not qualify for the 2014 World Cup finals. Poor results and organisational failures (e.g. the 'national swimming pool farce' before the Poland vs England match in Warsaw in October 2012; see Fifield, 2012) created an unfriendly atmosphere around the national team. However, things started to change in 2013.

The new coach, Adam Nawałka, was perceived as a highly skilled professional and hyper-perfectionist. He focused on trainings, training camps, tactics, mental training, massage, diets, etc. His successes came soon: the team qualified for EURO 2016 (where it made it to quarter-finals) and the 2018 World Cup (group stage). Robert Lewandowski became a global super star, and many other Polish players started to play for top European clubs. The national team, despite its failure at the 2018 World Cup and UEFA Nations League in 2018–2019, competes at the top European level.

Moreover, there have also been changes when it comes to the image of national football authorities. In late October 2012 Zbigniew Boniek was elected the president of PZPN and introduced the policy of professionalism in the Polish Football Association. He focused on professional relations with the players, media, sponsors and fans. The PZPN media communication has been improved (e.g. YouTube channel, social media). The relations with fans have been based on mutual cooperation – PZPN supports fan clubs, match tickets are cheaper, and there have been many grass-roots projects. As a result, fans no longer perceive the PZPN as their enemy. Their current relations involve cooperation rather than antagonism. Besides, Poland hosted many important events: the Europa League final in 2015 (Warsaw), the 2017 UEFA EURO U-21, the 2019 FIFA World Cup U-20, the Europa League final in 2019 (Gdańsk).

Professionalisation has also affected fans. Attending games of the Polish national team has become trendy. The stadiums have been full during the matches – qualifiers in Warsaw, and friendlies in other big cities: Poznań, Cracow, Gdańsk or Wrocław. Fandom has been mostly depoliticised and political slogans no longer appear at the stadiums. On the other hand, politicians eagerly appear in the terraces but they (mainly) do not seriously interfere in national team issues (e.g. President Andrzej Duda visited the players in the dressing room twice, in 2015 and 2017, to congratulate them on qualifying for EURO 2016 and the World Cup in 2018). Polish team matches have become a middle-class entertainment with a relatively large number of women and children in the stands.

On the other hand, there have also been some hooligan incidents; the most serious riots happened abroad. There were a few incidents in 2016–2017: clashes between Polish fans in France (during Euro 2016); street riots in Bucharest before the Romania vs Poland match in November 2016; fights between groups of Polish fans at the stadium in Yerevan, during the Armenia vs Poland game in October 2017; fights with the police in Denmark, before

198   *Polish national team supporters*

the Denmark vs Poland match in September 2017. Moreover, a group of fans chanted racist and anti-refugee slogans during Italy vs Poland match in September 2018; the UEFA imposed a 2,000 euro fine, closed one sector during the Poland vs Portugal match and requested the PZPN to display the 'EqualGame' flag at the stadium during the next game. All those incidents have affected the image of national team fandom.

Conclusion: two shifts

The key feature of Polish national team fandom is the internal dynamics. The fan community has been constantly changing in all the dimensions: the patterns of support, marketing patterns, the team's performance, etc. Different periods brought different social contexts and fans simply reacted to them.

One important aspect which affected fans was current politics. They were at the receiving end of political decisions rather than shaping the political reality, and their political commitment was influenced by two major factors. On the one hand, the current state of the political system influenced the position of fandom. Fans had a different role before the Second World War, under the communist regime and in democracy. The situation of supporters was shaped by the internal political reality, Poland's international relations and the social rank of the national team matched. On the other hand, there was a particular attitude of politicians towards football fans. In different periods fans were perceived as enemies, associates or neutral actors, which directly defined their involvement.

The above analysis of the Polish national team fandom indicates two major shifts. The first shift is from politicisation to depoliticisation. For many years the supporters of the Polish national team were an important element of political reality, not only as actors but also as the audience or even the 'set'. Fans were a vehicle for Polish national symbols or resisted the regime. However, the democratic transformation diminished their political role. Politics has been pushed out of the national stadium by marketing. Hardcore fans have avoided Poland games and 'new' fans have focused strictly on consuming the event. They have not been eager to engage in political issues, at least until now. Finally, it should be stressed that the depoliticisation of national fandom is a process opposite to the politicisation of club fans. When the former focus strictly on the team and the game, the latter increasingly proclaim political slogans more often.

The second shift is the transformation from individual fans/antagonist groups of fans to quite homogenous Polish national team fandom. The periods before EURO 2012 were times of the atomisation of fans, when they ascribed different meanings to national team matches: they provided an opportunity to show patriotism, hold anti-communist manifestations or have fights between hooligan groups. The EURO 2012 pricing out policy and the consumer revolution changed the situation. Traditional groups of fans have been pushed out of the stadiums. The remaining groups, despite their internal

Polish national team supporters 199

diversity, have had a common goal – to watch the game and support the national team. In this way, they have been driven by collective needs rather than very particular aims. Fans have become a fandom – a coherent community bound by weak ties of football consumption.

These two shifts describe the political evolution of Poland national team supporters. This process is, nevertheless, ongoing. There are many factors which currently affect the fandom, like political radicalisation, increasing populism or the elections in 2019 and 2020. The political commitment of fans could change completely even in this short time period.

References

Anderson, B. (1991). *Imagined Communities: Reflections on the Origin and Spread of Nationalism*. London: Verso.

Billig, M. (1995). *Banal Nationalism*. London: Sage Publications.

Castels, D. (2012). Euro 2012: Poland's 'dyed foxes' ready to defy critics against Greece. *The National*. Available at: www.thenational.ae/ [accessed 5 October 2019].

Chehabi, H. (2002). A political history of football in Iran. *Iranian Studies*, 35(4), pp. 371–402.

Dmowski, S. (2015). Football Sites of Memory in the Eastern Bloc 1945–1991. In: W. Pyta and N. Havemann (eds) *European Football and Collective Memory*. Hampshire/New York: Palgrave MacMillan, pp. 171–184.

Edensor, T. (2002). *National Identity, Popular Culture and Everyday Life*. Oxford: Berg.

Fifield, D. (2012). Farce as Poland-England qualifier is postponed after torrential rain. *The Guardian* [online]. Available at: www.theguardian.com/ [accessed 5 October 2019].

Fleming, M. (2010). *Communism, Nationalism and Ethnicity in Poland, 1944–50*. London/ New York: Routledge.

Foot, J. (2016). How Italian football creates Italians. The 1982 World Cup, the 'Pertini Myth' and Italian national identity. *The International Journal of the History of Sport*, 33(3), pp. 341–358.

Freeman, S. (2005). *Baghdad FC. Iraq's Football Story*. London: John Murray Publishers.

Gibbons, T. (2011). English national identity and the national football team: The view of contemporary English fans. *Soccer& Society*, 12(6), pp. 865–879.

Giulianotti, R. (1995). Football and the politics of carnival. An ethnographic study of Scottish fans in Sweden. *International Review for the Sociology of Sport*, 30(2), pp. 191–220.

Giulianotti, R. (2005). The sociability of sport. Scotland football supporters as interpreted through the sociology of Georg Simmel. *International Review for the Sociology of Sport*, 40(3), pp. 289–306.

Gońda, M. (2013). Supporters' movement 'against modern football' and sport mega events: European and Polish contexts. *Przegląd Socjologiczny*, 62(3), pp. 85–106.

Hughson, J. and Poulton, E. (2008) 'This is England'. Sanitized fandom and the national soccer team. *Soccer & Society*, 9(4), pp. 509–519.

Jawłowski, A. (2007). *Święty Ład. Rytuał i Mundialu* [The Holy Order. The Ritual and Myth of the World Cup]. Warsaw: Wydawnictwo Akademickie i Profesjonalne.

Jung, R. (2017). Around 'the Water Battle of Frankfurt'. On the political dimension of the Polish football team's performance in the 1974 World Cup. *Przegląd Zachodni*, 2, pp. 125–143.

200   Polish national team supporters

Kassimeris, C. (2012). Franco, the popular game and ethnocentric conduct in modern Spanish football. *Soccer& Society*, 13(4), pp. 1–15.

Kenney, P. (1997). *Rebuilding Poland. Workers and Communists, 1945–1950*. Ithaca: Cornell University Press.

Kersten, K. (1991). *The Establishment of Communist Rule in Poland, 1943–1948. Societies and Culture in East-Central Europe*. Berkeley: University of California Press.

Kill the referee [Les arbitres] (2009). [Movie]. Schaerbeek: Yves Hinant and Eric Cardot.

Kittleson, R. (2014). *The Country of Football. Soccer and the Making of Modern Brazil*. Berkeley: The University of California Press.

Kossakowski, R. (2017). *Od Chuliganów do Aktywistów. Polscy Kibice i Zmiana Społeczna* [From Hooligans to Activists. Polish Fans and Social Change]. Cracow: Universitas.

Kossakowski, R., Szlendak, T. and Antonowicz, D. (2018). Polish ultras in the post-socialist transformation. *Sport in Society*, 21(6), pp. 854–869.

Kowalska, M.Z. (2017). *Urban Politics of a Sporting Mega Event*. Hampshire/New York: Palgrave MacMillan.

Kramer, M. (1998). The Soviet Union and the 1956 crises in Hungary and Poland. Reassessments and new findings. *Journal of Contemporary History*, 33(2), pp. 163–214.

Lauss, G. and Szigetvari, A. (2010). Governing by fun. EURO 2008 and the appealing power of fan zones. *Soccer& Society*, 11(6), pp. 737–747.

Lepak, K. (1988). *Prelude to Solidarity: Poland and the Politics of the Gierek Regime*. Columbia: Columbia University Press.

Longman, J. (2002). Poland's top scorer gets a cold welcome. *New York Times* [online]. Available at: www.nytimes.com/ [accessed 5 October 2019].

Molnar, G. (2007). Hungarian football. A socio-historical overview. *Sport in History*, 27(2), pp. 293–317.

Montague, J. (2012). From clowns to Kings: When Poland (almost) ruled the soccer world. *CNN* [online]. Available at: https://edition.cnn.com/ [accessed 5 October 2019].

Nosal, P. (2009). EURO 2008 – koniec spektaklu narodów? [EURO 2008 – the end of national competitions?] In: T. Sahaj (ed.) *Pogranicza Współczesnego Sportu* [The Edges of Contemporary Sport]. Poznań: Wydawnictwo Naukowe AWF, pp. 187–205.

Press Association (2012a). Euro 2012: 183 arrests after fighting between Russia and Poland fans. Available at: www.pressassociation.com/ [accessed 5 October 2019].

Press Association (2012b). Euro 2012: UEFA condemns 'isolated' violence after 24 fans injured. Available at: www.pressassociation.com/ [accessed 5 October 2019].

Press Association (2012c). Euro 2012: Poland minister calls for severe sanctions on hooligans. Available at: www.pressassociation.com/ [accessed 5 October 2019].

Radziwiłł, A. and Roszkowski, W. (1995). *Historia 1945–1990* [History 1945–1989]. Warsaw: Wydawnictwo Naukowe PWN.

Riach, J. (2012). Euro 2012: Poland and Russia supporters clash before match in Warsaw. *The Guardian* [online]. Available at: www.theguardian.com/ [accessed 5 October 2019].

Saner, E. (2011). Is football pricing out the real fans? Interview with Mark Perryman and David Davies. *The Guardian* [online]. Available at: www.theguardian.com/ [accessed 5 October 2019].

Stadiums of hate (2012). [TV Programme] 1: *BBC*.

Studenna-Skrukwa, M. (2012). Fucking Euro! Protesty Społeczne na Ukrainie [Fucking Euro! The Social Protest in Ukraine]. *Czas Kultury*, 1, pp. 48–55.

Warwick, J. (2014). The rising price of football: the truth is fans just don't care. *The Telegraph* [online]. Available at: www.telegraph.co.uk [accessed 5 October 2019].

Wawrzyczek, I. (2017). Racist and neo-Nazi panic in the Euro 2012 coverage by the British press. A discursive failure in interculturalism. *Brno Studies in English*, 43(1), pp. 89–105

Williams, R. (2012). Euro 2012: Fairer ticket prices should be a Michel Platini priority. *The Guardian* [online]. Available at: www.theguardian.com/ [accessed 5 October 2019].

Woźniak, W. (2013). Sport mega events and the need for critical sociological research: The case of Euro 2012. *Przegląd Socjologiczny*, 62(3), pp. 31–50.

Woźniak, W. (2015). Euro 2012 i Kraków 2022. Polskie elity polityczne wobec wielkich imprez sportowych. *Przegląd Socjologii Jakościowej*, 11(2), pp. 60–83

Woźniak, W. (2019). Match-fixing in Polish football: Historical perspectives and sociological interpretations. *The International Journal of the History of Sport*, 35(2–3), pp. 247–263.

Zald, M.N. (1966). Politics and symbols. A review article. *The Sociological Quarterly*, 7(1), pp. 85–91.

10 Conclusion

Football fans and politics in Poland: between universality and peculiarity

Instead of introduction

On 20 July 2019, just as we were working on the final chapter of this book, organisations defending LGBT rights held the first ever local Equality March in the city of Białystok in the north-east of Poland (see: Santora and Berendt, 2019; Tara and Darwish, 2019). In the country where the rights of LGBT people are not recognised by the law, Equality Marches are the most visible manifestation of their ongoing struggle for recognition and respect in the legal and public sphere. Previously organised mainly in major cities, since the increase of anti-LGBT rhetoric in the narrative of the ruling Law and Justice party such marches have also been held in smaller cities and towns. Białystok is known in Poland for its strong far-right movements and numerous incidents involving violence against minority groups, which were documented by journalist Marcin Kącki (2015).

The march in Białystok was accompanied by a counter-demonstration registered with local and regional authorities. During the march, the participants were verbally abused and physically attacked by a few hundred counter-demonstrators, many of them wearing the colours of the local football club, Jagiellonia Białystok. The topic of political involvement of football fans hit the headlines once again, both in Poland and elsewhere, as the violence in Białystok was reported in mass media all over Europe.

For the liberal-left media, the aggression of people who identified themselves with the local club was a confirmation that they are an uncivilised mob. Some declared it an empirical proof for the growth of fascist tendencies among some segments of the Polish population. On the other hand, however, one of the most prominent leftist commentators (Żakowski, 2019) observed that ordinary thugs should not be confused with fascists. A prominent sociology professor, in turn, declared that different physical appearances explains the mental differences between the two groups of people in Białystok: 'Those are juicers, musclemen; they have a different physique. And on the other side there are faces, I'd say, of young, attractive people – or mostly young, attractive people. The difference is, I'd say, almost anthropological' (Śpiewak o uczestnikach, 2019).

The photos and footage showing violent attacks on young men and women taking part in the march were so gruesome that even right-wing politicians expressed their condemnation. The ruling Law and Justice party issued a statement condemning violence and asserting the right of assembly regardless of political ideas. However, right-wing media outlets were quick to attribute the violence to provocative behaviour of members of the LGBT movement. Like many other cases described in this book, this one has been treated by media and politicians both as a phenomenon *per se* and a symptom of more overarching processes occurring in Polish society, which confirms that this study is more topical than ever.

Since, as the case of Białystok proves, the political processes within and around football fandom in Poland are *in statu nascendi*, we make no definite and conclusive statements and we wish to withhold from formulating any forecasts other than those referring to the future of purely academic work in this field. Therefore, the generalisations below need to be treated cautiously, as they refer retrospectively to observations made over the years of empirical work.

Rather than summarise or repeat the arguments formulated elsewhere in this book, this chapter attempts to present several issues that emerged and were frequently discussed in the course of our work. We begin with observations on the topic of the political agency of football fans, and follow this by pointing out the main reasons why the left is not represented at all in Polish football stands. We also discuss to what extent Polish fans are unique, and to what extent, and under what conditions, we may extrapolate some of our findings. The next section is a modest exercise in developing a taxonomy of politically engaged football fans. In the final part, we briefly evaluate our experience of joint work and our discussions on the topic which was politically hot during the very period when we were working on this book. We also refer to the experience of our efforts to become publicly visible sociologists who share their expertise of researching politically and ideologically charged themes in an era of bitter divisions within Polish society, media and politics.

Are fans causative agents in the political sense?

As we have tried to present throughout this book, Polish football fandom is homogeneous in terms of political ideology. It seems amazing that fans manage to keep their ideological unity despite the fact that the surrounding social context is – naturally – more diversified. It would appear that this unity should be an excellent starting point for a political representation or organisation of some kind: it would guarantee no initial misunderstandings stemming from ideological differences. If we add here a well-organised style of 'human resources management' among fans, their coherent and cohesive structure, their authoritarian style of leadership, their will to fight for the sake of one another and their experience in 'guerrilla-type' resistant actions – we get an impressive image of a community with good predispositions for political engagement. Even though this engagement would probably not be very

204   *Conclusion*

significant in quantitative terms, it is definitely very consistent when it comes to radicalisation, a factor that has always attracted some – particularly young – individuals. Many leftist and liberal observers and commentators are prone to stating that fans are fertile ground for the emergence of a large and well-organised neo-fascist formation. Such comments mostly appear in reaction to politically charged banners displayed in the stadiums, or to cases of violent behaviour in the streets (like in Białystok). The pattern seems to be regular: fans engage in a display of political extremism, and follow-up comments warn against a new fascist movement. But things have never developed this way (at least until we concluded our work on this book).

As we have exhaustively investigated in this book, however radical and extreme fans are, they are not going to become a serious political formation for a number of reasons. Their political engagement mostly takes a performative form: presenting banners, chants and choreographies on the one hand, and attending national commemorative events (such as the Independence March) or provoking violent incidents in the streets on the other. This indicates that fans are well organised and can mobilise their resources very efficiently. But – we suppose – that is as far as they can go. There are many obstacles to the further development of their political involvement. Many local fan groups are controlled by small hooligan elites and mostly focus on financial resources they can gain. Since many hooligan groups are engaged in criminal activity, any political engagement would mean an additional risk to their operations. Other factors involve legal reasons. Many fans – even if they have right-wing sympathies – are mostly interested in football and fan culture: attending matches, being part of the community, rivalry with other teams. Some of them support conservative values as they find them important: they proudly sing the national anthem during the matches, they wear patriotic clothes and shout anti-refugee chants, for example. It seems, however, that this performative level of engagement is all they are willing to become involved in.

What is more, we assume that in the nearest future one should expect even less active forms of fandom in Poland. Since 2015 there have been fewer football fans taking part in the Independence March – mostly due to less likelihood of clashing with the police and the fact that the current Law and Justice government (as opposed to its liberal Civic Platform predecessor) is not viewed as a fierce enemy. Also, some reshufflings in the fan circles (mostly related to criminal deals between hooligan crews) have changed the atmosphere in the movement. Many fans are aware that the hooligan agenda is not about football or love for the club, which does not seem to have a positive impact on attracting new fans. We do not see much space for political development under such circumstances. There has been stagnation even in some social and charity activities – many supporters' associations are focused on a few types of actions which are easy to organise. As a result of all those hindrances, the human potential of fandom seems to be largely untapped.

The violent chants and behaviour of some Jagiellonia Białystok fans are not the sign of the advent of a fascist movement. Paradoxically, they can be a

Conclusion 205

sign of decline: fans are still capable of aggression and exerting violence but are unable to demonstrate more nuanced organisational power. The political climate that may encourage aggressive behaviour – or institutionalisation of political formations that may be interested in exploiting it – is not created by members of the fandom. The power of fandom can be regarded in terms of agency of (symbolic or physical) violence but not in terms of agency to develop and implement a structured set of political principles.

Where is the left side?

FC Sankt Pauli, SV Babelsberg, AS Livorno, Rayo Vallecano, Hapoel Tel-Aviv, Standard Liège, Sevilla FC, Beşiktaş, AEK Athens, Bohemians Prague 1905. For those interested in European fandom, this list of clubs has one common denominator – major organised groups of their fans are left-wing: anarchist, anti-fascist, openly communist or just embracing the progressive anti-homophobic and anti-capitalist agenda. Some would add to this list such globally renowned clubs with massive followings such as Celtic Glasgow, Olympique Marseille and Liverpool, where the fandom is obviously more heterogeneous, but left-wing groups of organised fans are also active and visible. To our best knowledge, until a grass-roots football club called AKS Zły (Alternative Football Club 'Bad') was established in Warsaw in 2015, there had been no single club in Poland whose fans would openly declare allegiance to these values. AKS Zły started from the lowest level of official football and is currently playing in the seventh league of local Warsaw games. As we mentioned in Chapter 8, the last organised anarchist fan group in more mainstream football operated in the terraces of Polonia Warsaw. The anti-fascist and anarchist group called the Black Rebels (black is the traditional colour of the club) was effectively silenced and pushed out of the stands in 2013 by their right-wing adversaries.

A reply to the question formulated in the title of this section may be found in a brief historical account of Polish transformation presented in Chapter 3. One reason behind the structural weakness of the left in Poland stems from the fact that the political parties declaring allegiance to the Solidarity movement unanimously supported the neoliberal pathway of economic transformation. The only declaratively left-wing formation which has ever made it to the government, the post-communist Democratic Left Alliance, had no major impact on the dominant discourse, which associated values of 'the left' with 'communism' or 'socialism'. Seeking recognition and forgiveness for their involvement in the pre-1989 political regime, post-communists neglected the symbolic spheres of memory policy and withdrew from any topics that could cause a serious conflict with the Roman Catholic Church.

The major clash observed in Polish politics since 2005 – between Law and Justice and Civic Platform – follows this pattern. The former party accuses the latter of 'leftist' tendencies when it declares its allegiance to the European Union. The latter uses the same label when criticising the generous social

206   *Conclusion*

spending of the party ruling since 2015. Prior to 2005, the two parties were allied against post-communists and jointly founded the Institute of National Remembrance, an institution which has had a great impact on official discourse. It strengthens a memory policy which frames 'the left' almost exclusively as a threat to Poland in the course of its history. Accordingly, Polish textbooks present very conservative narratives on Polish history and cultural issues. As elsewhere in Europe, the owners of football clubs look into the past of their teams, but as yet no club has openly declared that their working-class roots were anyhow associated with left-wing politics. As it was confirmed by the results of elections, left-wing parties and left-wing activism is weak. Consequently, introducing left-wing ideas among the new generations of fans may be difficult also because the 'elders' openly declare their right-wing sympathies. Additionally, the long decades of portraying football fans as uneducated, dangerous, uncivilised mob may discourage any attempts to promote different, more ideologically progressive narratives in the fan world.

Is the Polish case specific?

The analysis presented in this book provides a threefold characteristic of the relations between Polish football fans and politics.

At the first level, it provides illustrations of global trends in fandom. We describe a number of processes which currently affect supporters around the world, including Poland. The most important of them is the internal conflict in modern football – a rising tension between the top-down commercialisation and grass-roots politicisation of fans. The vision of commodified football assumes that supporters are merely passive consumers and not active co-creators of the social world of football. Their involvement in the match-day experience is supposed to be limited to cheering the team, purchasing franchised items and following the club and its players on social media. Fans who claim their right to political agency during the games clearly trespass on the limits of the role assigned to them by football associations, football management and their commercial partners. However, political activism is noticeable in most European countries, Latin America and North Africa, where political slogans, chants and banners often appear in the terraces. Besides, fans tend to participate in out-of-stadium political events: manifestations, protests, marches or even riots. The radicalisation of fandom is thus clearly apparent. The most politically active fan groups align with more or less radical right-wing politics. They declare themselves as patriots, sometimes openly formulate nationalist claims and frequently profess allegiance to conservative values. At the same time, even though we acknowledge that the terraces elsewhere are more pluralist than in Poland, the left is less visible and seems weaker in top national leagues than in lower echelons. Only a few groups in Europe openly profess liberal or leftist views (see Chapter 2). This situation makes the Polish case universal.

At the second level, the analysis stresses the peculiarity of the politicisation of the football scene in Central and Eastern European countries. Football fandom in different CEE countries has some crucial features in common. The main development factor here is the experience of the communist regime and democratic transformation, which has resulted in anti-leftist and anti-establishment attitudes (the former often involve belated anti-communism). Fans perceive themselves as opposition to the authorities, state institutions (e.g. the government, police) or the wider category of 'beneficiaries of the transformation' (e.g. businessmen, media, politicians). In effect, their *modus operandi* requires permanent conflict, contestation and resistance. This makes them important actors in politics: they act as an informal 'armed arm' during patriotic marches or protests. This type of engagement is typical for such CEE countries as Hungary, Czechia, Slovakia, Serbia or Russia (see Chapter 2).

At the third level, however, it appears that the Polish case is specific, as it is characterised by a number of features that distinguish it from a wider context, both global and that of other Central and Eastern European countries. The analysis of these peculiarities allows to notice certain specific patterns of the relations between fandom and politics in Poland.

Polish football fans use very specific symbols to define their own identity. In terms of ideology, it is a combination of conservative values: affirmation of some (Roman Catholic religiosity, patriotism, heterosexuality, machismo, etc.) and rejection of others (anti-leftist, anti-liberal, anti-Islamic, ethnic resentments, etc.). This political assemblage does not make Polish supporters unique: many right-wing fan groups propagate such ideas. However, they choose specific role models of this ideology. They rarely refer to figures from distant history – great monarchs, knights or holy figures (the exception here is Jesus) – and neither do they invoke Second World War heroes (the exception here are the Warsaw insurgents of 1944) or twentieth-century state-builders. The most praised figures in the Polish terraces are probably the Cursed Soldiers – members of underground resistance military formations fighting after 1945 (see Chapter 8). Football fans perceive them as anti-regime, anti-communist, fearless and steadfast freedom fighters. This reference defines the self-perception of a considerable part of the Polish football fandom: rightist and conservative on the one hand, and anti-systemic, militant and rejected on the other.

The figure of the Cursed Soldier explains to some extent the model of politicisation of fans in Poland, which can be called a reactive equilibrium. The ideological attitudes of fans are clearly articulated and generally constant. The agenda of their activity is quite stable: anniversaries of historical events, national holidays, cyclic marches. However, there are some – more or less unexpected – events that blur the routine and trigger their reaction: certain political decisions, international affairs or left-wing actions.

Polish fans do not perceive themselves as 'just political': it is more about being pro- or anti- particular issues. They are not strongly tied to any particular institutions or political parties, and the views they hold are 'worldviews' rather than strictly 'political views'. They are conservative but not in terms of party politics, rightist but beyond the political system. They are focused on promoting conservative values and cherishing selected elements of

208   *Conclusion*

collective memory. They do this for strictly ideological reasons and act without any hidden interests. In effect, fans work at the margins of the system but their engagement has a serious impact on its shape.

An important part of fans' engagement in politics is social performance: they are important actors displaying right-wing views in public. Groups of supporters visualise the key elements of the right-wing worldview in the stadiums, in the streets or during mass events. They make use of attendant symbols (flags, national colours, emblems, crosses) and slogans (which they chant or shout), and often literally fight for their values. In effect, this mode of right-wing involvement becomes eye-catching and spectacular. It also becomes a popular image of the right not only in the media but also in the social imaginary (e.g. pictures from the Independence March): radical fans embody the right wing. This kind of 'performative proclamation of rightist ideas' is impossible in the case of politicians, who use more formal communication channels. On the one hand, it is a great political strength of the fandom. On the other – it is an image challenge for the right to not be associated only with extreme political views.

Although the overview of Polish fandom presented in this book stresses its political potential, it cannot remain unnoticed that it is largely untapped. As has been mentioned above, while fans undertake political activities, they are not inspired by politicians. Of course, politicians set the agenda to which fans react (e.g. the refugee crisis), but their worlds are separate universes even if they share similar worldviews. Their paths may cross, but they still act independently: fans do not support any particular politicians, and there are no politicians who would openly support a particular group of fans (whether the club scene or the national team). This situation distinguishes the Polish case from many other CEE countries (e.g. Russia or Hungary): there are no strong links or (formal or informal) alliances between politicians and fans here. If it were to be otherwise, it could possibly lead to interesting consequences: fans' unequivocal support for particular politicians in elections; their engagement in political campaigns; well-organised groups of fans acting as the 'armed arm' of political parties; business opportunities in private security industry (e.g. fans as politicians' bodyguards); positive image of fandom in the public media, etc. Nevertheless, considering the peculiar nature of political commitment of Polish fans, any arrangements with politicians are hardly conceivable at all.

The question whether the case of Polish fans is specific should be answered as follows. On the one hand, the analysis clearly indicates the presence of global trends in Polish fandom, which means that the country is an inseparable part of the wider context – modern football and the globalised world. On the other hand, however, there are some peculiarities which make interrelations between Polish fans and politics quite exceptional. This comes as a result of a combination of different factors, especially the experience of the communist regime, unfinished consumer transformation and anti-establishment attitudes.

Conclusion   209

Towards a typology

Although this book is focused on a particular case, the collected data and analytical work enable an attempt to develop a more general typology of the political commitment of football fans. It is obviously inspired by the analysis of the Polish reality but the proposed categories aspire to be universal. We believe that they can be applicable in all contexts, although they certainly require future empirical tests.

The typology presented here is based on a combination of two key dimensions. The first axis is a distinction between more active and more passive political attitudes, which tries to capture the character of actions undertaken by fans. The description includes a wide scope of supporters' actions: from those which do not require special involvement (e.g. being a spectator in the stadium where political banners are displayed) to those engaging very strongly (e.g. participation in out-of-stadium political manifestations). Fans differ in the scale of their involvement – while some of them tend to be 'hot' in political terms, others are 'cold' (cf. Giulianotti, 2002).

The second dimension is the contrast between various channels of activity. On the one hand, there are grass-roots political activities. This kind of engagement is mainly informal in nature: the actions are located beyond political institutions or institutionalised democratic mechanisms. Fans proclaim their worldview in the free public sphere by means of slogans, chants, banners or protests and manifestations. On the other hand, there are many formal activities which are undertaken by supporters within the institutionalised democratic frame. This situation includes all official instruments of political participation – from voting to becoming a politician.

The combination of these two dimensions yields four types of fans' political commitment. The presented types are the extreme points on the scale. However, within the selected fields there is also a place for slightly less intense activities (some of them are mentioned in the following part). Another important assumption of this typology is that the person undertakes the analysed activities 'as a fan' (e.g. participates in a street protest dressed in a fan outfit).

Fans as silent supporters: This type of activity is confined to places where political manifestations occur, such as stadiums. Silent supporters are not leaders but marginal participants of the events. However, they are very important: their role is to enlarge the scale of the event – to magnify and reinforce it. They make a crowd and their 'being there' is pro- or anti- a particular issue. They become 'noders' – they echo the slogans shouted by the

Table 10.1

	Grass-roots	*Institutional*
More passive	Fans as silent supporters	Fans as voters
More active	Fans as civic activists	Fans as politicians

210   *Conclusion*

leaders. In effect, the protest or other ideological proclamation is more spectacular and thus may be perceived as more massive and serious.

Fans as civic activists: This category includes initiators or organisers of political events. They are not just 'commanding officers', the people who decide when, where and why the action is taken, including both the stadium (e.g. displaying a choreography, preparing banners) and out-of-stadium space (protests, manifestations, boycotts or even fights). Their engagement is definitely more intense. Civic activists manage the ideological aspects of the fan world. They set the political line of events, which means that they must be aware of current political issues. They both set the agenda and are involved in organisation. They also play the key roles during events: they lead the participants or supervise some strategic elements (e.g. chants, banners, pyrotechnics). Civic activists make fans' political postulates visible in the public sphere.

Fans as voters: Voting is the most basic expression of political activity. However, the analysis presented in this book indicates that in the case of fans voting is an ambiguous issue. First, fans are not really viewed as a group of voters that would require specific research. In fact, their voting preferences are not often studied and they are not treated as a group that would deserve attention during election campaigns. Second, fans are not the target of any specific political campaigns (at least in the positive sense) or addressees of electoral promises; their problems do not bother politicians. Third, fans' political views are stable and, according to available data, more rightist than in general society. Nevertheless, it should be stressed that their voting patterns are an important indicator of the more general fandom's political moods. Although those patterns do not provide knowledge about the nature of fans' engagement, they give an insight into their attitudes towards the idea of democratic elections and into their opinion on particular political candidates.

Fans as politicians: Direct involvement in elections and becoming a politician is probably the highest degree of institutional political commitment among fans. Entering the political world through involvement in party politics is often perceived as the most effective method of making changes. Regardless of the type of elections (local or general), the pathway is the same: the fan-politician has to make an effort to be selected as candidate and win the election. Although the success is a personal achievement of the candidate, in all instances it requires mobilisation of the entire fan community. It is thus important to notice that fan as politician is a phenomenon which concerns not only the engagement of a single actor but also a wider political mobilisation of fans. So far, this type of their political engagement has been the least common.

The presented typology has a number of limitations. All of the proposed types are theoretical constructs, 'ideal' or 'pure' types. The main aim here is to facilitate sociological analysis of the relations between fans and politics. In real life the lines dividing those types are blurred, and the political participation of fans falls along a two-dimensional continuum rather than into a clear-cut type. For example, participation in the Independence March is more active than passive and more grass-roots than institutional but it is not 'purely active' and 'purely grass-roots'. Moreover, many activities should be placed in-between the suggested types or at their crossroads. For example, participation of fans in a session of the city council in order to report a particular case is a grass-roots initiative undertaken within the institutional order. Nevertheless, the presented typology can be helpful in the mapping of political engagement of football supporters.

Final thoughts

Even the strongest political, axiological and moral assumptions of the researchers should not discourage them from getting first-hand knowledge about the phenomena they observe. Even adopting the constructivist perspective and withstanding attempts to recognise, describe and explain social phenomena 'neutrally', we should avoid our own perception biases interfere with our research and reasoning. On the basis of our own experience, we can observe that in research on football fandom this context has two principal aspects.

On the one hand, we had been engaged in various aspects of the social world of football long before we became researchers. We were fans, amateur players, sports journalists and therefore the outsider's perspective was completely beyond our reach in any way. Although this cannot be measured, a preliminary knowledge of this particular social world seems to be an important prerequisite before going into the field. It cannot be weighed whether this is a flaw that may cloud our judgements or, on the contrary, an indispensable qualification that enables a deeper understanding of observed processes and phenomena. We nonetheless hope that the approach derived from critical sociology – which both questions popular or common explanations dominant in media discourse and treats the existing scholarly narratives with suspicion – allowed us to formulate some fresh ideas and judgements.

Our position enables us to notice, feel, hear and understand more. However, participating in the social field, at least on an everyday basis, we often engage without rigorously following methodological principles of participatory observation techniques. Any attempt to objectify our judgements requires sociological imagination in the first place, but also, and maybe more importantly, a collective effort. We believe that teamwork was the only way to at least attempt to overcome these obstacles. During the writing process we constantly referred to one another's assumptions and challenged them. Sometimes, to our own surprise, final interpretations of many phenomena went far from our well-established original judgements. This would not have been possible if we had worked single-handedly. We are quite sure that this kind of permanent and rigorous researcher triangulation had a great impact on our joint effort.

On the other hand, we have our own political positions and moral values, which in some respects are in fundamental opposition to those embraced by the majority of the most active, hardcore football supporters. As part of our

212   *Conclusion*

research, some of us regularly took part in marches or protests organised by active members of the fan community. As citizens, in turn, we frequently participated in demonstrations which were contested, despised and sometimes verbally abused by some of them. We acknowledge that while attempting to explain the political choices of members of football fandom we may be (and in fact we sometimes are) criticised for lack of criticism or for too naïve understanding of motivations of radical football fans. Regardless of all the declarations, our understanding and explanation of their choices or motivations do not imply acceptance or even tolerance for some of those.

Researching the topic which is a recurring theme in the media and features in hot political debates also requires a deeper consideration of the role of sociologists in public debate. Engaging in public debate using research findings is particularly tricky these days. In the era of identity politics, when politicians, media and societies in general are so heavily conflicted, it is particularly difficult to voice a more nuanced diagnosis: this usually requires pointing out the deficiencies of all the conflicted sides. Academic analytical rigour is a very weak shield in deeply emotional public discourse. Public intellectuals in Poland are frequently expected to ally with one of the sides of the purely political conflict. Those who do not fulfil these expectations may be dismissed as incompetent or viewed as members of the enemy political camp.

Consequently, fans may view us as potential allies or, conversely, label as 'useful idiots' of liberal elites, when we pointed out clearly dangerous liaisons with far-right movements, notorious racism or xenophobia and criminal affiliations of certain parts of the fandom. Their derogatory labels are sometimes coupled with threats from members of the fan circles who felt inappropriately criticised. On the other hand, attempts to explain the wider context of fans' behaviour or to point out the ambivalent role of liberal media and liberal elites – who sparked the episodes of moral panics and distorted many facts about the scope of football-related violence – earned us the label of 'defenders of criminals, homophobes, chauvinists, etc.'.

It needs to be reasserted that in this book we have investigated political attitudes, actions and choices of the most active members of the fan community: 'die hard', 'hardcore' or 'industrial' fans (Antonowicz et al., 2015), for whom the football game will never be 'just' a sports event, and for whom collective identity is an essential part of their everyday life, and fandom – an essential platform of expression of their values. At the same time, however, we are certainly aware that – despite the hypervisibility of politically radical and right-aligning groups of organised fans – stadiums in Poland remain one of the few spaces of pluralism. In political terms, the silent majority does not engage in political football-related activism and represents a diverse spectrum of political options. In economic terms, even the growing commercialisation has not yet priced out those fans who in many other countries are not members of the stadium community anymore due to financial reasons.

Social and spatial segregation based on class divisions has been growing in Polish society throughout the last decades. To some extent, those divisions

Conclusion 213

overlap with the growing political tensions and divisions. This process of polarisation, particularly well visible since 2015, has narrowed the space where members of conflicted groups, tribes or political camps would not so much unite but just communicate and share the same experience. This is clearly apparent in the phenomenon of media, information and social media bubbles, where dialogue or even mere communication between the conflicted factions is limited. In our experience, stadiums may still fulfil this function: for many members of the football fandom their collective identity does not require subscription to the most visible and hence dominant political narratives.

Our book can be viewed as a local case study with references to a broader spectrum of Central Eastern Europe and to the general European context as well. The typology of fans' engagement in political issues which we present can be useful for researchers from other countries and may be adjusted according to local contexts. But our study can also be evaluated at an even more general level, one concerning a 'big question': should football be the arena of political spectacle? If yes – to what extent? If not – why not?

When it comes to institutions (organisations like UEFA, FIFA, national associations), it seems to be clear that football should be free from any political stances. The fines imposed on clubs by UEFA for presenting political statements by fans are proof of this strategy. But the question remains: who, and on the basis of what criteria, is eligible to decide what is political and what is not? Does a banner concerning the Warsaw Uprising feature politically unacceptable content? And, conversely, do banners devoted to the LGBT movement displayed by St. Pauli ultras present what is politically acceptable? What does it really mean that stadiums should be apolitical in the times when 'everything' can be political? Or, as Astrid Deuber-Mankowsky (citing M. Foucault) states: 'nothing is political, everything can be politicized' (2008, p. 135), which can be understood that 'being political' depends on the actors' interests, aims, assumptions and values. If we consider UEFA and FIFA's efforts to make stadium ideologically 'sterile', is it reasonable to state that their strategies are based on political economy of late capitalism, clearly oriented on consumer identity of football fans? Is it political? Many Marxist-oriented thinkers argue that it clearly is, and that such political actions are related to neoliberal tendencies in football (see Kennedy and Kennedy, 2016). This conviction is shared by some groups of fans who display banners 'Against Modern Football'. But still, these performative acts are an end in themselves and do not entail serious political engagement. Other actors – sponsors, media, governments – play the game set by football authorities.

The analysis provided in this book will help to map potential fields of further analysis. With no doubt, future studies can take into consideration political preferences of fans in terms of their voting attitudes. As we investigate the obstacles for more organised political involvement of fans, the question is what they look like in other countries. Are fans in other European regions (un)able to set political organisations which would go beyond performative spectacles? Has the commercialisation of football consistently stifled – step by step (fine by

214 *Conclusion*

fine) – all staunch political activities? What local and national (historical) circumstances make fans more rightist or leftist? What is the role of local politicians in flaring up political atmosphere in the stadiums? Can official politics offer some space for fans as political decision-makers? Although the Polish case can be investigated in terms of ethnological 'folklore', research on such local contexts draws attention to very serious topics concerning the political nature of football in general. And, even more broadly, if we consider fandom as part of society, we should ask more general questions, related to political transformation of society as a whole. And those are the next questions waiting to be answered.

References

Antonowicz, D., Kossakowski, R. and Szlendak, T. (2015). *Aborygeni i Konsumenci: O Kibicowskiej Wspólnocie, Komercjalizacji Futbolu i Stadionowym Apartheidzie* [Aborigines and Consumers. On Fan Community, Commercialization of Football and Stadium's Apartheid]. Warszawa: IFiS PAN.

Deuber-Mankowsky, A. (2008). Nothing is political, everything can be politicized: On the concept of the political in Michel Foucault and Carl Schmitt. *Telos*, 142, pp. 135–161.

Giulianotti, R. (2002). Supporters, followers, fans and flaneurs: A taxonomy of spectator identities in football. *Journal of Sport and Social Issues*, 26(1), pp. 25–46.

Kącki, M. (2015). *Białystok. Biała Sila, Czarna Pamięć* [Białystok. White Power, Black Memory]. Wołowiec: Wydawnictwo Czarne.

Kennedy, P. and Kennedy, D. (2016). *The Political Economy of Football: A Marxist Perspective*. Abingdon: Routledge.

Santora, M., and Berendt, J. (2019). Anti-Gay Brutality in a Polish Town Blamed on Poisonous Propaganda. *The New York Times*, https://www.nytimes.com/2019/07/27/world/europe/gay-pride-march-poland-violence.html [accessed 20 October 2019].

Śpiewak o uczestnikach marszu równości i kontrmanifestantach: Różnica niemal antropologiczna (2019). Available at: www.tvp.info/43609939/spiewak-o-uczestnikach-marszu-rownosci-i-kontrmanifestantach-roznica-niemal-antropologiczna [accessed 28 September 2019].

Tara, J., and Darwish, M. (2019) Polish city holds first LGBTQ pride parade despite far-right violence. *CNN*, https://edition.cnn.com/2019/07/21/europe/bialystok-polish-lgbtq-pride-intl/index.html [accessed 20 October 2019].

Żakowski, J. (2019). *To Są Zwykłe Oprychy, a Nie Faszyści* [There Are Only Hoods, not Fascists]. Available at: http://wyborcza.pl/7,75968,25021308,to-sa-zwykle-oprychy-a-nie-faszyci.html [accessed 3 October 2019].

Index

Page numbers in *italics* refers to an illustration

abortion 63–4
activism *see* football fan activism
Against Modern Football movement 28
AKS Zły (Alternative Football Club 'Bad') 205
Albania 33–4
All-Polish Youth 113
Anderson, Benedict 168
anti-communism 51, 56, 87, 88, 107, 152, 159–62, 163, 164, 169, 170, 207
anti-establishment 3, 106, 116, 153, 159–62, 168, 173, 207
anti-Semitism 75–7, 174
Antonowicz, Dominik 109, 175
army: football clubs' affiliation with 84–5
Arsenal Kiev (Ukraine) 12, 13

Balcerowicz, Leszek 52, 53
Balcerowicz Plan 56
Baltic States 16–17
banal nationalism 24, 163, 168–9, 182
banal patriotism 163, 170, 191
Bartkowski, Maciej 12
Beenhakker, Leo 192–3
Beiu, Adrian 20–1
Belarus 14–15; anti-Russian hostility 14; civic engagement of fans 14; fan protests 14
Besta, Tomasz 144–5
Bezlov, Tihomir 22
Białystok: March for Equality (2019) 177, 202–3
Bjelica, Duško 31
Black Rebels (anti-fascist group of Polonia Warsaw fans) 149, 150, 205
Bohemians Prague 17
Boniek, Zbigniew 85, 197

Boruc, Artur 157–8
Bosnia and Herzegovina 25, 28–30; ethnic context of conflicts between fans 29; impact of Yugoslav wars on 25
Brentin, Dario 27
Brimson, Dougie 16
Britain 109; war on hooliganism by Thatcher 109, 111
Bulgaria 21–2; hooliganism 22; Katounitza case (2011) 22; Lukov March 22; radicalisation of fans 22
Burski, Jacek 128
Bush, George W. 59
Bylina, Vadim 14, 15

Campbell, Sol 195
capitalism 99; football and wild 94–5
Catholicism 63–4; and fans 156–9
Cenar, Edmund 71
Central and Eastern Europe 4, 5, 11, 35, 206–7 *see also* individual countries
charity actions: by fans 130–1
Charvát, Jan 17
Chemicz, Stanisław 83
Children's Day 130
Chládková, Lucie 30–1
Chrobry Glogów 139
Cieślik, Gerard 186
Citizens' Militia 86, 88, 107
citizens' rights: and new rules 110–11
civic activists: fans as 210
civic engagement: and Belarus fans 14; and Czechia fans 17
Civic Platform (PO) 60–1, 121, 144; conflict with and hardline approach towards fans 115, 118, 136; conflict

216 *Index*

with Law and Justice party 60, 61, 205–6; *see also* Tusk, Donald
Cleland, Jamie 126
Cohen, Stanley 108
collective action 1, 34, 127, 139, 193; and resource availability 139
collective identity 127–8, 129, 157, 163, 177, 212, 213
collective memory 25, 27, 86, 208
Colović, Ivan 25, 26
commercialisation of football 126, 127, 155, 194, 206, 213–14
commodification: of football 102, 194, 206; of national team 190–1
communism/communist era 50–1, 57, 150–1; fall of 51–2, 188; football under 84–8; and football-related violence and hooliganism 86, 88, 96; national team and national team fans 186–7, 198; political engagement of fans during 87
community-based activity 127
Constructorul Chinău (Moldova) 23
corruption scandals 94, 103, 112, 193
Cracovia Cracow FC 77, 120, 131; establishment (1906) 72; rivalry with Wisła and games played against 75–6, 76, 82, 83
Cracow (city of) 71–2, 74, 75; football matches after liberation from German occupation 82–3; football teams *see* Cracovia Cracow FC; Wisła Cracow FC; underground football during Second World War 81–2
Cretan, Remus 20
crime: hard line-approach to by Law and Justice party 117; hooligans' involvement in 99, 125, 204
Crimea: Russian annexation of 13
criminal code/procedure reforms of 110
Croatia 25, 27–8; far-right political extremism of fans 28; impact of Yugoslav wars on 25; left-wing fans 28; relation between fans and Tudjman 27
Cursed Soldiers 163, 169–72, *170*, 207
Czarni FC 71
Czechia 17–18; anti-fascist reputation of Bohemians fans 17; civic engagement of fans 17; hooligans 17–18

Dąbski Cracow FC: execution of players/ staff by Nazis (1945) 82
DAC (Hungary) 19

democracy 54–5, 128
Democratic Left Alliance *see* SLD
Deyna, Kazimierz 85
Dinamo Bucharest 20, 21
Dinamo Minsk ultras 14
Dinamo Zagreb's Bad Blue Boys 24, 28
'division of functions' 127, 132, 134
Djordjević, Ivan 27
Dmowski, Seweryn 69, 84, 85
Dobrowolski, Maciej 119
Drzazga, Edyta 110
Duda, Andrzej 62, 163, 197
Dynamo Kiev (Ukraine) 13

Eberhardt, Adam 23
Edwards, Bob 139
elections 55, 59; (1989) 51; (2005) 59–60, 117; (2007) 60, 113; (2015) 4, 62, 106, 115, 117, 118; turnouts 55
Elias, Norbert 97
Engel, Jerzy 190
Equality March (2019) 177, 202–3
Estonia 16–17
Euro (2008) 192, 193
Euro (2012) 3, 61, 108, 111, 112, 118, 129, 194–6, 198; political legacy of 196; preparations for 194–5
Euro (2016) 197
Euromaiden movement 13–14
European Champion Clubs' Cup 85
European Convention on Spectator Violence 98, 109
European Court of Human Rights 117
European Cup Winners' Cup 85; (1983) 87
European Parliament elections (2019) 106
European Union (EU) 110; Poland's accession to (2004) 54, 55, 57, 59, 61, 129

Faje, Florin 19–20
fan-clubs: establishment of official 86; perishing of official 88
far right: attempts to infiltrate fan community by parties of the 112–13; rise of in the terraces 99–102, 108; victory of in 2015 elections 106; *see also* right-wing
FBK Kaunas (Latvia) 16
FIFA 112, 213
football clubs: in the 1990s 92, 102–3; affiliation with the army 84–5; and capitalism 94–5; fans' identity with history of 1–2; industrial affiliations

Index 217

85; and local authorities 121; mergers and renaming of; privatisation of 119–21; rescuing of by fans 133; rivalries 85; symbols seen as sacred 156; transfer market in 1990s 94; under communism 84–5

football fan activism 126–40; charity and social action examples 130–2, 139; dark side of 133–6, 139; factors explaining advent of supporters' associations 127–9; political *see* political activism/engagement; ''pro-club' 133; and whitewashing process 129–30

football fandom/fans: in 1990s 92–103; attempts to capitalise on relations with 112–15; beginnings of organised 86; collective identity 127–8, 129, 157, 163, 177, 212, 213; dealing with post-transformation anomie 92, 93; during communist era 86–8; effect of post-1989 transformation on culture 97–9; ethnic tensions 76–7; historical perspective 69–88; inter-war period 74–5; legislative attempts to control 109–11; and PiS 117–18; and political agency 203–5; political engagement *see* political engagement/activism; political and ethnic divisions in pre-World War II 74–80; professionalisation of 127–30; relations with PZPN 94, 193, 197; rise of the far right in the terraces 99–102, 137; shaping of by memory work 88; versus political elites 106–22

football players: naturalisation of foreign 191, 193; restrictions on top 85; transfers to foreign clubs 85

football policy 107–9

foreign players: naturalisation of 191, 193

'fork action, the' (2008) 117

Fornalik, Waldemar 197

free market ideology 145

Fshazi, Falma 34

Galicia 71–2, 74

Gazeta Wyborcza (newspaper) 161, 162

gender issues 3, 145, 175–6

Georgiev, Georgi 21–2

Germany: occupation of Poland during Second World War 80

Gierek, Edward 186, 187

Giertych, Roman 113, 115

Gilbert, Andrew 30

'git-people' subculture 86

Gloriozova, Ekaterina 15

Górnik Zabrze FC 85, 97, 98, 128, 195

Górski, Kazimierz 186

Gowarzewski, Andrzej 81

grass-roots activity 55, 106, 120, 139, 197, 206, 209, *209*, 211

Great Orchestra of Christmas Charity 131

Greater Poland 70

Greater Poland Uprising (1918–19) 71

Greater Poland's Association of Sports' Associations 70

Grodecki, Mateusz 109, 115, 116, 127

Guţu, Dino 20

Hakoah Vienna 77

Hałys, Jósef 71

Hamberger, Judith 19

hegemonic masculinity 176

Herberger, Sepp 78

history: fans' reference to 146–7

Hodges, Andrew 28

homo sovieticus 58

homophobia 176

hooliganism/hooligans (other countries): Bulgaria 22; Czechia 17–18; Republic of North Macedonia 32; Russia 15–16; Serbia 26

hooliganism/hooligans (Poland) 134–6; in 1990s 95–6, 98, 107–8;attraction of to young males 135; change in form 112, 115; clashes abroad 197–8; and communist era 88, 96; and criminal activity 99, 125, 204; dealing with by police 107–8; decisions over alliances with fans of other clubs 134; domination of in the fan world 134; legal regulations introduced to curtail 109–10, 189; parliamenterisation of 112; and preparations for 2012 Euro 195; professionalisation of 134; relationship with labour market situation 53; rise in 189; tackling 110; Tusk's zero tolerance policy towards 115–17, 129, 195; weak response to by the state in 1990s 107–8

'hot water in the tap' policy 4, 61–2

Hungary 18–19; political nostalgia for Great Hungary 19; ultras 18; v Poland (1939) 78, *79*

ideology (of football fans) 143–78, 207; absence of the left wing and reasons 149–52, 159; anti-communism 51, 56,

218 Index

87, 88, 107, 152, 159–62, 163, 164, 169, 170, 207; anti-establishment 3, 106, 116, 153, 159–62, 168, 173, 207; anti-refugees 173–4; Catholicism 156–9; dimensions of 155–77; factors influencing 178; gender roles 175–6; glorification of war heroes 172; nationalism 3, 4, 159–60, 162–9, 174; patriotism 148, 159–60, 162–9, 170; political 203–4; racism 172–3, 191; reverence of the Cursed Soldiers 169–72; right-wing orientation and reasons for 4, 10, 137, 143, 145, 146–9, 152, 204, 210–11; sexual identity 176–7

Independence March (Warsaw) (2011) 115, 137, 144, 164, 167–9, 204, 210–11

Institute of National Remembrance (IPN) 172, 206

institutionalisation of football 69

intelligentsia 56–7; split between working class and 58

Iraq war 59

Ishchenko, Volodymyr 13

Islam 174

Israel 84

Jacobsson, Kerstin 3

Jagiellonia Białystok fans 177, 202, 204

Jagiellonian University 71, 72

Jaruzelski, Wojciech 186

Jasna Góra: annual pilgrimage to by fans 156, 158–9

Jews 72, 75, 174; anti-Semitism 75–7, 174; fans' anti-attitude towards 174; and occupied Poland 82; sport clubs 84; under communism 84

'Jordan park' playgrounds 71

Jutrzenka Cracow FC 76

Juventus Turin 85, 160

Kąçki, Marcin 202

Kaczyński, Jaroslaw 62, 113, 117

Kaczyński, Lech 60, 117, 150, 192; death in plane crash (2010) 61, 165

Kamiński, A.Z. 55

Kania, Stanisław 186

Karpaty Lviv (Ukraine) 12

Katouniza case (Bulgaria) 22

Kempa, Beata 119

Kinder, Toby 29

Kłysiński, Kamil 14

Komorowski, Bronisław 62, 194, 195

Korolczuk, El◻bieta 3

Korona Warszawa FC 72

Korona Kielce FC 120, 165

KORWiN 143–4

Korwin-Mikke, Janusz 144

Kosovo 32–3; football as instrument of social integration 33; relationship with Serbia 32–3

Kossakowski, Radosław 86, 112, 144–5

Kotwas, Marta 169

Kowalik, Tadeusz 52

Krasniqi, Besnik 33

Krasniqi, Sanije 33

Krugliak, Maryna 12, 13

Krugliak, Oleksandr 12, 13

Kubik, Jan 169

Kukiz' 15 movement 115, 143, 144

Kukiz, Pawel 115, 144

Kušnierova, Daniela 18

Kwaśniewski, Aleksander 59, 195

Lalić, Dražen 25, 28

Lato, Grzegorz 193

Latvia 16–17

Law and Justice (PiS) 60, 61–4, 106, 114–15, 117, 144, 172, 173, 203; conflict with Civic Platform 60, 61, 205–6; and football fans 117–18; origins 117; victory in 2015 elections 173

Law on the Safety of Mass Events 98–9, 102, 109–11, 129, 189

League of Polish Families [*Liga Polskich Rodzin, LPR*] 113–14

Lech Poznań FC 120, 137, *138*, *150*, 165; anti-Lithuanian banner controversy 167; anti-refugees 173–4; celebrating Wielkopolska Uprising anniversary 165–7

Lechia Gdańsk FC 87, 93–5, 132, 134, 138–9, 160, 161; anti-communism 161; anti-refugee stance by ultras 174; collapse (2001) 138–9; match between Juventus Turin and (1983) 160

left-wing fans 10, 205–6; absence from Polish terraces and reasons 149–52, 159; Central and Eastern Europe 35; European clubs 205

left-wing political parties: weakening of 2

left-wing symbols 137

Legia Warsaw FC 84, 85, 118–19, 120, 138, 149; acquisition of by ITI 120; charity actions 13; commemoration of Warsaw Uprising (2017) 138, 162–3;

and religious symbols/values 156, 157–8, *157*; and 'the fork action' (2008) 117
legislation: attempts to control fans 98–9, 102, 109–11, 189
Levski Sofia (Bulgaria) 21–2
Lewandowski, Robert 197
LGBT community 176–7, 202; and Equality March (2019) 202
Lipton, David 52
Lithuania 16–17
ŁKS Łódź FC 73, *103*, 120, 121, 131–2
local authorities: and football clubs 121
local identity 167–8
Łódź (city of) 72, 73 *see also* ŁKS Łódź FC; Widzew Łódź FC
Lubański, Włodzimierz 85
Lviv 71
Lviv University 71

Maccabi World Union 72, 75
McCarthy, John D. 139
McDougall, William 159
Majewski, Stefan 193
Makkabi Cracow FC 76
Maksimir riots 25
Mazowiecki, Tadeusz 51
Manasiev, Aleksandar 32
March for Equality (2019) *see* Equality March
Marcinkiewicz, Kazimierz 60, 192
match-fixing 94, 112, 188
Mazowiecki, Tadeusz 52, 59
media 3; anti-attitude towards by fans 162; negative image of fandom by 133
memory, collective 25, 27, 86, 208
memory policy 63, 172, 205, 206
Mennell, Stephen 96–7
Merton, Robert K. 93
Michnik, Adam 161
Mills, Richard 24, 25, 29, 32
minority rights 64
Modern [*Nowoczesna*] party 144
Moldova 22–3; relations with Russia 23; tension between Transnistria and 22–3
Molnar, Gyozo 18
Montague, James 186
Montenegro 31
moral panic discourse 8, 108–9, 113, 115, 133, 195, 212
MTK Budapest 18

Muslims 174
Mustapić, Marko 27

National Democracy party 77
National Movement 115, 143, 144
national team: (1921–39) period 183–4; advancing professionalisation (2013–19) 197–8; advent of marketing (1997–9) 189; appointment of Beenhakker as coach 192–3; appointment of Wójcik as coach 189–90; commodification of (2000–2002) 190–1; and communist political propaganda machine 186–7; crisis of and defeats (2009) 193–4; and Euro (2012) 194–6, 195–6; first international game played (1921) 74, 183; Golden Age of (1970–89) 186–8; improvement in performance (1997–99) 190; intensive politicisation of (2003–09) 192; in multi-ethnic state during inter-war years 77–80; naturalisation of foreign players 191, 193; official pro-socialism of (1947–69) 184–6; organisational disorder 188; poor performance (1947–69) 185; poor performance (1986–2002) 94, 189; post-Euro 2012 crisis 197; vs Soviet Union (1957) 185–6; *see also* World Cup
national team fans/fandom 182–99; anti-communist manifestation during Poland vs USSR (1982) 187–8; effect of professionalisation on 197; and Euro 2012 preparations 194–5; and fan paraphernalia 190–1, 194; and hooliganism 189, 190, 192, 193, 197; and politics 182–3, 187, 198; and Poznań Pact 192; protest of (2009) 193–4; rarity of anti-Soviet attitude 186; transformation of (1990–96) 188–9; under communism 186
National Union of Supporters' Associations [*Ogólnopolski Związek Stowarzyszeń Kibicowskich*, OZSK] 129
nationalism 3, 4, 159–60, 162–9, 174; banal 24, 163, 168–9, 182
Nawałka, Adam 197
neoliberalism 57, 59, 60, 119–20
Never Again non-governmental organization 173
Nielsen, Christian Axboe 26
Niffka, Georg 80

220 Index

Nociar, Tomáž 18
nomenclature enfranchisement 56
Normania (later named Posnania)
  70, 71
Numerato, Dino 17

Olisadebe, Emmanuel 191
Olympic Games: (1924) 74; (1972) 186
Ost, David 58

Panorama (BBC Programme) 195
Partitions: beginnings of football under
  the 70–3
Partizan Minsk fans (Belarus) 14
patriarchal masculinity 176
patriotism 148, 159–60, 162–9, 170;
  banal 163, 170, 191
Paunović, Miloš 24
Pavlichenko case 12–13
Pekić, Relja 27
Perasović, Benjamin 27
Petrov, Ana 24
picnic fans 192, 194, 196
PiS see Law and Justice Party
PO see Civic Platform
Pogoń, Lviv FC 71, 83
Pogoń Szczecin FC 120, 131, 189
Poland: abortion issue 63–4; accession to
  the EU (2004) 54, 55, 57, 59, 61, 129;
  Balcerowicz Plan 56; civil society
  development 55; class divisions
  212–13; communist era 50–1, 57,
  150–1; conflict between Civic Platform
  and Law and Justice 60, 61, 205–6;
  decentralisation of administration 55;
  and democracy 54–5, 128; election
  turnouts 55; emigration 54; end of
  communism 51–2, 188; end of Second
  World War 84; from socialist welfare
  state to the retrenchment of the state
  53; GDP growth 54; German
  occupation of 80–1; 'hot water in the
  tap' policy 4, 61–2; income
  inequalities 53–4; increase in
  retirement age 51, 62; intelligentsia
  and restoration of the capitalist order
  56–8; middle class 57; multi-ethnicity
  of during inter-war period 75; NATO
  accession 59; neoliberalism 57, 59, 60,
  119–20; party politics and divisions
  58–60; pensions 53; privatisation 52,
  56; proclamation of martial law (1981)
  51, 86, 87, 160, 187; refugee policy
  173–4; regaining of independence

(1918) 69, 73, 183; relations with
  Russia 196; role of Roman Catholic
  Church 63–4; Russification of 72;
  socio-economic and political transformation 50–64, 102, 129, 188; Soviet
  domination of 184; split between
  intelligentsia and working class 58;
  suspension of martial law 160; transition to market economy 52; triumph
  of right-wing politics and demise of
  the left (2015) 62–4;
  unemployment 53, 54; working class
  57–8
police 107; dealing with hooliganism
  107–8; in stadiums 110
Polish Championships (1921–26) 74
Polish Cup: (1980) 88; (1983) 87
Polish Football Association see PZPN
Polish Football League, establishment of
  (1927) 74
Polish People's Party (PSL) 60
Polish United Workers' Party see PZPR
political elites: versus football fandom
  106–22
political engagement (Central and
  Eastern Europe) 11–36; Albania 33–4;
  Baltic states 16–17; Belarus 14–15;
  Bosnia and Herzegovina 28–30;
  Bulgaria 21–2; Croatia 27–8; Czechia
  17–18; Hungary 18–19; Kosovo 32–3;
  Moldova 22–3; Montenegro 31;
  post-Yugoslav republics 23–33;
  Republic of Macedonia 31–2;
  Romania 19–21; Russia 15–16; Serbia
  26–7; Slovakia 18; Slovenia 30–1;
  Ukraine 11–14; Yugoslavia 24–5
political engagement/activism (Polish
  fans) 1–4, 136–9, 140, 206–7; avoiding
  of involvement by fans and reasons
  137, 153–5, 155, 204–5; communist
  era 87; differences between Poland and
  other countries 207–8; different forms
  of 1; dynamic element 2; formal
  activities 209; grass-roots 209;
  involvement in Independence March
  115, 137, 144, 164, 167–9, 204,
  210–11,; and national team fandom
  182–3, 187, 198; obstacles to 204;
  performative form 204, 208;
  quantitative data on political
  preferences 143–5; role in shaping
  local patriotism 137–8; static element
  1–2; typology 209–11
political ideology 203–4

Index   221

political parties: fan support for 143–4
politicians: and fans 208; fans as 210
Polityka weekly magazine 108, 113;
  'League of Hooligans' cover 113, *114*
Polonia Bytom FC 86
Polonia Warsaw FC 72, 77, 120, 147,
  149–50; Black Rebels 149, 150, 205;
  clash between right-wing and left-wing
  fans (2013) 149–50
Popović, Stevo 31
populism 4, 159, 169
Posnania (was Normania) 71
post-Yugoslav republics 23–33
Poznań Pact 192
privatisation 52, 56; of football clubs
  119–21
pro-club activism 133
professionalisation 127–30
Prussian Partition 70–1
PSL (Polish People's Party) 60
punks 99–100, 147; confrontation with
  skinheads 99–100
Purs, Aldis 16
Putin, Vladimir 23
PZPN (Polish Football Association) 59,
  71, 74, 75, 94, 188, 189, 190; election
  of Boniek as president 197; election of
  Lato as chairman 193; establishment
  of (1919) 69, 74, 183; relations with
  fans 94, 193, 197; relations with
  government 112
PZPR (Polish United Workers' Party)
  50–1, 52, 184

racism 172–3, 191
Rangers 157–8
Raś, Ireneusz 111
Real Madrid 85
Red is Bad company 163
refugees 3, 4, 173–4
religion 156; Catholicism 63–4,
  156–9
religious education 63
religious metaphors 156
Republic of North Macedonia 31–2;
  ethnic conflict between fans 31–2;
  relation between politicians and
  football hooliganism 32
Reyman, Henryk 77
right-wing ideology 4, 10, 137, 143, 145,
  146–9, 152, 159, 204, 207, 210–11; *see
  also* far right
right-wing symbols 17, 100, 101, 137,
  152, 208

Rohloff, Amanda 109
Roman Catholic Church 63–4, 156–9
Romania 19–21; ethno-nationalism 20;
  impact of oligarchs on clubs 21; ultras
  movement 20, 21; violence of political
  activism of fans 20
Romaszewski, Zbigniew 118–19
Round Table Agreements (1989) 51, 56
Ruch Chorzów FC 70, 78, 80, 100, 134;
  hooligan element 134, 135
Russia 15–16; hooligan movement 15–16;
  pursual of political goals by fans 15;
  racist incidents 15–16; relations with
  Moldova 23; relations with Poland 196
Ruzhelnyk, Olga 12

Sachs, Jeffrey 52
Sarajevo, FK 29
Savvidi, Ivan 32
Scherfke, Fryderyk Eugeniusz 77, 78
Second World War 77, 162, 169; end of
  84; football during 80–3
Self-defence [*Samoobrona*] political
  party 59
Serbia 25, 26–7; and hooliganism 26;
  impact of Yugoslav wars on 25;
  left-wing fans 27; relation between
  fans and nationalism 26; relations with
  Kosovo 32–3; right-wing fans 26;
  tensions with Albania 33
sexual identity 176–7
SHARP movement 100
Shea, Alexander 26
Sheriff Tiraspol (Moldova) 23
Shprygin, Alexander 15
silent supporters: fans as 209–10
skinheads 99–102, 147–8, 164;
  confrontation with punks 99–100
Skonto Riga 16
Śląsk Wrocław FC 84, 120, 134, 159,
  161, 174; anti-establishment
  choreography performed by fans
  (2013) 161; and Cursed Soldiers 170;
  defence against Islam choreography by
  ultras 174
SLD (Democratic Left Alliance) 59, 60,
  62, 64, 205
Slovakia 18; conflict with Hungarian
  fans 19
Slovenia 30–1; homophobic incidents
  30–1; involvement in public protests
  by fans 31
Smolensk disaster (2010) 61–2
Smolik, Josef 17–18

222 Index

Sobczak, Kornelia 95
social mobilisation 131
social performance 208
socialism: and national team 184–7
Sofia (Bulgaria) 21–2
Sokół Pniewy FC 94–5
Solidarity, trade union [*Solidarność*] 51,
52, 58, 59, 87, 160, 187, 188, 205
Solidarity Electoral Action [*Akcja
Wyborcza Solidarność*, AWS] 117
Soviet Union 15, 50, 83, 84; collapse of 51
Soviet Union football team: vs Poland
(1957) 185–6; vs Poland (1982) 187–8
Spartak Trnava (Slovakia) 18, 19
Sport Analytics 144
Sroka, Marian 71
stadiums: attempt to control fans 110,
111; closure of as punishment of fans
116; police in 110
Stakovic, Peter 30
Staniszkis, Jadwiga 55
Staruchowicz, Piotr 118–19
Steaua Bucharest (Romania) 21
Sterchele, Davide 29–30
Stott, Clifford 107–8
supporters' associations 127–30, 132;
factors explaining advent of 127–9
Supporters United programme 130, 165
symbols 147, 165, 182, 207; commerciali-
sation of 163; left-wing 137; national
167; religious 156–7, 158; right-wing
17, 100, 101, 137, 152, 208;
'sacred' 156
Syryjczyk, Tadeusz 52
Szczepaniak, Władysław *79*
Sztompka, Piotr 58

Thaçi, Rrezarta 34
Thatcher, Margaret 109, 111
Third Way, The 165
Transnistria 22–3
Triad of the Great Cities [fans'
alliance] 134
Tudjman, Franjo 27
Tusk, Donald 3, 192; 'hot water in the
tap' policy 4, 61–2; war against
hooliganism 115–17, 118, 129, 136,
148–9, 161, 195
TVN broadcasting company 162

UEFA 112, 213
Ukraine 11–14; Euromaidan movement
13–14; Pavlichenko case 12–13;

right-wing and left-wing activism 12;
ultras movement 12, 13
ultras movement 12, 13, 164; anti LGBT
176; anti-communism 160; Hungary
18; Lithuania and Latvia 16; references to religious values/symbols 156;
Romania 20, 21; Slovakia 18; Ukraine
12, 13
Upper Silesia 70
ustawki 115

Vangelovski, Tome 32
Velez Mostar 29
Venetia Ostrów Wielkopolski 70
VfR Königshütte 70
Vienna, Congress of 72
violence, football-related 3; in 1990s
95–7, 98; communist era 86, 88,
96; interwar period 75; legal
regulations introduced to curtail
98–9, 102, 109–11; moral panic
surrounding 8, 108–9, 113, 115, 133,
195, 212; *see also* hooliganism/
hooligans
Volkava, Elena 12
voters: fans as 11, 210
voting 55
Vrcan, Srdjan 24–5, 25, 27, 28

Wałesa, Lech 59, 87, 160, 195
war heroes: glorification of 169–72
Warsaw 72; underground football during
Second World War 82
Warsaw Uprising 138, 162;
commemoration of by fans
162–3, 165
Warta Poznań FC 78
White Angels Zagreb 28
whitewashing process 129–30
Widzew Łódź FC 73, 85, 120, 121,
131, *132*
Wiechecki, Rafał 113, *114*
Wielkopolska Uprising 165–7
Wilimowski, Ernest 78–80, *79*
Wilson, Jonathan 78
Wisła Cracow FC 77, 84, 134; alliance
with Ruch Chorzów fans 134; and
Catholicism 76; establishment of 72;
and religious values/symbols 156–7;
rivalry with Cracovia and games
played against 75–6, *76*, 82, 83
Wnuk, Rafal 169
Wójcik, Janusz 189–90

women: political preferences 145; status of in fandom culture 175–6
Wood, Shay 25, 28, 29
World Cup 186; (1938) 77–8; (1974) 85; (2002) 190, 191, 192; (2006) 192; (2018) 197

xenophobia: use of as political tool 63

Yalta Conference (1945) 50
Yugoslav wars 25, 28–9, 30, 31
Yugoslavia 24–5

Žalgiris Vilnius' ultras group 16
Zarycki, Tomasz 56, 57
Zec, Dejan 24
Željezničar Sarajevo 29
Zenit Saint Petersburg fan club (Russia) 16
Zimbru Chinău (Moldova) 23
Zinoviev, Alexander 58
Żochowski, Piotr 14
ZPPN (Association of Polish Football) 72, 74
Zwicker, Stefan 17